THE READING SPECIALIST

SOLVING PROBLEMS IN THE TEACHING OF LITERACY
Cathy Collins Block, Series Editor

Recent Volumes

The
Reading
Specialist

SECOND EDITION

Leadership for the Classroom,
School, and Community

Rita M. Bean

THE GUILFORD PRESS
New York   London

Printed in the United States of America

This book is printed on acid-free paper.

Last digit is print number: 9   8   7   6   5   4   3   2   1

Library of Congress Cataloging-in-Publication Data

Bean, Rita M.
  The reading specialist : leadership for the classroom, school, and
community / Rita M. Bean.–2nd ed.
      p. cm.–(Solving problems in the teaching of literacy)
  Includes bibliographical references and index.
  ISBN 978-1-60623-406-8 (pbk.)–ISBN 978-1-60623-407-5 (hardcover)
  1. Reading teachers—United States.   2. Reading—Remedial teaching—
United States.   I. Title.
  LB2844.1.R4B43 2009
  428.4′071—dc22
                                                      2009011350

About the Author

Rita M. Bean, PhD, is Professor Emerita in the School of Education at the University of Pittsburgh. Prior to joining the University of Pittsburgh, she taught at the elementary school level and also served as a reading supervisor for grades K–12. Dr. Bean has developed elementary and middle school reading curriculum materials and has published in many different journals and monographs on the topics of reading curriculum; assessment and instruction in reading; professional development; and the role of reading specialists and literacy coaches (K–12).

Dr. Bean developed and directed a program at the University of Pittsburgh that places certified teachers in classrooms for a year to serve as reading specialist interns while they take the coursework required for the reading specialist certificate. She served as Director of the Reading Center at the University for 25 years. During the past 5 years, she conducted research on the role of literacy coaches in schools and their role in improving literacy instruction.

Dr. Bean is a member of the Reading Hall of Fame and served as a member of the Board of the International Reading Association (IRA) from 2003 to 2006. She was Chair of the IRA's Commission on the Role of the Reading Specialist, which resulted in a position statement approved by the Board; she also served as Chair of the IRA Standards 2010 Committee for Specialized Reading Professionals. Dr. Bean received the University of Pittsburgh's Chancellor's Distinguished Teaching Award and the University's Distinguished Service Award for her community and outreach efforts in improving literacy.

Preface

T*he Reading Specialist* is written for the many reading specialists, literacy coaches, and principals currently working in schools to improve the reading performance of individual students and the effectiveness of reading programs for all students. It is also written for those individuals who are enrolled in programs that prepare them to become reading specialists or literacy coaches. In this second edition, I build on the framework established in the first edition—current research and knowledge in the field—to address important educational issues of the day.

The book then identifies and describes the many roles that reading specialists at all levels (kindergarten through grade 12) may be asked to fulfill. My goal in the first edition as well as in this one was to write a book that offers many practical ideas for those working in the field, based on the research and literature about the roles of reading specialists/coaches. I want reading specialists to be able to take the book from their bookshelves as a quick resource to use when a question or issue arises. At the same time, the book can be used as a textbook for those enrolled in reading specialist or literacy coaching programs. Likewise, those involved in professional development programs designed to build leadership skills will find the book helpful.

The book continues to focus on the central issues related to the role of the reading specialist: instruction, assessment, and leadership. The major changes or additions in the second edition include the following:

- *Response to intervention (RTI)*. Given the impact of this federal initiative on the role of reading specialists who have major responsibilities for helping teachers differentiate instruction for all students, I have included information about RTI, what it is, and what reading specialists can do to assist in the implementation of programs and procedures that help school personnel differentiate instruction for students. I also discuss in more depth how classroom data can be used for instructional decision making.

- *Middle and high school efforts.* I listened to readers who asked for more information about how reading specialists can function at these levels and have added information about how reading specialists/ coaches can work at these levels. Furthermore, there are vignettes from a middle school coach and a high school reading specialist that provide concrete examples of how individuals function at these levels. There is also a specific section with ideas for developing school reading programs at the secondary level.

- *Literacy coaching.* This edition has an additional chapter about coaching. I provide a framework for thinking about coaching and discuss important aspects of each of the elements of that framework. Ideas for "getting started" are described, as well as ideas for coaching individual teachers. This edition also includes specific forms or tools that coaches can use as they visit classrooms.

- *Ideas for course instructors or workshop leaders.* Several colleagues who used the first edition talked with me about the possibility of an "instructor guide." I hope those who use the text for teaching a course or a series of workshops will find this section to be helpful. Included are activities that I have used with my graduate students or with practitioners in professional development workshops.

There are some aspects of the first edition that remain, given positive feedback from readers:

- "Think about This"—a set of questions placed in each chapter to stimulate thinking about various issues being discussed.
- Reflections—a set of questions placed at the conclusion of each chapter to provide opportunities for self-reflection or group discussion.
- Follow-up Activities—suggested activities that can be used in a study group setting or in a course listed at the end of each chapter.
- Vignettes—written by practicing reading specialists who represent the high caliber of exemplary reading specialists working in

schools, they bring to life the excitement, passion, and commitment of these dedicated professionals.

From the early days of my career, I have been interested and involved in areas of research and teaching that relate to the role of the reading specialist. This book is based on my own experiences as a reading specialist, struggling to meet the needs of students and teachers (K–12). In addition, it is based on my many interactions through the years with other reading specialists faced with similar challenges. Many of the recommendations and ideas for working with others come from the interactions I have had with reading specialists and literacy coaches in the field.

As mentioned previously, I have had the opportunity to prepare reading specialists for many years. These potential reading specialists have taught me a great deal. They have shared their experiences in schools working with struggling readers and with teachers to improve the reading program. I have strived to make their voices heard in this book.

The field is a dynamic one; the work of reading specialists has never been more important, given the emphasis on literacy as a key to future success. It is my hope that this book will serve as a resource for reading specialists that will enable them to address questions or issues they face as they strive to improve student literacy learning by providing the leadership essential for developing effective literacy programs in schools.

Acknowledgments

I have been fortunate to work with colleagues in schools and universities across the country who are also committed to improving reading instruction for students, pre-K–12. These colleagues have influenced my thinking about the role of the reading specialist and the literacy coach. They include many different faculty colleagues from institutions across the United States. I mention only a few here, recognizing that there are many more who have had profound effects on my work. Naomi Zigmond, a friend and colleague at the University of Pittsburgh, with whom I have conducted research for many years, has challenged my thinking and helped me to think more broadly about struggling readers and how to help them succeed. Likewise, I have been fortunate to work with and learn from Isabel Beck, who has conducted cutting-edge research on reading instruction. The members of the International Reading Association's (IRA) Commission on the Role of the Reading Specialist played a critical role in developing the framework for the role of the reading specialist that serves as the basis for topics discussed in this book, and members of the IRA Standards 2010 Committee continue to raise issues and consider alternatives to identify what reading specialists need to know and be able to do to effect student learning.

As influential as faculty colleagues have been in shaping my thinking, students in the reading specialist certification program at the University of Pittsburgh whom I have had the pleasure of teaching, and the reading specialists and literacy coaches with whom I have worked, have had a profound effect on the contents of this book. I have learned much from these individuals, not only about what they do in order to be successful in their role, but also about the questions and concerns that they have about their positions and how to best serve the students, teachers, and administrators in their schools.

I also want to acknowledge the contributions of Katy Carroll, Jennifer Juriga, and Antonette Saul for writing the vignettes that appear in the book and Sandra Akers and Marsha Turner, former students in the reading specialist program at the University of Pittsburgh, for permitting me to include their work. I thank my mentor and colleague, Robert Wilson, Professor Emeritus at the University of Maryland, with whom I coauthored a text that highlighted the importance of the leadership and resource role of reading specialists, *Effecting Change in School Reading Programs: The Resource Role* (IRA, 1981). Certainly, we have learned a great deal about the leadership role since then, but many of the ideas in that text have withstood the test of time.

I thank my family for their support and encouragement. Thank you, Erin Eichelberger, Derek and Barbie Eichelberger, and Ethan, Ava, and Dylan (our grandchildren who are just beginning their school journey!). And finally, I thank Tony Eichelberger, my husband and best friend, for his encouragement, critical reading, and constant reminder that there was a need for the messages that this book conveyed.

Contents

1

The Role of Reading Specialists in Schools, Classrooms, and Communities

Much has been learned about how to teach reading to all students, yet the evidence is clear; there are students in schools at all levels (pre-K–12) who are not learning to read or who are reading below grade-level expectations. Across the United States, legislators and policy makers, those in the business community, parents, and educators alike have been searching for ways to address this dilemma. The federal government has invested in large-scale prevention programs such as Head Start and Reading First, the professional development initiative of No Child Left Behind (U.S. Department of Education, 2002a), to support primary reading instruction. Likewise, they have funded initiatives such as Striving Readers, developed as an intervention program, to address the literacy needs of adolescents, especially those who struggle with reading. The 2004 reauthorization of the Individuals with Disabilities Education Improvement Act of 2004 (Public Law 108-446, 2004) promoted a response-to-intervention (RTI) model for identifying and instructing students who may be at risk for learning disabilities. RTI has great implications for reading specialists, as well as for general and special education teachers. It encourages schools to prevent academic failure by identifying students who are in need of supplementary or intensive instruction and then designing and implementing programs for those students. The goal of RTI is to provide instruction that might prevent students from being identified as needing special education services. These federal initiatives as well as others developed by states or local districts require that teachers have an in-depth understanding of how to teach reading. Furthermore, in order to reach the goals of these various

1

initiatives, there is a need for reading specialists with dual roles: They must be able to work with struggling readers and provide support to classroom teachers so that all students are successful. The instructional role of the reading specialist is an important one given that it increases the opportunity for students to receive appropriate and differentiated instruction. The leadership role, in which reading specialists work with classroom teachers, has been evolving, especially since the early 2000s, with many schools hiring literacy or reading coaches to work with teachers in the schools to improve classroom instruction. As cited in Hall (2004), "the concept of literacy coaching dates back to the 1920's—but they are increasingly in demand in 21st century schools" (p. 11).

Yet, the dual role of the reading specialist is not a new one. In 1981, Bean and Wilson, in their book, *Effecting Change in School Reading Programs: The Resource Role*, wrote about the need for reading specialists to work as partners with teachers, parents, and administrators, and that "this partnership must be based on mutual trust and respect" (p. 7). In 1998, Snow, Burns, and Griffin reinforced this stance, stating, "every school should have access to specialists ... reading specialists who have specialized training related to addressing reading difficulties and who can give guidance to classroom teachers" (p. 333). It is this dual role that is addressed in this book. This role requires that reading specialists have expertise with reading assessment and instruction as well as possessing the leadership skills that enable them to work with other adults, such as classroom teachers, other professionals (e.g., speech teachers, special educators), and the community (e.g., parents, volunteers, universities, community agencies). This introductory chapter, which provides an organizational framework for the other chapters, begins with a brief history of the reading specialist in the schools, especially in regard to compensatory programs such as Chapter or Title 1. A discussion of what is known about the role of the reading specialist, based on research in the field, follows. I conclude by discussing what I believe are factors that will affect the work of the reading specialist in the coming years.

Where We Have Been

The presence of specialists in schools dates back to the 1930s when they functioned essentially as supervisors who worked with teachers to improve the reading program. It was after World War II, in response to the raging criticism of the schools and their inability to teach children to read, that "remedial reading teachers" became fixtures in many schools, public and private, elementary through secondary. The primary responsibility of the specialist was to work with individuals or small groups of children who were experiencing difficulty in learning to read. Briggs and Coulter (1977) stated, "Like Topsy, these remedial reading services just 'growed,' aided and abetted by government at all levels and by private foundations quick to provide grants of funding for such programs" (p. 216). Even the International Reading Association (1968), in their *Guidelines for Reading Specialists,* strongly supported the remedial role: Five of the six functions described for the "special teacher of reading" related directly to instructional responsibilities. However, there were those educators who began to see the difficulty of reading specialists serving only an instructional capacity. Stauffer (1967) described the remedial role as one of working in a "bottomless pit" and supported the idea of the reading specialist serving as a consultant.

Support for reading specialists serving in multiple roles continued throughout the next several decades. As mentioned previously, in 1981, Bean and Wilson wrote about the resource role of the reading specialist, emphasizing the importance of interpersonal, leadership, and communication skills for those in reading specialist positions. However, various factors helped to define the roles of reading specialists, including the source of funding that provided support for these specialized personnel, and, indeed, research that contributed to new ideas about reading instruction and assessment.

The Role of Reading Specialists in Compensatory Programs

Since 1965, a large percentage of reading specialists have been funded by Title 1 of the Elementary and Secondary Education Act (1965). This large compensatory program, funded by the federal government, was developed to provide supplemental support to students who are economically deprived. In the initial conceptualization of this program, policies and procedures were developed to ensure that the appropriate students were receiving support provided by these funds. Reading specialists who were funded by Title 1 were, therefore, required to work solely with eligible students and to purchase and use various resources and materials for those students only. Such policies led to what is commonly referred to as "pullout" programs; that is, large, separate, and distinct programs for designated students. By separating the Title 1 program from the "general" school program, it was easier for school personnel to maintain fiscal compliance. However, these programs generated many problems. Often, there was little congruence or alignment between the classroom program and the supplemental program, so students with reading difficulties, who could least handle this lack of alignment, received two different programs, with no "bridges" connecting them. Some reading specialists were not knowledgeable about the instruction students were receiving in their classrooms (Allington, 1986; Slavin, 1987), nor did they share what they were doing with the classroom teachers! Moreover, when students who received Title 1 services returned to their classrooms, they were then asked to learn from materials that were too difficult for them or to use strategies or skills different from those they were learning in their pullout program. Another problem was that, too often, students in these supplemental programs spent their time doing workbook-type, skill-related activities. There was little opportunity to read nor was there much direct instruction (Allington & McGill-Franzen, 1989; Bean, Cooley, Eichelberger, Lazar, & Zigmond, 1991). And some classroom teachers seemed to think that the reading specialists had sole responsibility for teaching these students to read, even though the instruction provided by the specialists was identified as *supplemental.*

At the same time, teachers resented the "swinging-door" dimension of pullout programs; their instruction was interrupted by students coming into and going out of their classrooms. This feeling is illustrated in an article from a newsletter published by a teachers' organization:

> Over the past few months I've been noticing that my class has been quietly disappearing. They leave one by one, or in small groups. They come late due to dentist appointments and leave early for eye exams. They are being remediated, enriched, guided, weighed, and measured. They are leaving me to learn to speak English, pass the TELLS test, increase sight vocabulary, develop meaningful relationships, and to be PEP'd or BEEP'd.
>
> They slip in and out with such frequency that I rarely have my whole class together for any length of time on any given day. I don't know when to schedule a test anymore. I've considered administering them during lunch when I'm on cafeteria duty—but then again the "packers" aren't sitting with the "buyers"—so we are still not all together.
>
> One day I accidentally had the whole class in my room. As soon as I discovered it, I quickly gave them their language pretest and posttest! If it ever happens again, they're getting their final exam.
>
> When the office calls for one of my students, I try to be fair about it. My policy is—if they can find them, they can have them. I find you can get one small advantage from all this coming and going, if you work it right. You seat your talkative kids in between the frequent remedials and half the time they'll be next to empty desks.
>
> I am learning to deal with the disappearances. I teach in bits and pieces to parts of the whole. But you can help me out, if you will. If you even run into any of my meandering students, say "hi" for me—and take them over their time tables please. (Anonymous, 1986)

Another problem was the stigma associated with leaving the classroom; students were viewed by their peers as being dumb or different, creating a lack of self-esteem in these students. Also, Allington (1986) and others were concerned that pullout programs that provided minimal reading instruction (e.g., 35–40 minutes, several times a week) did not address the serious needs of students.

The results of large-scale evaluations of Chapter or Title 1 were not always positive, although Borman and D'Agostine (2001), in their meta-analysis of Title 1 program effects, indicated that "there has been a positive trend for the educational effectiveness of Title 1 across the years of its operation" (p. 49). They contended that, without these services, students would have fallen farther behind academically. The evaluation of Title 1 has been difficult because it is essentially a funding program, not one that requires specific instructional foci, and there are many variations in the ways that it is implemented in districts across this nation. At the same time, the great expectation for Title 1—that it close the achievement gap between at-risk, poor students and their more advantaged peers—has not been met.

Many changes were recommended in the literature and in the new legislation of 1988. These changes included recommendations for additional collaboration with classroom teachers and special educators and more emphasis on programs in which reading specialists worked in the classrooms with teachers. These recommendations certainly influenced the role of reading specialists, making it essential that they be able to work well with other adults. Although this movement generated more interaction between teachers and reading specialists, it was not always a "marriage made in heaven"; both partners had to learn to work collaboratively in new and different ways. (I address this further in Chapter 2.)

Changes in Reading Assessment and Instruction

In the early days of Title 1 programs, reading specialists carefully documented the reading achievement and reading expectancy of students who might be eligible for compensatory services. Reading expectancy was calculated in various ways, from obtaining the intelligence quotient of the students to administering a listening comprehension test. Teacher judgment, at times, was used. Only those students who were identified as "discrepant"—that is, their test performance revealed a gap between achievement and potential—were assigned to receive reading services. With growing recognition of (1) the limitations inherent in scores achieved on intelligence and standardized tests and (2) possible test bias in identifying students, the use of a discrepancy formula was eliminated, and students were identified based on their actual reading achievement.

This criticism of standardized testing also led to the identification of new indicators of success for students and Title 1 programs, with a primary emphasis on how well students performed on "authentic" measures and indicators of success in the classroom, such as grades in subject areas. Schools, therefore, found themselves in the position of creating their own measures, identifying what they want students to know and be able to do at various grade levels. And, often, reading specialists found themselves in the position of working with classroom teachers to develop such instruments.

Likewise, changes in reading instruction influenced the work of reading specialists. As mentioned previously, Allington and McGill-Franzen (1986) and Bean and colleagues (1991), who studied Chapter 1 programs, found that reading specialists often spent their time using "skill-and-drill" methods. Students completed worksheets or participated in specialized programs that emphasized skill instruction. Little time was spent on reading itself. Yet research evidence and theorists in the field were advocating the teaching of more explicit reading strategies and increased opportunities for students to engage actively in reading and writing tasks.

The changes described previously and the results of Title 1 evaluations led to a period in the 1990s when school districts eliminated or downsized the number of reading specialists in their schools. One reading specialist summarized the situation as follows:

> Our grant from Title 1 is substantial; yet rather than use the expertise of reading specialists in the district's reading program, the number of specialists has dropped in the last several years from 14 to 4. Reading specialists have been assigned to classroom teaching positions or have not been replaced from attrition. Blame for dropping reading scores has been laid at the Title 1 door; reading specialists are an expensive liability. Reading specialists are being replaced with many, many inexpensive aides. (personal communication, May 1991)

Various programs and strategies were implemented to address the problems of struggling readers: increasing the competence of classroom teachers, reducing class size, using technology in the classrooms, adding after-school and summer programs, and employing volunteers and aides to work with students. All of these strategies, though they can be beneficial, did not seem to produce the desired results, however.

In 1995, the International Reading Association, encouraged by its members, established a commission to investigate the role and status of reading specialists in schools. The commission was given three tasks: (1) analyze the literature and research about the role of the specialist,

(2) conduct a survey of members to determine what reading specialists were actually doing in schools, and (3) investigate the role of reading specialists in exemplary schools. This work is reported in three articles found in *The Reading Teacher* (Bean, Cassidy, Grumet, Shelton, & Wallis, 2002; Bean, Swan, & Knaub, 2003; Quatroche, Bean, & Hamilton, 2001). Some of the key findings of the commission are reported below. The work resulted in a position statement, *Teaching All Children to Read: The Roles of the Reading Specialist* (International Reading Association, 2000b).

National Survey of Reading Specialists

The survey of reading specialists (Bean, Cassidy, et al., 2002) revealed interesting and, in some ways, disturbing information. Completed questionnaires were returned by 1,517 individuals who identified themselves as reading specialists. The respondents were 97% white and 98% female; they were also experienced educators, with 86% having served as classroom teachers. More than 90% worked directly with students on a daily basis, providing instructional services either in the classroom or on a pullout basis. Interestingly, pullout instruction was still prevalent, although respondents indicated that one of the changes they saw in their position was a move to more in-class instruction. Most reading specialists worked with primary grade students. Respondents also reported a greater expectation that reading specialists function as a resource to teachers and that they plan instruction for students with classroom teachers on a regular basis.

One of the disturbing findings of the survey was the virtual absence of men and minority groups among the reading specialist population, a problematic finding given the need to provide good role models for students who themselves may be male or from a minority group. Likewise, the lack of specialists at the intermediate, middle school, and high school levels reduces the potential for maintaining performance of students and helping content teachers at those levels understand how they can help students read informational text more effectively. Finally, although respondents did indicate that they planned lessons with teachers, many also indicated that they had little time for planning because they were scheduled to teach large numbers of students almost every period of the day.

Reading Specialists in Exemplary Schools

The study by Bean, Swan, and Knaub (2003) provided the most provocative information about the role of the specialists. First, principals in the exemplary schools selected were extremely positive about the importance of the reading specialist to the success of their reading program, with 97% indicating that specialists were "extremely" or "very important" to its success. These specialists were experienced teachers (all but one of them worked directly with students), all of them also served in a leadership role, and all of them saw the leadership role as an essential part of their work. These specialists identified the following capacities and qualities that they also believe characterize the ideal reading specialist:

- Teaching ability
- Knowledge of reading instruction
- Sensitivity to children with reading difficulties
- Knowledge of assessments
- Ability and willingness to fill an advocacy role
- Ability to work with adults
- Knowledge of reading research
- Lifelong learners
- Ability to provide professional development
- Ability to articulate reading philosophy
- Energy

THINK ABOUT THIS

Which capacities and qualities do you believe are most important? Why? Notice that the qualifications include those that relate to the instructional capabilities of the reading specialist and their leadership skills. Are there others that you would add?

The 2000 position statement adopted by the Board of Directors, International Reading Association, calls for reading specialists to apply their expertise in the areas of assessment, instruction, and leadership (see Figure 1.1). In the following chapters, the role of reading specialists in each of those areas is explored and ideas for working effectively are provided.

Where We Are: The 21st Century

There are several movements in today's schools that have affected the role of the reading specialist: These include literacy coaching as professional development, research-based instruction, accountability, a

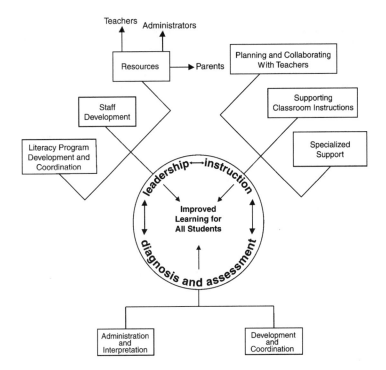

FIGURE 1.1. Graphic from the International Reading Association (2000, September). Teaching all children to read: The roles of the reading specialist. *The Reading Teacher, 54*(1), 115–119. Copyright 2000 by the International Reading Association. Reprinted by permission.

greater focus on secondary or adolescent literacy, and emphasis on pre-school education. The current emphasis on improving reading performance of all students and the recognition that high-quality instruction is related to student learning have led to a call for teachers who are better qualified and prepared to teach reading—and with that call came support for individuals who can serve as coaches or mentors for teachers in the schools. The passage of Reading First, with its stipulation that participating schools have well-designed professional programs, led to the hiring of reading or literacy coaches in schools across the country that received such grants. Likewise, common concerns about the reading performance of students at the secondary level, and the need to help secondary content teachers understand literacy and its place in the academic disciplines, was addressed in a paper prepared by Sturtevant (2003) for the Alliance for Excellent Education. Sturtevant highlighted the need for such coaching support at these upper levels and indicated that at least 10,000 reading coaches would be needed to fill the available positions. This phenomenon of "coaching" has led to changes in the role of many reading specialists across this country, with some who originally worked only with students now assuming a leadership role that requires them to help teachers improve classroom instruction. This new role of coaching requires individuals with not only an in-depth knowledge of reading instruction and assessment, but in addition, knowledge of adult learning, and excellent interpersonal, communication, and leadership skills. This movement has generated consternation for some reading specialists whose "first love" is working with struggling readers, or who feel unqualified to serve as coach.

Second, the present focus on research-based reading instruction has implications for reading specialists. They must have an understanding of research results about evidenced-based practices and be able to interpret what the findings mean for reading instruction. Reading specialists may also need to address misunderstandings or misinterpretations of such research. For example, although the National Reading Panel Report (National Institute of Child Health and Human Development, 2000) found evidence that supported oral fluency practice for improving reading performance, evidence was not available about the best type of material (e.g., decodable text, authentic text) to use. Yet, too frequently, decodable texts were thought to be the only source for such fluency practice.

Third, accountability issues also loom large in the schools. Certainly, there is a need for accountability; all who work in schools should recognize the need to evaluate the work they do. However, at times, the emphasis on accountability has led to "teaching to the test," and reading specialists (as well as classroom teachers) find themselves in the position of providing narrow, focused instruction only. In a more positive vein, the focus on accountability has made it critical that reading specialists understand how to assess reading growth, interpret results of various assessment measures, and communicate results to others. The use of data to make instructional decisions has certainly influenced what specialists do in schools. They often help teachers administer and analyze test data throughout the year, and most importantly, they are responsible for helping teachers think about how to use these test results to differentiate instruction through the use of different materials, approaches, and/or small-group instruction.

Fourth, the concern about reading achievement at all levels, especially with the standards movement that requires students to pass various literacy tests at middle school and high school levels, has generated interest in placing reading specialists at upper levels. These specialists need skills that enable them to work effectively, not just as teachers of struggling readers, but with content area teachers who are being asked to incorporate reading and writing strategies into their instruction as a means of developing student learning of academic content and helping them read to learn.

Fifth, the recognition that appropriate literacy and language activities at preschool levels can reduce or eliminate future literacy and learning problems has generated a great deal of focus on the instruction that goes on in preschool and day-care settings. There has been a call for better preparation of preschool teachers and for better transitional programs bridging preschool and kindergarten (Snow et al., 1998). In turn, these issues call for well-prepared reading specialists who can work cooperatively with preschool educators so that there is a better understanding of what students need to know and do when they arrive in kindergarten—and so that kindergarten teachers have a better idea of what students are learning in preschool settings. This movement also calls for more partnering among all individuals and agencies involved in the education of young children: parents, teachers, preschools, libraries, and community agencies. The reading specialist in today's schools must work effectively with all of these groups.

Where We Are Going: A Crystal Ball?

Although the issues mentioned above—coaching, evidenced-based practices, accountability, and emphases at all levels of schooling—will most likely continue to influence the roles of reading specialists, there are several other factors that will affect the role in the coming years. First, I suspect that we will see some changes in how literacy coaches are prepared and in how they work in schools—given the results of research currently underway. The coaching movement continues to gain momentum and schools across this country regardless of location, poverty, or achievement status, have begun to think about ways to improve professional development for teachers by employing literacy coaches to work collaboratively with teachers. But funding concerns and other issues have created some dilemmas for schools. Specifically, there is a call for evidence that addresses questions not only about qualifications and roles, but about whether coaching as a professional development effort is effective in creating changes in classroom practices and improving student learning. Funding agencies, including school boards, want to know whether employing a literacy coach is cost-effective. Is it the best way to promote student literacy learning? I believe that in the near future, we will gain access to more knowledge about what literacy coaches should be doing at various levels (pre-K–12), who should serve as coaches, and whether and how coaching has an effect on teacher instruction and student learning. In addition, we will learn more about how reading specialists can serve in the coaching role, perhaps while also assuming some responsibility for the assessment and instructional roles. The Professional Standards 2010 being developed by the International Reading Association have the potential to help those preparing reading specialists to understand better how future reading specialists can handle the multiple tasks of assessment, instruction, and leadership.

A second initiative, however, that will most likely affect the ways in which reading specialists work in schools is RTI (IDEA, 2004). This legislation encourages schools to use an approach different from the traditional discrepancy approach for identifying students with learning difficulties. RTI supports early intervention to reduce the numbers of students qualifying for special education by promoting differentiated instruction that will enable all students to be successful. The initiative necessitates collaboration among classroom teachers, reading specialists, and special educators with each professional bringing to the table ideas for how to make instructional adjustments. Classroom teachers will need instructional support from reading specialists (e.g., a reading specialist may be responsible for providing supplemental comprehension instruction to a small group of students). For example, he or she may provide explicit instruction on how to summarize or how to predict to students who seem to have difficulty even after the classroom teacher has presented these lessons to the entire class. Or the specialist may be assigned to deliver specialized or targeted instruction to a small group of readers who seem to be making little or no progress in the classroom, even after modifications have been made by the classroom teacher. Thus, the instructional role of the specialist will continue to be important, but it may require different responsibilities from those expected of reading specialists in the past.

Technology will also affect the role of reading specialists. They will need to be more knowledgeable about and able to evaluate the software that is available, and, in addition, understand the influence of the "new literacies" (Leu, Kinzer, Coiro, & Cammack, 2004; Leu, Mallette, Karchmer, & Kara-Soteriou, 2005) on students, especially adolescent readers. Furthermore, they must understand how to use the capabilities of the computer and the Internet to help students become critical readers. Moreover, technology will continue to influence the ways in which reading specialists themselves are prepared for their positions; I suspect that there will be more opportunities for reading specialists and reading coaches to receive at least some of their preparation through online programs.

A fourth issue that will affect the role of reading specialists is that of the increasing diversity of students in classrooms across the country, specifically students whose primary language is not English. Between 1979 and 1999, the number of language-minority students in the United States nearly doubled from 6 million to 14 million and it is predicted that the percentage of children who arrive at school speaking a language other than English will continue to increase (Kindler, 2002). Because these second-language learners are demonstrating significantly lower levels of academic achievement as compared to native English-speaking students in the United States, classroom teachers and reading specialists need to gain the skills that enable them to provide effective language and literacy instruction for these students.

Finally, as we learn more about school change and the need to work with others, if we are to improve schooling for all, there is recognition of the importance of collaboration, not only in the school setting but also with external partners (e.g., parents, community agencies, universities). Reading specialists need to have the necessary knowledge and skills to work collaboratively to build those partnerships. This focus on collaboration, and on what I see as a new wave of school reform, will also affect the ways in which reading specialists work in schools.

THINK ABOUT THIS

Do you agree or disagree with the factors that have been identified above—relative to how reading specialists might function in schools? Are there factors that you think should be added?

Summary

The role of the reading specialist has continued to evolve over the past decades. Currently, we are experiencing a greater emphasis on the leadership or resource role. Some of these changes have occurred in response to research findings on reading instruction and assessment practices. Other changes have emerged on the heels of criticism about the results of compensatory programs that lacked congruence between classroom and supplemental instruction. New emphases in reading instruction and increased demand for scientifically based reading instruction have created demands for reading specialists to assume an increased leadership role. Reading specialists, however, will continue to fill multiple roles that require individuals to have an in-depth knowledge of reading instruction and assessment and the ability to work well with other adults. The coaching movement, an emphasis on improving literacy instruction for all students, pre-K–12, and technological capabilities will generate the need for new skills and new roles. Moreover, reading specialists will need to have an understanding of how the organization in which they work affects what they do and how they can collaborate with others to create changes that facilitate student learning.

Reflections

1. What skills and abilities do you think are essential for working successfully as a reading specialist in an instructional role? Leadership role? Assessment role?
2. With which role are you most comfortable? What concerns do you have about the other roles?
3. What are the implications of the following issues for reading specialists and their role: placement in the middle or secondary school, increased emphasis on working with preschool providers, focus on research-based reading instruction, and focus on accountability?

Activities

1. Analyze your own skills in relation to the three areas of expertise required of reading specialists: instruction, assessment, and leadership. Write a summary of your thoughts, indicating your strengths and where you think you may need to gain additional experience or knowledge.
2. Interview a reading specialist, asking questions about how he or she fulfills responsibilities in the following areas: instruction, assessment, and leadership. You may want to use the questions in the following section.

Interviewing Reading Specialists

1. What are your responsibilities as a reading specialist? (Ask the person to describe what he or she does in his or her school/program.)
2. How do you determine the goals and content of your instruction? (Ascertain *what*—and *who*—determines the instruction.)
3. Which assessment instruments do you find to be particularly helpful in assessing students' needs?

4. How do you use assessment results?
5. In what ways do you serve as a resource to teachers? Do you have any other coaching responsibilities, and if so, what?
6. If you were able to develop your own assessment program, what would you emphasize or change?
7. What are some of the major difficulties experienced by students in your school?
8. In what ways do you facilitate parent involvement?
9. What are the major issues you face as a reading specialist?
10. How well prepared were you for the position you now hold?

2

An Overview
of the Instructional Role

Although reading specialists have multiple roles, one of the key roles is that of instructor, working with students who are struggling with reading. There are students in schools who need additional or supplemental support from teachers who have specialized training. Classroom teachers, who have multiple demands on them, also value having reading specialists provide supplemental support to help students with specific needs. Moreover, as mentioned in several studies, reading specialists themselves value the instructional role (Bean, Cassidy, et al., 2002; Bean, Swan, & Knaub, 2003). Working with students enable reading specialists to gain a better understanding of what is occurring in the classroom and help them establish credibility with teachers. This chapter discusses approaches that have been used successfully by reading specialists in working with struggling readers—from working in pullout programs to working with teachers in the classroom. In this chapter, given its relevance to reading specialists, I also provide an overview of the RTI initiative, given its relevance to reading specialists.

There is no single model of the instructional role for reading specialists to follow. Those who work in Title 1 programs may find themselves in classrooms, in pullout models, or both. Those at middle school and secondary levels often focus on reading in the content areas, and although they frequently work in the classroom with teachers, they may also have responsibility for a class of students needing supplemental reading support. Often reading specialists work with small groups of children; however, there are also specialized programs such as Reading Recovery (Clay, 1985) and Success for All (Slavin, Madden, Dolan, & Wasik, 1996) that require individual instruction or tutoring of students.

What is essential is that the reading specialist who is generally responsible for working with struggling readers understand the critical elements necessary to promote reading success for these students. Foorman and Torgeson (2001) provide an excellent summary of the research on effective classroom instruction and on effective instruction for children at risk for reading failure. They identify three critical components of instruction for struggling readers: such instruction "must be more *explicit and comprehensive*, more *intensive*, and more *supportive* than the instruction required by the majority of children" (p. 206, original emphasis). They describe the need for both cognitive and emotional support. In other words, these students need more scaffolded instruction that helps them complete tasks successfully, and in addition, they need "encouragement, feedback, and positive reinforcement" (p. 209). The importance of emotional support at all levels cannot be understated, and such support is essential for those working with adolescent students whose sense of self and feelings of academic adequacy are critical elements to consider in developing reading or literacy interventions for them. When reading the sections below, it is important to think about how reading specialists can organize their instructional work to best address the needs of struggling readers.

What Reading Specialists Need to Know about Working in an Instructional Role

Need for Collaboration

Regardless of the approach and where the instruction is being delivered, reading specialists must communicate and collaborate with the teacher who is providing the "first" instruction to students. Only if the reading specialist knows what the classroom teacher is doing, and vice versa, can the most appropriate instruction be provided for students. Much has been learned about the problems that typically arise when struggling readers are faced with fragmented instruction that increases their confusion—and anxiety. Likewise, adjustments need to be made so that these readers are not asked to do the work required by both the classroom teacher and the reading specialist. Students should not be made to stay in during recess or take assignments home because they did not complete the work required by the classroom teacher (because they were receiving instruction from the reading specialist).

Reading specialists and classroom teachers have been ingenious in finding ways to communicate and collaborate. Often this is done "on the fly," since schools do not always provide the time essential for such planning. Indeed, this lack of collaborative planning time was one of the greatest concerns of reading specialists who participated in the national survey conducted by the Commission on the Role of the Reading Specialist (Bean, Cassidy, et al., 2002). Ogle and Fogelberg (2001) asked reading specialists to describe a successful collaboration and the reasons for its success. The respondents identified, among other factors, the need for an effective school climate or culture that permits teachers to experiment with new ways of teaching. Creating environments that facilitate and reward collaboration among educators, thereby promoting learning communities, is the ideal. In the following sections, I discuss practical ideas for promoting collaboration.

Written Communication

Simple forms that can be completed by both teachers and reading specialists enable them to determine quickly what is being emphasized by each venue in a particular week or unit. These forms also serve as a paper trail that can be useful in decision making as well as to provide detailed information to parents and other educators (see Figure 2.1). Some teachers actually share or exchange copies of lesson plans. Reading specialists can ask teachers to identify the skills or strategies they are working on that week and can plan their lessons to coincide with them.

Oral Communication

SCHEDULED MEETINGS

School districts have designed many different approaches to providing needed planning time for teachers and reading specialists. For example, specialists may meet with grade level or subject area teachers once a week during a designated planning period. During these meetings, participants can discuss common needs, particular issues, and those students who may need supplemental help. One of the advantages of these meetings is that reading specialists and teachers learn from each other; such meetings also tend to encourage teamwork among teachers and specialists. Moreover, they foster the notion that students are the responsibility of all teachers—not only the classroom teacher or the reading specialist. Too often, in the past, classroom teachers believed that they had little or no responsibility for teaching struggling readers; rather, it was the reading specialists' task to work with these students.

Teacher: _____ Grade: _____

What selection are you reading? _____
_____

What are the key words being taught? (Attach list, if available.)_____
_____

Are you working on any specific skills or strategies?_____
_____

What letters/sounds are being taught?_____
_____

Do you need me to help you with something special when I come in for in-class instruction?
_____
_____

What day would be best for our in-class session?_____
_____

Do you need help with a specific lesson? (Identify.)_____
_____

Are there any students about whom you have concerns?_____
_____

Anything else?

FIGURE 2.1. Coordination Form.

Likewise, reading specialists will be involved in ways that affect the learning of all students, from those who are excellent readers to those who are experiencing difficulty.

Some districts hire a substitute teacher to manage a classroom for one period for each participating teacher, and the reading specialist meets with individual or groups of teachers during the entire day. For example, in one school district that is implementing an RTI program, substitutes are hired for one day every marking period (four times a year); they teach classes while the reading specialists and teachers from each of the grade levels meet for 90 minutes to review assessment data and make instructional decisions about content, grouping, and how the reading specialist will support the teachers at a specific grade level. Although this approach may seem costly, it provides the opportunity for in-depth discussions about specific students and how personnel can collaborate to meet student needs. It is also an important source of professional development in which reading specialists and teachers share ideas about resources, materials, and various approaches for differentiating instruction.

Reading specialists may also meet with individual teachers either before or after school, or during a designated time for teacher planning/preparation. However, some teachers may be reluctant to give up this time during which they plan for the following day and, if so, school leadership must develop procedures that provide opportunities for interaction between teachers and specialists.

INFORMAL CONVERSATIONS

There may be opportunities to talk briefly when students are working independently. However, this is not an approach that allows for long periods of discussion, since teachers need to be available to teach, assist—or watch—as students are working. Many times teachers talk informally during their lunch break or in the halls. Knaub (2002), in her study of collaborative work between specialists and classroom teachers, found that teachers and reading specialists who worked together became familiar with various types of lessons (e.g., Cunningham & Hall's [1994] *Making Words*) and were able to coordinate their teaching effectively and with little planning. Knaub (p. 50) coined the phrase "impromptu partnering" to convey the ease with which reading specialists and teachers often collaborate. We found this same sort of conversation occurring between literacy coaches and teachers; such "opportunistic" discussions provided the basis for later, more intentional work (Bean, Belcastro, Jackson, Vandermolen, & Zigmond, 2008).

Need for Support from Administration

Without administrative support, there is less chance that meaningful collaboration will occur. Schedules that provide teachers and reading specialists with opportunities to plan and policies and procedures that encourage collaboration are necessary for developing an effective program. Likewise, reading specialists need schedules that enable them to be in specific classrooms during the teaching of appropriate subjects. Even the placement of students needs to be considered carefully. As noted by Ogle and Fogelberg (2001), in some schools, struggling readers at the same grade level are placed in two or three classrooms only so that they can receive services from the reading specialist. Administrators can also show their support by providing staff development for all teachers participating in collaborative teaching. It is not sufficient for reading specialists alone to understand how to work collaboratively; all teachers can benefit from experiences that heighten their understanding of what collaboration means and how to do it. This is especially important as schools attempt to implement programs that meet the recommendations of the RTI initiative, which requires collaboration among classroom teachers and other available specialized personnel (e.g., reading specialists, special educators, etc.).

Need for Clear Procedures

Both classroom teachers and reading specialists must know and understand their roles in the classroom, else the lack of clear procedures leads to problems. Reading specialists may feel as though they have no clear instructional responsibility and therefore "float" around the classroom, trying to anticipate what might be helpful. This type of role seems to generate the feeling in reading specialists that they are "aides" in the classroom and that their expertise is not useful or valued. Classroom teachers also experience frustration because they do not know exactly why the reading specialist is even present. Only with the establishment of clear expectations can teachers both enjoy and recognize the benefit of an additional person in their classrooms. However, establishing those clear expectations is not easy, given the culture that has existed in schools in which each teacher is assigned a group of students and is responsible for the academic success of those students. Teachers have been accustomed to teaching in isolated settings, planning and implementing instruction that they deem best. Figure 2.2 identifies questions that the classroom teacher and reading specialist can ask each other as they think about how to work together.

	Yes	No
1. Do we come to class with prepared materials/ideas?	_____	_____
2. Do we signal our students to come to us when it is time?	_____	_____
3. Do we follow through on plans made at joint planning sessions?	_____	_____
4. Do we provide feedback on students' lessons to each other regularly and frequently?	_____	_____
5. Do we bring materials to joint planning sessions?	_____	_____
6. Do we share new strategies with the other teachers?	_____	_____
7. Do we engage in self-reflection after teaching a lesson?	_____	_____
8. Do classroom teachers try to help the reading specialist "fit in" with the flow of the classroom?	_____	_____
9. Do we invite feedback on students/lessons from each other?	_____	_____
10. Do classroom teachers share expectations for student behavior?	_____	_____
11. Do we try to keep a schedule? (Does the reading specialist arrive on time? Does the teacher plan to be ready for the collaborative lesson?)	_____	_____
12. Do we discuss other classroom teachers/reading specialists or students with others in a professional manner?	_____	_____
13. Do we "keep up" on reading instruction information and read professional journals?	_____	_____
14. Do we demonstrate respect for each other?	_____	_____

FIGURE 2.2. Classroom teacher/reading specialist self-reflection questionnaire.

THINK ABOUT THIS

Would you feel comfortable using the questions in Figure 2.2 in a conversation with teachers? How can you use these questions effectively?

The following scenario describes how Shala, a reading specialist, and David, a third-grade teacher, planned their lessons for a week, using a framework that builds on the classroom instructional program. It also discusses how Shala works with some of David's students in a pullout setting to provide supplemental instruction for them. (See Figure 2.3.) The schedule calls for Shala to be in this classroom 3 days a week—Monday, Wednesday, and Friday—for 30 minutes each day. This week, the class is reading the selection *Mom Can't See Me* (1990) by Sally Alexander. David and Shala team-teach to introduce the selection on Monday, focusing on vocabulary and prior knowledge. Then, to help students who are working with vocabulary in pairs, both the reading specialist and teacher circulate around the classroom. Shala also takes 5 minutes to talk with a new student about his previous school experience and to listen to him read a grade-level text so that she and the teacher have a better idea of the child's reading performance.

On Tuesday, the entire class reads the selection together and participates in a discussion with the classroom teacher. Students are also assigned to various learning centers where they are given activities that relate to their specific needs while the teacher monitors their work. (Shala had helped David design these centers by providing him with

Monday	Tuesday	Wednesday	Thursday	Friday
In-class (30 minutes)	*Pullout*	*In-class (30 minutes)*	*Pullout*	*In-class (30 minutes)*
Team-teach (introduction to selection)	Targeted instruction for several groups of third-grade students (two from David's room)	Targeted, small-group instruction based on student needs	Targeted instruction for several groups of third-grade students (two from David's room)	Targeted, small-group instruction based on student need; monitor with teacher
Participate in guided and independent practice (monitor with teacher)				

FIGURE 2.3. Shala's weekly schedule with David and his students.

ideas and resources). While the students are working in centers, David provides 20 minutes of supplemental instruction to a small group of three students who need more explicit instruction focused on decoding multisyllabic words. (During this center time, Shala works in a pullout setting with two students from David's class and three students from another third-grade classroom who are having decoding difficulties. She is providing instruction that is more explicit, structured, and multisensory to help these students develop stronger decoding skills; these students also do partner reading in each lesson so that they have opportunities to apply what they are learning to actual reading.

On Wednesday, the goal is fluency practice. Three groups are formed, with Shala working with a group of students identified as needing additional assistance with reading the text, the classroom teacher working with another group, and the third group engaging in partner reading. Shala asks students in her group to read and reread a specific section of the selection. First, she models fluent reading (and disfluent reading); she then has various students read the section orally (e.g., the boys, the girls, the students with red shirts). She also reviews some of the concepts and understandings that were addressed in the discussion during the previous day. Students in David's group also read orally, but his group is focused on finding and reading parts of the selection that answer specific comprehension questions.

On Thursday, the classroom teacher presents a specific skill suggested in the anthology to the entire class and also introduces a writing task to the students: "Write a letter to the author telling [her] what you liked about the story and raising questions that you would like to have her answer." Students again are assigned to centers; David monitors their work and also spends about 15 minutes providing supplemental instruction to a small group of students who need some reinforcement of the vocabulary taught that week. (And again, as she did on Tuesday, Shala works with the same five students in a pullout setting to work on their decoding skills.)

On Friday, students continue to write the letter and they are also given time to read additional materials that are available in the classroom. The reading specialist and teacher are holding conferences with students, helping them to think about what they have written and how they might revise or edit their work. The focus is on writing a friendly letter to an author. For 10 minutes, Shala, the reading specialist, also pulls aside a small group to review strategies for identifying multisyllabic words because she and David had noted that some students were having difficulty with such words.

Shala and David use a mutually agreed-upon framework in planning each week's lesson. Shala knows that she is going to help students as they work with vocabulary on Mondays (she may also work with a small group to do some review work); on Wednesdays, the focus is on rereading the selection, and Shala often works with the group experiencing the most difficulty; on Fridays, there is an emphasis on some follow-up activity (e.g., writing, art, or creative dramatics). Shala assists with this activity, or she may work with a small group to provide additional reading practice or review specific strategies or skills. Then she also helps students in David's classroom by providing the intensive support they need by pulling them from their classroom and working with them in a small-group setting. This set of procedures is, of course, only one example of how the reading specialist and teacher may work together. Many different approaches can be used; the approach selected may depend on the curricular demands or the needs of the students.

THINK ABOUT THIS

What do you see as the strengths of this framework? Do you have any concerns about it? What skills and abilities do the reading specialist and classroom teacher need to make this framework effective? What other procedures do you think might work?

Approaches to Collaboration

In this section, I describe five approaches to collaboration that are based on the literature (Bean, Trovato, & Hamilton, 1995; Cook & Friend, 1995; Hamilton, 1993) and on observations made of reading specialist interns and classroom teachers (Bean, Grumet, & Bulazo, 1999). Some of the approaches require in-class teaching, whereas others might occur either in class or away from the classroom; all require collaborative planning. Table 2.1 provides a summary of the approaches and lists the advantages as well as potential problems of each (Bean, 2001).

Station or Center Teaching

Both reading specialists and teachers can develop stations or centers for teaching, based on the needs of the students and their own expertise or interests. Such stations can be used to provide independent work for some students while the specialist and teacher are teaching others, or a teacher, specialist, or instructional aide can be assigned to work with students at a center. The classroom teacher might be responsible for leading a center on writing, while the reading specialist guides a

TABLE 2.1. Approaches to Collaboration

Model	Advantages	Potential problems/dilemmas	Location
Station or center teaching	Students have opportunity to work with both teachers Attention to individual/group needs or interests Small-group work Teachers have some choice (utilizes teacher strengths and interests) Teachers share responsibility for developing and teaching	Time consuming to develop Noise level in classroom Organizational factors Management factors	In class
Targeted teaching	Focuses on individual or group needs Small-group instruction Specialized instruction Utilizes talents of teachers to meet needs of students	The need to know both classroom reading program and specialized approaches Rigid grouping	Either in class or pullout
Parallel instruction	Pacing/approach can vary Small-group instruction Same standards/expectations for all students Easier to handle class	May not meet needs of students Noise level in classroom	Generally in class (can be pullout)
Teach and monitor	Same standards/expectations for all students Immediate reinforcement or help from monitor Opportunity to do "kid watching" (assessment) Teachers can learn from each other (demonstration)	One teacher may feel reduced to aide status Lack of attention to specific needs of children	In class
Team teaching	Same standards/expectations for all students Utilizes strengths of both teachers Teachers share responsibility Students have opportunity to work with both teachers Attention to individual/group needs or interests Small-group work	Lack of common philosophy or approach to instruction	Generally in class

Note. From Bean (2001, p. 357). Adapted by permission of the author.

review center for phonics or vocabulary development. This method enables both teachers to work with all students as they rotate through the centers. Such centers can be used two or three times a week, thereby facilitating a flexible, heterogeneous grouping of students. Activities provided in the center can be such that students rotate through all centers (writing center, listening center), or tasks may be differentiated and students may be assigned to specific centers (phonics center for students who need additional practice, fluency center). The best centers include activities that provide for the differentiated needs of students and promote independent work. One of the advantages of learning centers is that teachers can design activities for areas of literacy in which they have specific expertise or interest. They can also focus their energies on a specific area of reading, thus reducing preparation time. Although the development of activities for centers is time consuming, once developed, they can be used at future times or in different classrooms. Moreover, activities can be shared across grade levels. Two key resources for center activities at the elementary levels include Florida Center for Reading Research (*www.fcrr.net*) and Diller's (2005) *Literacy Work Stations for Grades 3–6.*

To implement these centers effectively, teachers need to have excellent organizational and classroom management skills. Furthermore, both teacher and specialist must work collaboratively. Some teachers may have difficulty with the noise level that occurs in their classrooms as the centers are functioning; hence the need for collaboration in establishing classroom rules for moving through the centers.

Targeted Teaching

Classroom teachers who have responsibility for a large number of students may not be able to focus or target instruction to the extent necessary for some students to achieve success. The reading specialist can address specific needs of individual or small groups of students, selecting supplemental materials that provide for reinforcement of learning; adjusting the level of material used, for example, practicing fluency with material at students' instructional level, or reteaching a skill or strategy. They may choose to use a specific reading program developed for students who are having difficulty learning to read, for example, Wilson Reading Program (Wilson, 1996) or Reading Recovery (Clay, 1985). Students who need additional exposure to the vocabulary of a story (perhaps even before the story is introduced) may be grouped for instruction, while other students work on their writing projects or do independent reading. In one school district, reading specialists work with selected primary children individually for short 10-minute mini-lessons, asking them to read orally, working with a word or words that present difficulty for them, and then providing opportunities for students to compose a sentence that can be read, cut into strips, reordered, reread, and taken home for practice (along with the book that has been read). In another school, in the intermediate grades, reading specialists work with small groups of students who need additional support with comprehension; their major focus is helping students understand and use specific comprehension strategies such as those described in *Explaining Reading* (Duffy, 2009). At the high school level, reading specialists may work with students who need more help with study skills or with reading their science textbook. They may also be assigned to teach two or three classes of students who have been identified as needing reading support; these students most often are required to take this class, possibly in lieu of an elective or study hall. Although the reading specialist generally takes responsibility for these targeted lessons, at times, the specialist may work with other students while the classroom teacher is given the opportunity to teach these focused or targeted lessons.

Parallel Instruction

Parallel instruction provides opportunities for reducing the size of the class. Both teachers teach the same lesson and the same content but with a different group of students. Such instruction enables teachers to change the pace and the instructional techniques, depending on the needs of the students. For example, both teachers may focus on comprehension, using the same materials, but teach in ways that reflect the different needs of the students. In one group, the teacher may move quickly through the story and focus on the comprehension strategies that enhance and extend students' understanding of the selection after the reading. In the other group, more time may be spent providing explicit instruction about a specific reading strategy, for example, using prediction before, during, and after reading. This type of instruction, done in the same classroom, can be difficult because of the noise level, with two direct lessons occurring at the same time. Teachers tell me that students seem to adjust nicely to the noise, but they have more difficulty adjusting.

Teach and Monitor

In this approach, one teacher presents the lesson while the other moves around the room, helping and supporting children who need assistance. As mentioned previously, it is this approach that has created frustration for some reading specialists who feel that they have become nothing more than aides in the classroom. When the reverse occurs and the reading specialist assumes the instructional role, a few classroom teachers may see this as a time for them to complete other tasks, marking papers or calling parents, causing concerns for reading specialists who notice this type of behavior. Nevertheless, there are many opportunities and advantages for such teaming in the classroom. For those working with young children, an extra pair of hands and eyes can be extremely beneficial. For example, reading specialists may teach a lesson requiring first-graders to manipulate letter cards as they "build words." The second teacher can be extremely effective in making sure children have the right cards in the right place. Likewise, writing and reading workshops may require monitoring (and conferencing) by both teachers. Another advantage of this approach is that classroom teachers can observe the reading specialist using a specific strategy with which they may not be familiar. If the classroom teacher is teaching, the reading specialist can observe students with reading difficulties and note how they behave in a group setting ("kidwatching").

Team Teaching

Team teaching may include aspects of each of the models described above. In this model, both teachers plan how they will conduct instruction, whether for a particular lesson or over time. The previous scenario of the third-grade teacher and reading specialist (David and Shala, respectively) describe several approaches to collaboration. Both teachers have specific roles based on their expertise and interests. Each works with the entire group as well as with small groups or individuals within that group. Such collaboration requires time for planning, a good working relationship between the two individuals, and common beliefs/ideas about reading instruction and classroom management.

Helping Students Succeed in the Classroom While Developing Needed Skills and Strategies

One of the dilemmas faced by reading specialists is that of determining where to put their focus: Should they emphasize helping students succeed in the classroom, or should they help students to achieve those skills/strategies that they are missing, based on assessment results? There is no simple answer. In fact, the only solution is that of doing *both*. Students who are reading below grade level and struggling with the material in their classrooms deserve to receive the help they need so that they can achieve some degree of success. At the same time, these students may benefit from opportunities to work in small groups or individually, so that the reading specialist can review and reteach the specific skills with which these students are having difficulty.

Focus on Classroom Success

The need for congruence between classroom and reading specialist instruction is recognized as important when working with struggling readers (Allington & Shake, 1986; Walp & Walmsley, 1989). Allington (1986) decries the fact that struggling readers, who are least able to make accommodations, may experience two separate and distinct instructional programs. Reading specialists can promote congruence by reteaching or reviewing a specific skill or strategy important for classroom performance. They can also provide additional practice with specific vocabulary words needed for a selection, guide students in repeated readings of selections, and help with specific assignments.

Although this emphasis is important in the primary grades, it is especially essential for students at upper levels where they are using reading to learn new concepts in various subject areas. What skills and abilities will help the middle school student read and comprehend his or her social studies textbook more effectively? What are the note-taking skills and review strategies that students in a biology class can use so that they are prepared for the unit test? When reading specialists address these questions, they are most likely to prepare instruction that can be used as part of the ongoing procedures in the content classroom. For example, the reading specialist may choose to demonstrate the use of an anticipation guide (Buehl, 2009) with tenth-grade students in a biology class. Such a lesson helps students think about what they know and might learn before they read a chapter in their textbook. It also demonstrates for the teacher an approach that can be used to build and activate students' prior knowledge in preparation for reading of text. In this case, the reading specialist works in the classroom with the teacher to promote successful classroom performance.

Focus on Meeting Specific Needs

Students who have not learned various skills or strategies need to have opportunities to develop them; otherwise, they may always have difficulty with reading. Thus, for students in the intermediate grades who have weak phonic skills, targeting instruction on those skills can be extremely useful. Likewise, if students are assigned to read from textbooks that are above their reading level, they need many opportunities to read silently and orally in books that are at or slightly below their instructional level. O'Connor and colleagues (2002), in a study with struggling readers, found that students made more improvement when they were taught using material at their instructional reading level than with materials at their specific grade level. The bottom line is that struggling readers need opportunities to achieve success—and providing instruction at an appropriate level will enable them to experience it.

Reading specialists at the secondary level may wish to organize a specific class in which they can work with small groups of students who are struggling with reading. During that class, they can alleviate some of the difficulties the students are facing by reviewing or reteaching specific strategies or skills. For example, such students may benefit greatly from lessons that help them learn various Latin and Greek roots and how to improve their vocabulary with such knowledge. Such lessons should, of course, help students see the relationship between what they are learning in this small-group setting and the subjects they are taking. No matter the emphasis of the specialist, students must be helped to see the relevance of what they are learning and how it can help them to read effectively and achieve success in their classrooms.

Response to Intervention

What, Why, and How

A federal program that is having a major impact on how schools differentiate instruction for all students is RTI, or response to intervention (sometimes thought of as response to instruction). This initiative, which emerged from the reauthorization of IDEA (Individuals with Disabilities Education Act, 2004) has implications for how schools identify and work with students who are experiencing learning difficulties. The goal of RTI is to reduce the number of students being identified as needing special education, by providing early identification of needs and immediate intervention. Mesmer and Mesmer (2009, p. 283) discuss five important steps in the RTI identification process: (1) establish benchmarks for literacy performance and appropriate assessment measures to identify students at risk, (2) implement scientifically based interventions for those who need them, (3) monitor the progress of students receiving intervention, (4) provide more intensive interventions for students who continue to need help and continue to monitor progress, and (5) if a student is not making progress, begin a decision-making process to determine eligibility for special education. Such a program requires involvement of all the professionals—classroom teachers, reading spe-

cialists, and special educators. It also requires schools to think differently about how reading instruction occurs in schools. Schools use a
multilevel model for differentiation similar to the three-tiered model
developed at the University of Texas at Austin (2003). As illustrated in
Figure 2.4, such a framework might include the following:

- *Tier 1:* high-quality comprehensive instruction at the classroom
level that should meet the needs of most students in that classroom.
Most frequently, schools adopt some sort of core program that is used
by all students, although some schools have developed their own "homegrown" program. This instruction should include whole-class, small-
group, and individual instruction and is generally provided by the

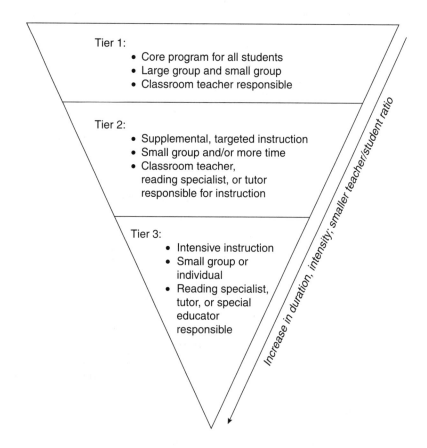

FIGURE 2.4. Response-to-intervention framework.

classroom teacher. In the example above, Shala, the reading specialist, assists teachers with their Tier 1 instruction by working in the classroom with them.

• *Tier 2:* supplemental instruction that can include small-group work and often additional time. This instruction is an extension of the Tier 1 instruction; it provides for more explicit and structured reteaching, and additional practice. Schools plan for this instruction in different ways: They provide this specialized instruction within the reading or language arts block while other students are involved in centers or doing work appropriate for them (similar to what Shala was doing when she pulled students from the two third-grade classrooms). For some students or in some schools, additional time is provided for reading/language arts instruction and all students are assigned to learning tasks appropriate for them; in other schools, students who need Tier 2 instruction receive it during a nonreading period. Most often this instruction is provided by a reading specialist or a tutor trained to implement such instruction.

• *Tier 3:* intensive instruction that requires additional time, very small group, and possibly one-on-one tutorial instruction. This instruction can be provided by the reading specialist or someone who has specialized training. In some schools, Tier 3 instruction is provided by the special education teacher for students who are not responding to Tier 2 instruction.

All three tiers necessitate careful assessment of skills and progress monitoring to determine students' success and needs. Assessment is discussed more thoroughly in Chapter 9.

Some Issues and Unknowns

Although there is great hope that an RTI model will help schools identify students who are experiencing difficulty earlier, provide support to prevent further difficulties, and reduce the number of students identified as needing special education, there are still some unknowns and a need for additional research. Important questions include: What sorts of Tier 2 instruction are best for students? How long should students receive Tier 2 instruction before being recommended for Tier 3 instruction? Does the number of tiers make a difference? For example, how soon should students be recommended for special education placement? As Shanahan (2008) indicates, "there are lots of variants in what counts as RTI.... There are three-tiered RTI models and four-tiered models, and even with those models not everyone agrees as to what the different tiers may refer to (p. 106). A question also arises as to whether these tiers are linear, that is, must a student go through each tier, or can a student go from Tier 1 to Tier 3, skipping Tier 2? In other words, is important support being denied students because they must go through each of the tiers before receiving the intensive instruction needed by them?

Another important question addresses the use of RTI in middle and high schools: What sorts of programming is possible at these levels for schools wishing to use an RTI model for these adolescent readers? More work has been done at the elementary level, although some secondary schools are attempting to use this model to support their struggling readers (H. Duffy, 2009; Samuels, 2009). The assessment component of RTI can be useful to high schools since it promotes important screening and monitoring of student progress. There are schools, also, that are attempting to add the instructional support for students who need it. Some schools add courses for these students or they adopt intensive programs for these students, for example, Read 180 (Scholastic, 2002) or Language! (Green, 1996). Other schools have developed tutoring centers or provide after-school support. Other schools have focused their efforts on providing professional development, often with coaching, to help content area teachers provide high-quality instruction. But there is much we do not know about how to implement RTI at the secondary level, and the extent to which such efforts are effective. Recently, the U.S. Department of Education awarded a grant for a partnership between the University of Kansas and the Illinois Education Department to develop systems for implementing RTI (H. Duffy, 2009), which should provide much needed information.

What should be obvious is that classroom teachers alone—even the very best—would be hard-pressed to meet the expectations of this approach. The demands are great in terms of assessment and instruction. Reading specialists as well as school leadership must become familiar with the goals of RTI so that there is a clear understanding of what it means—and does not mean. As stated by Allington (2006), some schools think they can address RTI by purchasing three different reading programs, with students at Tier 2 participating in two of the programs, and students identified as needing Tier 3 instruction, actually participating in three programs! Such an approach flies in the face of what is known about congruent instruction. Allington suggests that the keys to successful implementation of RTI requires schools to build in additional time and/or more personalized instruction to improve upon or extend classroom reading instruction. Moreover, RTI requires experts such as reading specialists who can "identify just where the reader has gotten off-track and then ... design instruction that moves the reader back onto an accelerated track of development" (p. 20). This does not negate the possibility that students may benefit from a special (and different program), especially those at Tier 3. Certainly, this type of intervention would reflect the notions in the International Reading Association's position statement, Making a Difference Means Making it Different (2000a). But, if such programs are used, "there should be clear articulation about how such an approach complements or reinforces what is being taught in the classroom" (Bean, 2008, p. 20).

In the following section, I discuss an issue that has generated controversy in the past for reading specialists—that is, whether instruction should be in the classroom of the students or in pullout situations. Given the RTI initiative, I believe that the notion of having multiple teachers in the classroom has become more accepted, although actual implementation is still problematic. Most frequently, there is a need for both in-class and pullout instruction, and determination of the location of supplemental and intensive instruction—as well as who teaches those students—is dependent on the context of the school, including its human resources and the needs of struggling readers.

Pullout or In-Class Instruction: Is That the Question?

In a national survey of reading specialists (Bean, Cassidy, et al., 2002), one of the greatest changes that reading specialists observed was the shift from pullout to in-class instruction. As discussed in Chapter 1, this change has occurred for many reasons. This emphasis parallels the inclusion focus of special education, which stresses the importance of providing help to students in their own classrooms. At the same time, the success that has been attributed to various tutoring programs, such as Reading Recovery (Clay, 1985) and the tutoring component of Success for All (Slavin et al., 1996), has led to an increase in programs in which students are tutored individually and away from their classrooms.

In this section, I discuss the benefits and limitations of each setting and what is needed if each is to work. Table 2.2 identifies bridges and barriers of in-class, pullout, and combination models as described by principals, teachers, and reading specialists (Bean et al., 1995). The benefits of these models can be thought about in three ways: What are the advantages for students? What are the advantages for teachers? How does each model improve classroom instruction as a whole?

TABLE 2.2. Instructional Setting: Identification of Bridges and Barriers

Setting	Principals	Reading specialists	Classroom teachers
		Bridges	
In class	• *Provides more opportunities for collaboration, cooperation, and communication.* • Provides less isolation for students.	• *Provides more opportunities for collaboration, cooperation, and communication.* • Could serve more students.	• *Provides more opportunities for collaboration, cooperation, and communication.* • Provides congruence. • Discourages the labeling of children.
Pullout	• *Provides students with a place and opportunities to feel special.* • Serves more students.	• *Provides a special environment for young students.* • Requires collaboration and cooperation to be successful. • Provides positive learning experiences in small groups.	• *Provides a comfortable environment in which students can try new strategies.* • Provides opportunities for students to develop positive self-esteem and self-confidence. • Provides special/ individualized attention for students.
Combination	• *Provides the flexibility to do what is best for the students.*	• *Provides flexibility of setting when students' needs are better met outside of the classroom.* • Provides flexibility for personality and philosophical differences between specialist and teacher.	• *Provides flexibility to change settings when necessary.* • Mirrors the needs of the people and children involved.
		Barriers	
In class	• *A reading specialist acting in the role of an aide.* • Reading specialist permitted to work with Chapter 1 students only.	• *A reading specialist acting in the role of an aide.* • Increases the distractibility of students. • Collaboration, cooperation, and communication are difficult. • Provides little flexibility for personality and philosophical differences between specialist and teacher.	• *A reading specialist acting in the role of an aide.* • Team teaching is difficult. • Encourages a pullout model within the classroom. • Improper scheduling provides no time for cooperative planning.

(cont.)

TABLE 2.2. *(cont.)*

Setting	Principals	Reading specialists	Classroom teachers
Pullout	• Reading specialist's room is in an undesirable facility. • Could serve fewer students.	• Teacher penalizes student for going to Chapter 1—such as making up work during recess.	• Resentment on the part of students for being pulled out—they miss a lot of classwork. • Does not fit integrated approach. • Improper scheduling provides no time for cooperative planning. • Promotes labeling of students.
Combination	• None expressed.	• None expressed.	• None expressed.

Note. Italicized text indicates trends across groups. From Bean, Trovato, and Hamilton (1995, p. 211). Copyright 1995 by the College Reading Association. Reprinted by permission.

In-Class Models

Benefits

In-class instruction is much more efficient in that students are not pulled from their classroom, so they lose neither time (for travel to instruction) nor focus (the emphasis is on what is needed in the classroom). Furthermore, there may be less stigma when students are not pulled from their classrooms; in other words, students are not identified as "different" from others. Additionally, students who are not targeted for assistance also may benefit from the instruction occurring in those classrooms.

When an in-class program is working effectively, teachers often feel that they learn from each other and that the quality of instruction is greater as a result of the sharing of ideas and materials. Some instruction is much more effective with two teachers in the classroom—for example, writing or reading conferences, monitoring work of young children who are using manipulatives, and content teacher and specialist coteaching to address the literacy and content needs of students at the secondary level. By working in the classroom, the reading specialist can observe how the targeted students perform in this setting.

Over time, communication and collaboration between the two teachers occur more naturally, with each having a better understanding of the other's expectations. And importantly, the reading specialist and teacher accept responsibility for the reading performance of all students in the classroom.

The emphasis during the past 5 years on the use of data to make instructional decisions has led to even more emphasis on the in-class model, with various professionals (e.g., reading specialist, special educator, aides) present in the classroom to assist the classroom teacher in differentiating instruction for students.

Potential Problems

Given the benefits discussed above, why have in-class programs in some schools been problematic? As mentioned previously, past traditions and our current model of schooling have not promoted such collaboration and shared teaching. We are more accustomed to the traditional model in which each teacher is responsible for his or her classroom. As we discuss each of these potential problems, we consider them in relation to students, teachers, and classroom instruction.

Some students may have difficulty learning in a whole-class setting and may need the privacy and quiet afforded by a pullout model. They may also need more intensive work in a one-to-one setting. Likewise, the in-class setting may not afford opportunities to work on the skills/strategies that particular students need; rather, the focus may be on helping students to achieve in that particular classroom. Moreover, students may still be identified as "different"—especially if *pullout* has simply been changed to *pull aside* or *pull back*!

Probably the greatest difficulty with in-class programs is that of differing and conflicting philosophies of teaching or even classroom management. Some teachers do not appreciate (and cannot tolerate) the noise and activity that an additional teacher brings. Neither teacher may have the knowledge and skills necessary for undertaking such a venture. This problem is especially likely to occur when mandates are issued and teachers and specialists are thrust into such programs without the necessary professional development. There are also concerns that reading specialists are not used appropriately (i.e., they feel like an aide) or are assigned to so many classrooms and students that they cannot work efficiently or provide *enough* support to students.

Finally, some classrooms are too small or contain so many students that the specialist cannot work effectively. In some schools, reading specialists are not provided with a place to work effectively with students in the classrooms or they find themselves moving from one section of the classroom to another, trying to find a place in which to conduct their lessons.

Critical Factors for a Successful In-Class Program

1. Teachers and reading specialists have consistently stressed the importance of scheduling common planning time so that they can implement a successful in-class program. Although some reading specialists and teachers, over time, learn to plan effectively via written communication or "on the fly," these approaches are not as effective as two or more teachers sitting down and planning together.

2. Both the reading specialist and the teacher must be willing to "share" the students. This willingness occurs only when the two have respect for each other and are able to agree on, and enforce, consistent rules for classroom management and student behavior. The two teachers must also talk openly with each other about their beliefs and instructional practices. Such conversations can lead to successful compromises regarding how the in-class model operates.

Pullout Programs

Benefits

One of the benefits of pullout instruction is that students, when pulled, get the specific instruction that they need (e.g., strategies for improving their comprehension skills, word-attack skills) in a small-group or individual setting, where they can focus on what they are learning. There is evidence that individual tutoring (Pikulski, 1994; Wasik & Slavin, 1993) and small-group instruction are beneficial to students (Elbaum, Vaughn, Hughes, & Moody, 2000; Manset-Williamson & Nelson; 2005; Sackor, 2001) and that such instruction, when provided by a well-prepared teacher, can improve students' reading achievement. Classroom teachers may feel that they can better focus their instruction to address the needs of the remaining students. Reading specialists can certainly focus their instruction; they do not have to worry about creating a distraction in the classroom and they have the materials they need to implement their lessons.

Potential Problems

One of the criticisms of the pullout model is that students lose time as they move from one room to another. One reading specialist commented: "I've had to develop an incentive program to encourage children to arrive at my room on time. It's amazing how they can dawdle as they move through the halls, stopping at the water fountain, the bulletin board, or just wandering along." Another criticism is the stigma that occurs when students leave their classmates to receive special instruction. At times, classroom teachers have been critical of the pullout model, feeling that students are missing important instruction, or disliking the disruption that occurs when students leave or enter the classroom. The anecdote in Chapter 1 (pp. 3–4) certainly speaks to teacher concerns about pullout programs. Reading specialists too may feel that they are less aware of what is going on in the classroom, both in terms of how specific students perform and how teachers are presenting the literacy curriculum to their students. Finally, especially at the secondary level, students may have little success in transferring what they are learning in these pullout classes to the work that they do in the content area.

Salinger, Zmach, Tanenbaum, Thomsen, and Lefsky (2008), in discussing the impact of several intervention programs at the ninth-grade level, found limited results and identified several difficulties with such programs, including problems with overreliance on commercial programs. Research about intervention or pullout programs at the secondary level, as well as research about programs in which content teachers work more closely with specialists or reading coaches, is a definite need.

Critical Factors for a Successful Pullout Model

In order for pullout models to work, there must be careful planning and collaboration between the reading specialist and classroom teachers. Reading specialists should be aware of what is occurring in classrooms, even though they are teaching students away from the classroom. One suggestion is that reading specialists spend some time in the classroom, observing students and teacher instruction. This experience provides the reading specialist with a better sense of how his or her students perform and behave when in a large-group or classroom setting. Moreover, it should be clear as to whether the instruction received in the pullout setting is supplemental or serves as the core program for students.

Ideas to Foster Effective Collaboration in Instructional Roles

Regardless of whether the reading specialist works in a pullout setting or goes into the classroom (or both), the following ideas have been helpful to reading specialists in fostering effective collaboration.

1. *Time.* Teachers appreciate the fact that the reading specialist is in their classroom as scheduled (even if the teachers are not quite ready for him or her). In talking with teachers about reading specialists, one of their primary complaints was that specialists did not arrive in their classroom when expected. Arriving and leaving on time are critical, as is adhering to the schedule when taking students from the classroom.

2. *Be prepared!* Have everything needed to teach a lesson, including magic markers, scissors, dictionaries, books for practice, and so on. If going into the classroom, do not assume that the teacher will have the material needed—or be willing or able to take the time to find it. Reading specialists who teach in classrooms have developed ingenious systems for organizing and carting materials, from using luggage with wheels to movable carts to milk carton containers.

3. *Discuss and establish responsibility.* The reading specialist and classroom teacher must decide early in the process who will be responsible for giving grades, writing report cards, and making telephone calls to parents about student performance.

4. *Offer to help.* As the reading specialist with expertise, think of ways to be helpful in the classroom. Perhaps the teacher is covering a special unit in which students need to take notes—this would be a great time to give a mini-lesson on note taking to the entire class. Or the teacher may be doing the midyear assessments with his or her students and need some help with students who have been absent.

5. *Meet your commitments.* Teachers have difficulty when reading specialists make changes in their plans, even if there are legitimate reasons for such changes (e.g., need to attend an Instructional Support Team meeting to discuss the needs of a specific student or a meeting requested by the principal). These unforeseeable occasions do happen, but to the degree possible, reading specialists should alert the teacher as soon as possible and make arrangements to reschedule.

6. *Be flexible!* Although the reading specialist may be on time and prepared, teachers and their classes may not be ready or even present. Assemblies, fire drills, health examinations, and many other events compel teachers to change or adjust their plans. These occurrences are, of course, frustrating to the reading specialist but may not be avoidable. *Adjusting* is the only helpful response. If some change needs to be made in the lesson (e.g., the teacher did not complete yesterday's lesson and wants to work with the entire group), the reading specialist can volunteer to assist by helping the students who may have difficulties completing the task or try to rearrange his or her schedule so that the plans can be implemented at a different time. Or it may be a time that the reading

specialist returns to his or her office or room to do some additional planning, or an opportunity to assess a child new to the school.

7. *Discuss the progress of the students with whom you are working.* This is especially important when working with students in a pullout setting. Let teachers know what students are learning and the success they are having. Such conversations help teachers better understand the needs of these students, and may open the door to more extended discussions about what can be done in the classroom to facilitate learning.

Summary

Although most reading specialists have instructional responsibilities, the way in which they fulfill them may vary. The key to enacting an effective instructional role is collaboration. Reading specialists must know how to work collaboratively with their colleagues to ensure effective instruction for students. There are many different ways of working collaboratively, some of which are more effective when working in the classroom and others more appropriate in pullout settings. Deciding where to work (in class or pullout) is not the key question to ask regarding instruction for struggling readers. Rather, reading specialists need to think about and identify their instructional goals and how best to achieve those goals, given the climate and culture of the school and the needs of the students. Moreover, the RTI initiative has generated the need for all school personnel to be involved in collaborative efforts to meet the differing needs of students.

Reflections

1. What do you think are the skills and abilities that reading specialists need if they are to work effectively in the classroom? In pullout settings? Both?
2. What skills and abilities do teachers need to work with reading specialists? In what ways are the skills and abilities needed by reading specialists and teachers the same? Different?
3. What types of lessons would work best with each of the approaches to collaborative teaching?

Activities

1. Observe a reading specialist in an in-class setting. Write a description of what he or she and the classroom teacher are doing. Which approach or approaches to collaborative teaching are used? What are your responses to these approaches?

2. Observe a reading specialist teaching students in a pullout setting. Write a description of what he or she is doing with students. (Be sure to ask the specialist how he or she made decisions about the instruction.)

3

The Instructional Role
Initiating, Implementing, and Evaluating

Chapter 2 provided a broad overview of the instructional role, focusing on the need for collaboration, approaches to collaborative teaching, and the strengths and limitations of two settings for instruction (i.e., in class and pullout). It also discussed the RTI initiative and what it means for reading specialists. This chapter explores ideas and issues that reading specialists need to address at various stages, for example, starting a new program, ongoing implementation issues, and evaluating results of the instructional program. When implementing an effective program, reading specialists need to understand (1) the culture of the school, (2) the importance of congruence between their instruction and that of the classroom teacher, and (3) approaches to scheduling that permit effective use of their time. The instructional role of reading specialists at the primary or beginning reading level, intermediate or middle school level, and the high school level is examined, and the need for obtaining feedback or evaluating the instructional program is explored.

Starting a New Program

In most instances, newly hired reading specialists step into a program that is already developed and most likely understood by faculty at the school. However, there are situations in which new reading specialists, or those who are working in a school, need to change or modify the current program. This has certainly occurred during the past several years as schools have attempted to implement approaches that meet RTI guidelines. Also, reading specialists often ask for suggestions about how to begin a new program; most often they are interested in how they can change from a pullout program to an in-class program or in how to coplan more closely with classroom teachers. In this section, I discuss ideas for those who are faced with such situations.

Getting the Evidence

Regardless of the type of program under consideration by the school administration, reading specialists and others associated with a possible change should read the literature and research that will help them substantiate their views. They must also share the literature with the classroom teachers who will be directly affected by the change(s). The information discussed in Chapter 2 should help reading specialists address ways to think about differentiating instruction to meet the needs of all students, and the advantages and limitations of pullout and in-class programs in relation to their own school and its student body.

Sharing the Evidence

As mentioned above, classroom teachers need to be part of the decision-making process. They should have opportunities to read the literature and talk with their colleagues and the reading specialists about how the new program will operate. They should feel free to raise their concerns and make suggestions about how the new program might function more effectively. At this time, scheduling teacher visits to other schools to observe ways in which these schools structure their programs are often helpful.

Getting Started

The best way to start a new program, especially an in-class one, is to begin with those who want to do it. Begin with volunteers! Once other teachers see that the program is an effective one for students, they will feel more comfortable about the changes. In school districts that have mandated changes in the instructional program (e.g., moving from pullout to in class), change is much more difficult. By working with volunteers, the reading specialists and the involved teachers can work out the "bugs," and the program will improve as it is expanded into other classrooms. One of my colleagues who worked with administrators often made the statement, "Make haste slowly"; I have become more convinced that this statement makes a great deal of sense!

At the present time, given the focus on accountability and RTI, which means meeting the needs of all students, teachers are becoming more accustomed to working collaboratively with support personnel in the school, not only with the reading specialist, but with special educators, volunteers, and paraprofessionals. Therefore, there tends to be more acceptance or at least acknowledgement that adults, other than the classroom teacher, will have some responsibility for working with students.

Ongoing Staff Development

Classroom teachers and reading specialists should participate in staff development, through which they learn more about how to collaborate and how to work effectively in the classroom. The school district may choose to bring in someone from outside the district who is familiar with the work of reading specialists or the importance of collaboration in providing for the instructional needs of all students. Or, a reading specialist and a classroom teacher who are working together could discuss and share with other teachers the work that they are doing in the school. They may also invite classroom teachers to observe them as they are working in the classroom. Again, teachers may be asked to read pertinent materials, for example, "IRA Commission on RTI: Working Draft of Guiding Principles" (2009), available on the International Reading Association's website (*www.reading.org*), in which six important notions about RTI are described. Or, they may wish to read articles that discuss collaboration between reading specialists and teachers (e.g., Ogle & Fogelberg [2001] or Bean [2001]), so that they are prepared to discuss the potential of any new approach to collaborative teaching and their role in it.

Again, regardless of whether specialists are initiating a new program, working with a school administrator who is undertaking such an effort, or working in an established program, they need to think about the culture of the school and the classrooms, the need for congruence between classroom work and special reading programs, and scheduling that maximizes the use of their time. These areas are discussed in the next sections.

The Culture of the School and Classrooms

Because reading specialists generally work with many different teachers in a school, they must become familiar with the school and its procedures, personnel, and climate. Reading specialists, for example, should have an effective working relationship with the principal, given the key leadership role of that position. How knowledgeable is the principal about reading instruction? How does he or she view the role of the reading specialist? How supportive of that role is he or she? A lack of understanding or agreement between the reading specialist and the principal regarding the specialist's role can create serious problems. In my work with Reading First in Pennsylvania, reading specialists serving in the role of literacy coaches indicated that they were successful in their roles only if a principal understood and supported them in their efforts (Zigmond & Bean, 2008). For example, the principal who lacks knowledge about the importance of collaboration may not arrange schedules that promote planning between specialists and classroom teachers. Or, a principal who asks reading specialists to evaluate or supervise teachers, especially those who are experiencing some teaching difficulties, may generate situations that limit the specialists' effectiveness in working collaboratively with teachers.

Likewise, reading specialists should have an understanding of teachers' expectations. Teachers who are not accustomed to an in-class approach may not be receptive to the presence of the reading specialist in their classrooms. Teachers do not always understand how they can or should function when there is another adult in the classroom. Some teachers have difficulty "giving up" their students; they are accustomed to providing all the instruction in the classroom. I am reminded of one teacher who told me how she planned for a specific story (one that she loved), including the "costume" she wore to introduce the story and the dramatic entrance that she made! Lacking an understanding of how an in-class model might work, she was distraught to think that some of her students would not have an opportunity to be part of her planned experience. Teachers who are insecure in their role might be threatened by the presence of another professional in the classroom. On the other hand, most teachers, given the staff development needed to learn how to teach collaboratively and the rationale for such instruction, are willing to try the new procedures, and again, given the demands in today's schools, more and more teachers are becoming accustomed to partnering with others.

Reading specialists and their teaching partners need to think carefully about the many different issues related to effective collaboration, especially if coteaching in the classroom is planned. Cook and Friend (1995) identify nine different topics that reading specialists and teachers should discuss on a regular basis: instructional beliefs, when and how to plan, parity issues, confidentiality issues, noise levels, classroom routines (instructional and organizational), discipline, feedback, and pet peeves.

Congruence or Alignment

As mentioned in the previous chapter, one of the concerns about pullout instruction is the lack of congruence or alignment between the
instruction provided by the reading specialist and that provided by the
classroom teacher. Such congruence is important for helping students
achieve in their own classrooms, which gives them a sense of self-worth
and satisfaction (i.e., "I can do it!").

Walp and Walmsley (1989) discuss three types of congruence:
philosophical, instructional, and procedural. They indicate that the
easiest form of congruence to achieve is *procedural*, where teachers
decide when and how they are going to work together in the classroom. How many times per week and for how long will the specialist be
there? What are the classroom management procedures? Who will do
what section of the lesson? How often will the reading specialist meet
with classroom teachers? How will they share information about students? *Instructional* congruence is more difficult to achieve, given the
need for both teachers to think reflectively about the strategies and
skills needed by students, how the teachers will present them, and what
materials they will use. Questions such as the following can be asked:
How will specialists work with specific students; for example, what
materials, approaches, and activities? What data are available to provide information to make decisions? What will the classroom teacher
be doing and with whom? Of course, *philosophical* congruence is most
difficult. Often, teachers working in the same school have similar goals
and objectives for each grade level and therefore are able to compro-
mise or agree to an approach that is best for students. But if each
teacher has deep-rooted beliefs about how reading should be taught
and these beliefs are not congruent, teachers may encounter extreme
difficulties working together. For example, a classroom teacher who is
deeply committed to a whole-language approach in which he or she
uses multiple texts and generates skill instruction based on student
needs, may be able to implement a successful reading program, using
this set of beliefs, in a manner in which *most* children in his or her
classroom are successful in learning to read. However, this teacher
may have difficulties working with a reading specialist who wants to

provide more structure and explicit instruction for those students who are not making progress.

Furthermore, in addition to differences in beliefs about instruction, teachers and specialists may have differences of opinion about how students should be disciplined and in procedures for classroom management. Some of the problems raised by specialists are those that relate to a few teachers' low expectations of students with learning problems and the disrespect shown toward these struggling readers. It is difficult for specialists to work in a classroom in which such behavior occurs, given that they have little authority or opportunity to intercede or change behavior.

Walp and Walmsley (1989) make clear that reading specialists and teachers within a school need to discuss the term *congruence* and what it means. They indicate, for example, that congruence may *not* mean "more of the same," nor does a "different" approach necessarily hinder congruence (p. 366). In fact, in some schools implementing RTI programs, students who are having more serious difficulties (often those identified as needing Tier 3 instruction) are taught using a more explicit approach; for example, Wilson Reading (Wilson, 1996) and the Sonday Reading System (*www.winsorlearning.com*). The key to effective congruence may be the ability of the teacher and specialist to discuss and share knowledge about their philosophical or theoretical approaches to reading instruction and why certain approaches to reading instruction may differ, depending on students' needs and abilities.

THINK ABOUT THIS

What do you think can be done when there are philosophical differences between teacher and specialist in their beliefs about reading or their approaches to classroom management?

The answers to this question are not easy or definitive. Sometimes the specialist can make a difference just by serving as a model. The fact that the reading specialist is an advocate for struggling readers may also make a difference. If there is serious concern about how teachers treat students, specialists may need to consult with supervisors regarding what can or should be done. Specialists, too, must have someone with whom they can share their experiences and problems.

Overall, teachers and specialists alike want to do their best to help students learn; therefore, it is infrequent that specialists find them themselves in unworkable situations. Nevertheless, they should be aware that such a situation can occur.

Making a Schedule

There is no easy solution for developing an effective schedule. It depends on the number of students with whom the reading specialist is required to work, the number of classrooms in which these students are placed, and the type of program the reading specialist wants or is required to develop. It also depends on the time allotted to the reading specialist for instruction. In some schools, reading specialists are assigned to instruction for every period of the day (except for the usual planning period and lunch). In other schools, reading specialists work with students for part of a day, and the remainder is used for various other activities, such as working with teachers or addressing assessment needs.

In the study of reading specialists in exemplary schools, the number of students with whom reading specialists worked varied from 20 to 80, with a mean of 52 (Bean, Swan, & Knaub, 2003). Certainly, the specialist assigned to 20 students can design a schedule that is very different from one responsible for working with 56 students. Issues that need to be addressed include the following:

- How often per week can the reading specialist meet with certain students (how should this vary, given the specific ages or difficulties of students)?
- Which students should be worked with in a pullout setting?
- In which classrooms can the reading specialist function effectively (or for what part of the lessons can the reading specialist function within the classroom)?

Working at Various Levels

In the following section, I describe the work of three reading specialists, each working at a different level. It will become obvious that the roles they fill have many similarities, even though there are also differences in how the specialists schedule their time and where they put their emphases.

Yvonne: A Reading Specialist in the Primary Grades

Yvonne is a certified Reading Recovery teacher and also serves as a reading specialist for kindergarten and first-grade students in one school in her district. During the afternoon, as part of her Reading Recovery role, she works with four first-grade students who have been identified as needing individualized support. She follows the procedures and strategies required as part of the Reading Recovery program, seeing each student for 30 minutes a day.

In the morning, Yvonne schedules her time so that she can work in the classrooms of the three kindergarten and first-grade teachers (see Figure 3.1). She also meets with each grade-level team once every 2 weeks, during which time she and the teachers discuss (1) the specific skills, strategies, and content that teachers will be presenting; (2) any data the teachers have about students; and (3) specific students who are experiencing difficulty and what instruction might help them.

Yvonne works in each of the first-grade classrooms three times a week. On 2 days, she assists the classroom teacher who is presenting an activity-based phonics lesson to the whole class; this activity requires children to manipulate letter cards on their desks. She walks around helping individual students who are having difficulty. In one of the first-grade classrooms, she conducts the lesson so that the teacher, new to the district, can learn the procedure. In this classroom, the teacher monitors the students' work. Often, if there is time after this mini-lesson is completed, Yvonne pulls aside a few students and asks them to read material in which they can apply the skills they are learning. (The other students write their new words in a journal or complete assigned work.) One day, Yvonne works with a small group that needs additional review of the skills taught that week. While she is teaching that group, the teacher is either holding reading conferences or teaching another group that may also need additional help with some strategy or skill. The groups change each week, depending on the needs of the students.

In the beginning of the year, in the kindergarten classrooms, Yvonne and the teachers focus on phonemic awareness activities. Either she or

Time	M	T	W	Th	Fri
8:30–9:10	Gr. 1-A	Kdg. A	Gr. 1-A	Kdg. A	Gr. 1-A
9:15–9:55	Gr. 1-B	Kdg. B	Gr. 1-B	Kdg. B	Gr. 1-B
10:00–10:40	Gr. 1-C	Kdg. C	Gr. 1-C	Kdg. C	Gr. 1-C
10:45–11:15	Planning Time 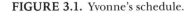				
11:20–12:10	Lunch				
12:15–3:30	Reading Recovery/Planning/Preparation Period				

FIGURE 3.1. Yvonne's schedule.

the teacher teaches the lesson while the other assists and reinforces the students' work. These lessons last only 15 minutes. Then Yvonne works in one of the centers that has been set up in the classroom, generally assisting students who have been identified as needing help with letter recognition or concepts of print. Yvonne also helps when there is a writing activity, taking dictation as students tell her what they want to say. Yvonne and the kindergarten teachers have also agreed that there is a small number of students in each of the kindergarten classrooms who would benefit from additional small-group or Tier 2 instruction for more focused oral language and vocabulary experiences. Yvonne is revising her schedule so that she can work with these six students for 15 minutes, 2 days a week, using a form of interactive reading, ELL Storybook Intervention, that she read about in the Walpole and McKenna book, *Differentiated Reading Instruction: Strategies for the Primary Grades* (2008).

THINK ABOUT THIS

What do you think are the strengths of this plan for the reading specialist?

What do you see as potential problems with Yvonne's schedule?

In what ways is Yvonne supporting the professional growth of teachers?

How can Yvonne change her schedule to make room for this small-group instruction with kindergarten students?

Greg: A Reading Specialist at the Intermediate Level

Greg works in a setting where the intermediate teachers, grades 4–6, teach either the language arts block or math, science, and social studies. His major role is to provide instruction for struggling readers. At the same time, the principal has asked him to serve as a resource to teachers and has allowed him to develop a schedule that provides him with that opportunity (see Figure 3.2). Greg works in the classrooms two times a week with the six teachers responsible for teaching the language arts block. This schedule necessitates careful planning so that when he is in the classroom, he can work productively. During his time in the classrooms, he works with small groups needing additional support with vocabulary or comprehension skills. He may also assist by holding conferences with students about their writing. On Fridays, Greg's schedule allows him to work where needed. He may work with students who have special needs or with teachers who are addressing a specific issue or

Schedule	M	T	W	Th	F
Period 1	Gr. 4-A	Gr. 4-B	Gr. 4-A	Gr. 4-B	float
Period 2	Gr. 5-A	Gr. 5-B	Gr. 5-A	Gr. 5-B	float
Period 3	Gr. 6-A	Gr. 6-B	Gr. 6-A	Gr. 6-B	float
Lunch					
Period 5	Work with math/science/social studies teachers, assessment/planning with teachers				
Period 6	Same as period 5				
Period 7	Planning ⟶				

FIGURE 3.2. Greg's schedule.

topic (e.g., outlining). He also uses this time to assess students about whom the teachers are concerned.

Greg works with the content area teachers to help them incorporate literacy instruction in their content teaching. He has gone into classrooms to work with students on study skills or to conduct mini-lessons requested by the teachers. He did a lesson on writing a research report (how to organize it) for the sixth-graders who were given this assignment in social studies. He also did a demonstration lesson, introducing the students and the teacher to the "know, want to know, learn" (K-W-L) strategy (Ogle, 1986) as a means of activating prior knowledge, and creating enthusiasm and an organizational framework for the unit on machines and how they work (for the fifth-grade science teacher). At times, Greg plans with the various content teachers during his afternoon periods. Greg is now planning to work with Kelly, a sixth-grade social studies teacher who has admitted that she spends too much time "talking at kids" and wants to improve the way in which she uses small-group discussion in her classroom. Greg shared with Kelly information from Alvermann and Phelps's text, *Content Reading and Literacy: Succeeding in Today's Diverse Classrooms* (2002) about how to hold effective small-group discussions that recommended assigning clear and manageable tasks, preparing and guiding students, setting limits, monitoring and assisting group work, holding a whole-class follow-up, and serving as a model (p. 289). After discussing these points, Greg and Kelly decided that they would collaborate in introducing this approach to the students, with Greg leading the way for the first two lessons; both would monitor and assist the students in their groups. For the third lesson, Kelly would introduce and present the discussion tasks while Greg observed since Kelly wanted some feedback about how well she was able to lead such discussions. Both agreed that it would be important for them to work together for at least four or five lessons over the next month.

THINK ABOUT THIS

What skills do you think are essential if Greg is to be successful in this situation? What problems does Greg face with this schedule? What are your responses to the work that Greg is planning to do with Kelly; the pacing and structure? What additional knowledge and skills does he need to lead these discussion groups? Any possible pitfalls?

Brenda: A High School Reading Specialist

Brenda is the *only* reading specialist in a large high school, making her job a very difficult one. She has a flexible schedule, except for three periods each day when she teaches small groups of ninth-graders who scored at a low level on a reading assessment measure given at the beginning of the school year, or those recommended by teachers as needing help to pass the state competency test given in the spring. During the other periods, Brenda makes arrangements to work with a small number of teachers while they are teaching a specific unit. She believes that spending more time in a particular classroom (perhaps almost every day while the unit is being taught) gives her the opportunity to become better acquainted with the students and their needs and with the teaching style and goals of the classroom teacher. Thus, during one 4-week period, Brenda team-taught with the civics teacher a unit about American democracy. In one lesson, Brenda presented information on note taking, after which the teacher gave a short lecture to the class about the topic of voting rights and responsibilities. Brenda and the teacher then had the students work in small groups to compare their notes and to discuss how note taking had helped them organize the material. Brenda also did a mini-lesson, using the classroom textbook. Her goal was to help students develop a better understanding of how the text was organized, the ways in which the author identified important information, and how they could take annotated notes that would improve their understanding of the text. During this same time period, Brenda worked with a biology teacher using the same collaborative model.

Brenda's other responsibilities include assessing students at the request of teachers and working informally with teachers who want to talk to her about students or instruction that facilitates students' understanding of text material. Brenda also shoulders the major responsibility for making presentations to faculty that address how they might improve their instruction by using various reading strategies. Next month, she will give a short presentation on how teachers might help students write summaries of what they have read. She will also volunteer to demonstrate this strategy in classrooms. Just this week, the principal and other members of the school's leadership team met to discuss the importance of literacy across the curriculum as a means of improving student learning overall. The school has the opportunity to participate in a funded project in which volunteer teachers and members of the leadership team could attend workshops on literacy and how it can improve content area teaching. Brenda is excited about this opportunity and the chance to work more closely with teachers from the various academic disciplines, but she wonders how she will be able to manage this work, given her teaching responsibilities.

THINK ABOUT THIS

What skills and abilities do you think Brenda needs to be successful in her position? One of Brenda's difficulties is finding the time to work with all the teachers who have requested her assistance. What suggestions or recommendations would you make to Brenda? What are some possibilities that Brenda can consider that may enable her to work more closely with teachers as they begin to implement this new approach to content area teaching?

Henwood, a reading specialist at the high school level, described her role as a collaborative one (1999–2000). Although she works with students, she most frequently works alongside the teacher in planning and implementing lessons. She sees herself as a resource for both teachers and students. Henwood stated empathetically that she does not want colleagues to regard her as an expert giving advice. "Instead, I needed to be considered a partner in improving the learning of all students, one who complemented the teacher's knowledge of content with knowledge of the learning process that I possessed as a reading specialist" (1999–2000, p. 317). Her instructional work is based on the needs of the students as identified by the teachers. She has opportunities to work with many different teachers and students. For example, she describes helping students learn to write a research paper, assisting one teacher who wanted to change her classroom practice from teacher centered to student centered, and helping another teacher convince students that their reading ability could be improved.

Reading Specialists at the Middle and High School Levels

What should be obvious from the schedules of the reading specialists described above is that all, primary through high school, have some instructional responsibility. All need to know how to work with struggling readers either individually, in small groups, or as a class. And all need to know how to work collaboratively with the classroom teacher to identify student needs regarding what is required in the classroom curriculum and which strategies or skills the students might need to become successful readers.

As we move through the grades, however, there are differences in how reading specialists function. There is much more emphasis on reading to learn in the intermediate and upper grades; therefore, the reading specialist at those levels needs to be extremely knowledgeable not only about how students learn to read but about how students use reading to learn. They must also be comfortable working with content area teachers who are generally experts in their specific field. Frequently, as mentioned by Henwood (1999–2000), reading specialists at the high school level actually serve more in a resource capacity to teachers than in a direct instructional role. Given that high school reading specialists work with so many teachers, often they work with students only indirectly. Chapter 4 provides additional information about serving as a resource to teachers.

Indeed, there are many middle schools and high schools in which there are no reading specialists. However, given the national data that indicate that there are still large numbers of adolescents experiencing reading difficulties (Biancarosa & Snow, 2004; International Reading Association, 1999), there is clearly a need for professionals with expertise in teaching reading to work with students and their teachers. The adolescent position statement published by the International Reading Association (1999) recommends that individual students who have difficulty learning how to read be served by reading specialists; services should include the following:

> providing tutorial reading instruction that is part of a comprehensive program connected with subject matter teachers, parents, and the community;
>
> structuring challenging, relevant situations in special reading classes and in subject matter classrooms where students succeed and become self-sufficient learners;
>
> assessing students' reading and writing—and enabling students to assess their own reading and writing—to plan instruction, foster individuals' control of their literacy, and immediately support learners when progress diminishes;

teaching vocabulary, fluency, comprehension, and study strategies tailored
to individuals' competencies;

relating literacy practices to life-management issues such as exploring
careers, examining individuals' roles in society, setting goals, manag-
ing time and stress, and resolving conflicts; and

offering reading programs that recognize potentially limiting forces such
as work schedules, family responsibilities, and peer pressures. (p. 8)

This list of services should be useful to specialists who are working in
middle and high schools as they think about their own job descriptions
and how they function in the schools.

In the vignette on pages 60–63, Jennifer, a high school reading
specialist, describes her role, discussing the fact that her major role is
instruction, although she works informally with teachers to help them
think about how to improve their content area teaching to address the
literacy needs of students. On the other hand, Katy, whose vignette
appears in Chapter 7 (pp. 151–153), who is assigned to work as a literacy coach at a middle school, has little responsibility for instructing
students. Most of her time is spent working with teachers, using data to
help them think about how to plan and implement appropriate instruction in the classrooms.

Getting Feedback (Evaluating the Program)

It is important for reading specialists to solicit feedback about their
work so that they have the information they need to improve. I suggest
that reading specialists think of ways to gather feedback from teachers
on a regular basis. For example, midway through the year, the reading
specialist might ask teachers to complete a simple questionnaire that
raises questions important to the successful functioning of the program (see Figure 3.3). Or, the reading specialist might choose to talk
with individual teachers about the program. In that case, the questionnaire in Chapter 2 (see Figure 2.2) might provide the impetus for such
discussion. The specialist may also want to discuss the program with a
supervisor or the principal and other specialists. Reflecting on what has
been successful and what has not is an important process for program
improvement.

A more formal evaluation might involve analyzing the impact of
the program on the students. At the end of the year, reading specialists can review the achievement data on the students with whom they
have worked. How much progress have these students made? Has the
program been a successful one for them? If so, in what ways? Chapter 9
provides ideas for assessing student performance.

Dear Teacher:

I am interested in getting feedback from you about the program that you and I are implementing. Both of us want to help students learn to read successfully. Therefore, I would appreciate your response to the following questions. If you would feel more comfortable discussing these with me, I would certainly be happy to sit down with you.

1. Have you seen any improvement in the performance of struggling readers in your classroom?

        None   Some   A lot

Please elaborate:

2. Have you seen any improvement in the attitude of struggling readers in your classroom?

        None   Some   A lot

Please elaborate:

3. How easy has it been for you to make a schedule that enables us to work together?

        Easy   Not easy

4. What can be done to make scheduling easier?

5. What has been the most positive part of our working together?

6. What has been the most difficult aspect of program implementation?

7. Any suggestions for program improvement?

Thank you,

_____
Reading Specialist

FIGURE 3.3. Getting feedback from teachers.

Summary

Reading specialists must be able to initiate new programs and work effectively in those that are ongoing. They may be assigned to work in an instructional role at various levels in the schools. Regardless of the level at which they work, specialists need to have an understanding of the culture of the schools to which they are assigned and a good working relationship with school personnel. Likewise, given the need to work collaboratively with teachers, the issue of instructional congruence is an important one; struggling readers need experiences that will help them integrate what they are learning from several teachers. Reading specialists at all levels need to be experts on reading curriculum, instruction, and assessment. Reading specialists at the upper levels need to have an understanding of how students use reading to learn. At all levels, specialists must be able to work collaboratively with other adults. Getting feedback from those with whom they work can provide a basis for program improvement.

Reflections

At what level would you feel most comfortable working? What qualifications do you have that made you choose that level?

Activities

1. Ask a reading specialist to share his or her schedule with you. How similar is that schedule to the ones described in this chapter? What are the specialist's views about his or her schedule (e.g., any problems, why the schedule developed in that way, what is helpful about the schedule, etc.)?

2. Discuss the following scenario with other reading specialists or classmates. As a reading specialist, you have been assigned to work with several intermediate-grade teachers who teach reading in an in-class program. You have heard other teachers talk about one of them, Frank, as a really tough teacher who makes his students "toe the line." You see yourself as a teacher who "lets kids have some fun." You give students permission to talk informally and share personal stories, believing that struggling readers need a low-risk environment in which to succeed. You are worried! What do you think you should do? (Remember, there is no right answer in this situation; what might work best as you begin your work with Frank?)

Jennifer: Reading Specialist in an Urban High School

Some questions to think about:

What lessons can be learned about the role of the reading specialist from this vignette?
What questions come to mind from reading this vignette?
What key characteristics make Jennifer an effective reading specialist?

I am a reading specialist at a charter high school. As a charter school, we have a diverse student population as students come from both urban and suburban school districts as well as private schools. City High has a population of about 550 students with a cap of 156 students per grade level. The school design provides for grade-level teams that follow the same class of students through the 4-year high school cycle. When I am with the ninth and tenth grades I teach a reading support class, Reading Strategies, and when I am with the eleventh and twelfth grades I teach English electives, administer reading assessments, and provide support to the English teacher who is assigned to the Reading Strategies class. As the only reading specialist in the school and also a classroom teacher, I have multiple roles that keep my days very busy. I discuss my responsibilities related to assessment, instruction, and leadership below.

Assessment

In the first days of every school year, I help organize the informal assessment of all ninth-grade students, collaborating with the math support teacher. We have a short window of time—2 days—to assess all students and determine whether they should be scheduled into a foreign language elective or our Reading and Math Strategies elective, where they can receive support in the skill development that they need to succeed in high school. We administer Globe Fearon's Secondary Reading Assessment Inventory (2000) in a 1-hour time frame. The assessment is a quick reading comprehension assessment with reading passages on varying grade levels. Students are asked to read a passage as many times as they want and then answer comprehension questions without using the passage. It is not the ideal assessment to determine the skill deficiencies of students but when you only have 1 hour to assess, it is a quick way to get an overview of students' reading ability. The math support teacher also administers a skills inventory and the data of the two assessments are compared to determine scheduling.

Once a student is scheduled into our Reading and Math Strategies class, each student is evaluated in more detail. I work with another English teacher in the mornings, who helps assess the students who have been placed in the class I teach. Our goal, through assessment, is to get a better idea of each student's strengths and weaknesses so that I can make individualized decisions for instruction. The process I have instituted for the individualized assessments includes a review of students' transcripts from their previous school for classes that they were in, their grades, and absences; and a brief interview with the students about their background, feelings about reading, and what they see as their strengths and weaknesses in reading. I then administer the Qualitative Reading Inventory (Leslie & Caldwell, 2006) and the Slosson Oral Reading Assessment (Slosson & Nicholson, 2002). At times, if a student is at a very low reading level, I also use the Developmental Reading Assessment Grades 4–8 (Beaver & Carter, 2003) to get a better idea of the specific areas he or she is struggling with.

Upon completion of the assessment process, the classroom teacher and I create a personal reading profile of each student that summarizes the data we collected and the standardized testing data (if it is available). Each profile addresses specific suggestions for instruction and also contains an area for informal notes about instructional strategies that have seemed to promote progress, and decisions that have been made for future support. Using specific data about each student definitely impacts instruction as it can become more tailored to students' specific needs as teachers follow their progress.

Classroom Instruction

The largest part of my role as a reading specialist is to teach two sections of Reading Strategies in ninth grade and two sections in tenth grade every day. Each of our trimester grading periods runs 13 weeks. The math support teacher and I split each section in half, to give us smaller classes, and teach our half for 6.5 weeks; then we switch. So we are both teaching the same prep two times each trimester per section. It provides for more work in planning but it also gives us the flexibility of individualizing instruction, given the small number of students we have. Most of the classes have around 20 students total, so we have about 10 or fewer students for the 6.5-week period.

Most of my students think that reading is "orally reading something" and that comprehension will just occur naturally. I am constantly telling them that they can't just read something quickly and hope it sinks in but instead need to be active to really understand. Any student, regardless of reading comprehension level, can benefit from being more active while he or she is reading. Because I do not have time to pull students to work on remediation of basic skills, teaching them the skills to be "actively engaged" in reading is my main focus in all of my classes.

In the ninth-grade class, I begin with a preview, setting a purpose by posing questions, using a note-taking key while reading, asking questions while reading, and pulling all of the information together in the end to fully comprehend what was read. I use one novel in the class per trimester that is high interest, lower reading level that supports the themes in the English classes, for example, we read *Autobiography of My Dead Brother* by Walter Dean Myers (2005) when the English teacher was focusing on *Identity*.

The note-taking key I teach is a simple three-symbol key and the students love it when I show them my own books completely marked up with the same three symbols. These keys are

! next to anything that is part of the main idea or is a main event

? next to anything the student does not understand when they come up with a question while they are reading

✓ next to anything that they want to respond to in a personal way (I usually tell them that this is something they agree with, disagree with, or somehow relate to)

New vocabulary is also a focus; I emphasize using context clues and connection to prior knowledge as ways to learn unknown vocabulary. Another important part of the curriculum at both the ninth- and tenth-grade levels is a trimester-long independent reading project. Each student chooses an overall goal for the project, at the beginning of the trimester, such as understanding more while reading or improving his or her oral reading skills. Every Friday, after completing a formal assessment for the week, the students choose a specific goal for the day that relates to their overall goal, such as asking more questions while they read or stopping at the end of each paragraph to make sure they understand what they have read before moving on. Students choose from reading materials that I provide such as novels, graphic novel collections, magazines, or reading material they have brought from home. The students then have the rest of the class period to read and complete their goal for the day. Each Friday, they complete a summary sheet for what they read that includes the goal they chose, the title of what they read, how many pages they read, whether they reached their goal or not, how they know whether they reached their goal, and three important pieces of information they learned from what they read. At the end of the trimester the students put together a summary of whether they met their overall goal, what went well, what they want to improve next time, and what evidence they have from their weekly goal sheets that support their findings.

My goal for the independent reading project is for the students to be able to choose material they want to read, be more self-aware of what they need to improve, allow them to take steps on their own to improve those areas, and also to enjoy reading. Most of my students do not enjoy reading because they have struggled for so long with reading in school. When they are able to be honest with themselves about what they need help with and choose their own reading material, something tends to click. They realize that it doesn't have to be a burdensome process and they can enjoy reading in and outside of school. It is my view that I am not just supporting students who struggle with reading to improve so that they can get higher grades or do well on a standardized test, but most importantly I am trying to give them the self-motivation to read more and read for enjoyment. If the students are reading more with the strategies that I am teaching, then they will improve and may begin to view reading as less of a chore and more of a process that is everywhere around them; one that does not need to intimidate them.

Leadership

The biggest area I struggle with as a reading specialist, is as a leader. My schedule is so packed with the four classes I teach, the assessments I administer, the personal reading profiles I write for each of my students, and all of the other general school responsibilities I have, that I do not get to coach or support teachers directly. I consider myself a quiet leader who does things behind the scenes and not as overtly as other teacher leaders. I am a resource for information about students and their abilities when someone has a question about how to help them. I provide ideas, graphic organizers, and book-choice ideas to teachers who are planning classes that have students with a wide range of reading abilities. I have mentored two English teachers who help with reading assessment and then teach a strategies class, similar to what I teach. I believe that leadership does not always have to be direct and obvious to the outside observer. I try to serve as a leader by working away at what I do and being a good example. This seems to work better than if I try to tell others what they should do.

Words of Advice

I love what I do even on the days that it is very difficult. As a reading specialist, the days are never predictable. Flexibility and willingness to work "on the fly" is vital in the classroom with students or when supporting teachers. The dynamics are constantly changing and one needs to go with it at all times! Sometimes I find myself confused and at a loss for what to do for a student who is "hitting a wall." When I first started as a reading specialist, I beat myself up often in those situations. I thought if I was an expert in reading, then I should know what to do. The bottom line is that every student is different. Students will have good days, bad days, will catch on to concepts easily one day, and on the next day, give up and put their heads down! I've found that I don't always have an immediate answer as to what to do for a student. Sometimes it takes a day, week, or month to figure out how to best help a student. The one thing that I try to do every day for every student is to be a source of understanding, support, and encouragement. Many struggling readers feel so bad about themselves and their ability that having someone who is there for them will likely impact their overall progress more than the best mini-lesson on using context clues ever could.

JENNIFER JURIGA, MEd
Reading Specialist
City Charter High School
Pittsburgh, Pennsylvania

4

Leadership of the Reading Specialist
What Does It Mean?

> You can accomplish much if you don't care who gets the credit.
> —RONALD REAGAN

These words of wisdom have been attributed to several leaders; they are important ones for reading specialists who find themselves in a leadership position. The instructional role of the reading specialist seems to be a given, accepted by administrators, teachers, and reading specialists themselves; generally, it is clearly understood by all. Less clear-cut, however, is the leadership role that must be assumed if the reading specialist is to have an impact not only on individual students but on the school as a whole. As mentioned in Chapter 1, the position statement accepted by the board of the International Reading Association (2000a) calls for leadership by reading specialists, suggesting that in that role, they can exert an influence on the overall reading program and reading performance of all students in the school. As also indicated previously, in a study of reading specialists in exemplary schools (Bean, Swan, & Knaub, 2003), 100% of the principals in those schools indicated that specialists were important to the success of the reading programs. In addition, in follow-up interviews with a number of the reading specialists, they indicated that they spent much of their time in leadership activities, such as serving as a resource to teachers, conducting professional development, leading curriculum development efforts, and working with other professionals and community members to improve the students' achievement. All but one of the reading specialists interviewed had instructional responsibilities; nevertheless, in varying degrees all were very much involved in leadership activities.

64

Moreover, at the present time, reading specialists at all levels are being recruited to fill coaching positions in their schools, which requires excellent leadership, interpersonal, and communication skills. Also, International Reading Association Standards 2010, currently being developed, are putting more emphases on this leadership role, given the demands of the field.

In the position statement about the Role of the Reading Specialist (International Reading Association, 2000a), leadership is divided into three components: serving as a resource to others, professional development, and literacy program development and coordination. This chapter discusses qualities and characteristics of effective leadership, working with groups, and serving as a resource to others. Chapter 5 focuses on professional development; Chapters 6 and 7 on coaching as a specific way of serving as a resource to teachers and providing "job-embedded" professional development, respectively; and Chapter 8, on the development of school reading programs.

What Is Leadership?

Given the many different ways in which individuals define leadership, offering yet another definition is not an easy task. Some think of leadership in terms of the role an individual fills, such as the role of principal. Others see it as synonymous with control or influence, suggesting that anyone who can require or influence certain behaviors in others, has leadership qualities. For example, teachers may be influenced by an experienced teacher who is well respected by peers for his or her ability to teach and willingness to state his or her position about various school issues. Others see leadership as a set of behaviors; an individual can be a leader by exhibiting certain behaviors associated with leadership, such as solving problems creatively, obtaining commitments from others, or resolving conflicts. Certainly specific traits or qualifications enhance leadership (e.g., ability to communicate well with others, effective interpersonal skills). Likewise, style (e.g., democratic, laissez-faire, authoritative) can influence the way in which one leads. A specific principal might be characterized as very demanding or known as someone who "leads in a top–down manner" (authoritative); another principal might be someone who involves teachers in decision making and aims for consensus of teachers for solving problems. Leadership in this text is defined as any activities or set of activities associated with working with others to accomplish a common goal: that of improving student learning, especially as related to literacy. This definition is closer to the notion of "shared leadership" described by Lambert (1998). She stated that everyone in the school setting has "the potential and right to work as a leader" (p. 9) and that informal leadership in schools can greatly influence school change efforts. Reading specialists often are expected to lead by influence or by their own personal power (Kaser, Mundry, Stiles, & Loucks-Horsley, 2002).

In fact, most reading or literacy coaches, employed as instructional rather than administrative personnel, do not have the "authority" to require teachers to make changes. Most often they suggest or recommend possible instructional changes. And, although some reading coaches lament this lack of authority, most who write about coaching view the coach's role as collegial rather than evaluative or authoritative.

But reading specialists whose major responsibility is instructing struggling readers can also serve effectively in a leadership role. Say, for example, the school wants to select a new reading textbook. The reading specialist has worked in classrooms with teachers and is well aware of the strengths and limitations of the current textbook. He or she also is familiar with most of the available series, has experience in serving on textbook selection committees, and knows the research on reading instruction. The reading specialist, therefore, may well be the best person to serve in a leadership role on a committee to select a new textbook. Another reading specialist may take the lead in helping several new teachers who have questions about the most effective ways to use flexible grouping in their classroom, while a reading specialist at the middle or high school level may lead the study group meetings being scheduled to discuss literacy across the curriculum. Leaders are those who promote positive change and inspire and empower others to participate in the process. They lead not only by the power of persuasion but by the power of example. As Covey (2004) states, "Leadership is communicating to people their worth and potential so clearly that they come to see it in themselves (p. 98). In other words, leadership sets into motion leadership in others.

Characteristics and Qualifications of Leaders

"I think everyone can be a leader. The key is for people to see themselves as being someone who can make a difference."
"One of the important things about leadership is being yourself!"
"True leaders are loyal to those who are under them."
"You have to be reliable. When you tell someone you are going to do something, you need to do it!"

THINK ABOUT THIS

Think of a leader you know and respect. What qualifications or traits does he or she exhibit? What impact does/did that individual have on your behavior? Do you agree with the four statements above about leadership? Why or why not? What traits or characteristics do you associate with effective leadership?

The statements above reflect thoughts about characteristics of effective leaders. Just as the definitions of leadership vary, so too do personal views of it, some emphasizing a focus on directing an activity or group, and others seeing it as facilitative behavior. The key is that in schools, everyone—teachers, specialists, and administrators—can serve in a leadership role. When a teacher chairs a committee to select a new textbook, he or she is assuming a leadership role. When reading specialists sit down with a new teacher to discuss how to teach struggling readers in the classroom, they are serving in a leadership role. So too when teachers work with a group of volunteer tutors or with student teachers assigned to them for their field experiences. The following five qualifications are seen as contributing to effective leadership: ability to communicate, teamwork, empowerment, goal seeking (having a vision or direction), and respect for others.

Communication Skills

Active Listening

Seek first to understand, then to be understood.
—COVEY (1989, p. 235)

Covey (1989), in his book *The 7 Habits of Highly Effective People*, presents this notion as one of the important principles designed to help individuals work with each other effectively. Of course, we know how to listen; we do it all the time! However, as Covey (2004) indicates, too often, individuals listen from "within their own frame of reference" (p. 192). He describes a listening continuum that includes "ignoring, pretend listening, selective listening, attentive listening, and empathic listening—only the highest, empathic listening, is done within the frame of reference of the other person" (p. 192). Too often, we listen from our own frame of reference because we are busy evaluating, interpreting, or preparing our responses rather than trying to understand what the person is attempting to communicate. Active listening is one of the key skills of an effective leader. It shows respect and creates trust, essential for effective communication. The following behaviors contribute to active listening:

1. *Focus on the speaker's message.* Listen to the message for both content, what the speaker is saying, and feelings. Look for cues that indicate how the speaker feels (e.g., facial expression, body language, posture). For example, a teacher who is telling the reading specialist about the negative classroom behavior of a particular student, in describing the behaviors, may be feeling confused, unhappy, or even angry about the situation. The active listener understands both the content and the feelings of the message.

2. *Test your understanding by rephrasing in your own words what you heard the speaker say.* You may also need to ask questions, especially when you are not certain that you have understood the message. Covey (1989) suggests that the listener (1) mimic content (i.e., repeat what is said), (2) rephrase content, and (3) rephrase content and reflect feelings (pp. 248–249). In other words, there is a need to *clarify* and *confirm* what we are hearing as well as acknowledge the feelings we are perceiving.

3. *Provide nonverbal indications of active listening.* Effective listeners understand the importance of nonverbal indicators of active listening: They smile and acknowledge that they are listening by nodding in agreement. They sit in ways that show their interest in the subject and in the listener. Some researchers have indicated that much of effective listening has to do with these nonverbal aspects. Think about an experience you've had, perhaps in talking with a salesperson, or trying to get information when your airplane flight has been cancelled. It's very easy to determine whether that individual is engaged in active listening!

4. *Encourage elaboration.* When listeners are asked to "say more," or to expand on what they are saying, they are more likely to share in-depth their concerns or issues. They will also recognize that they can trust the individual with whom they are speaking.

5. *Stay away from interrupting the speaker or finishing sentences*! In their book *Joining Together: Group Theory and Group Skills*, Johnson and Johnson (2003) emphasize the importance of nonevaluative listening, indicating that one of the barriers to effective communication is the tendency of individuals to make judgments as they are listening to a speaker. Have you ever found yourself thinking about your reply while another is speaking? Or interrupting a speaker before he or she has finished a sentence? Such behavior is not part of active listening; it not only limits the listener's understanding of the message but can create a negative attitude on the part of the speaker.

Clear, Congruent Speaking

Johnson and Johnson (2003, p. 140) provide important insights about sending messages. Their list is adapted below.

1. *Own messages by using first-person-singular pronouns.* If you have a particular feeling or opinion about an issue, make certain that you indicate this directly, for example, by saying, "I really have problems with ability grouping; these are the reasons."

2. *Make your verbal and nonverbal messages congruent.* As mentioned previously, nonverbal communication is important. Even though you may have a positive message to relate to others, a frown on your face or lack of expression may reduce the impact of that message to others. Listeners attend to more than words: They notice the tone and the nonverbal cues. I had an interesting experience in observing a second-grade teacher. Although the lesson was effective, the teacher never smiled or expressed any emotion, even when she complimented certain students on their performance. After the lesson, I asked the teacher whether she still enjoyed teaching (she had taught for many years). Interestingly, she responded, "Oh, yes, I just have a permanent frown on my face. My students understand that I care." In other words, she was well aware of the nonverbal message that she sent, but she also believed that her students saw past her expression to her unexpressed caring. I wonder, however, about the impact of this behavior on students, especially those who were struggling in her classroom. And I was fascinated to discover that she quickly related my question to her facial expressions! (Had others mentioned this to her?)

3. *Ask for feedback about the message.* Taking the time to ask listeners to restate your message or to ask for questions tells you whether you and your listeners are "on the same page" and whether any confusion exists.

THINK ABOUT THIS

Think about your own communication skills. What do you think are your personal strengths? Possible trouble spots? What communication qualities do you appreciate in others?

Teamwork

None of us is as smart as all of us.
—BLANCHARD, BOWLES, CAREW,
    AND PARISE-CAREW (2001, p. 60)

The ability to work as part of a team is an especially important competency for reading specialists, because most frequently the leadership role is one of influence rather than authority. In other words, the reading specialist must be able to motivate others to work together to improve the school reading program. Reading specialists often work with groups or teams of teachers (e.g., committees, grade-level groups, subject area groups). The following standards can be used in shaping effective teamwork:

- The atmosphere is comfortable and relaxed.
- Everyone feels as though he or she has an important role in the group, and everyone participates.
- Group members listen to each other.
- Leadership shifts from individual to individual, depending on experience or expertise.
- The group works effectively as a unit to achieve its tasks.
- Group members are conscious of how the group is functioning (i.e., they are aware of the interpersonal and communication skills between and among group members).

I recommend Johnson and Johnson's (2003) *Joining Together* for those who want to read more about working with groups. They discuss in a clear manner the importance of attending to both *task* and *maintenance* responsibilities of a group. That is, there is a goal to be met, and group members need to work in ways that enable them to focus on that goal. If the group is not staying on task, someone in the group must remind members of their goal; often this is the designated leader. The leader must also be conscious of the importance of maintaining a climate that enhances the members' ability to work comfortably and effectively with each other. Ideas and comments made by members should be received in a receptive manner; all members must be encouraged to participate in the conversation.

When reading specialists are asked to work with groups, they must remember that it takes time for the members to begin to think and work as a group, and to move from divergent to convergent thinking. Often, leaders become disappointed or disillusioned when, after one or two meetings, it appears as though no progress is being made. All groups go through what Kaner, Lind, Toldi, Fiski, and Berger (1996, p. 20) call "a groan zone," before they begin to function effectively; they move from divergent to convergent thinking.

Empowerment

The most effective schools are those in which teachers feel as though they have a voice in what happens; they feel a sense of ownership or empowerment. There are several ways in which leaders can empower others. First, they can recognize the work of others, thus identifying colleagues as leaders. They can also encourage others to actively participate, thus promoting leadership behaviors. For example, the reading specialist may ask an individual teacher to lead a workshop session in which he or she discusses classroom management. In a group setting, the reading specialist as leader may solicit ideas and thoughts of particular group members, especially those who tend to be reticent to speak but who often have great ideas to share. The reading specialist also can provide opportunities for decision making that require group consensus or participation. For example:

> We've come up with three different ideas about how we want to promote parent involvement in our schools. Let's talk about each of these, and what they mean in terms of planning and implementation. I think all of us as a group need to decide whether we will attempt to do all of these or will focus on just one. After listing pros and cons, we should try to come to a consensus as to our future direction.

Achieving Goals

This characteristic of effective leadership is what some would call "the bottom line": the ability of the leader to get the job done. Without a sense of direction, a goal, or a vision, little can be accomplished. When a decision is needed (e.g., about materials or a curriculum issue), the leader must be able to work with others in ways that ensure one is made. First and foremost it is essential to establish (1) a clear understanding of the goal to be achieved and (2) a commitment of the group to achieving that goal. In addition, leaders must make certain that those with whom they are working have the skills and resources they need to achieve those goals. Finally, there must be recognition and support every time a step is taken that moves the group toward goal achievement.

Respect for Others

Effective leaders respect those with whom they work. They seek and value ideas of others; they recognize their own limitations. So, although effective leaders have a sense of vision and work aggressively to reach that vision, they also are respectful of others. They are honest and fair in their dealings with their colleagues. Leaders who are seen by colleagues as "having all the answers" will soon find themselves without anyone to lead!

Meeting with Groups

All reading specialists, regardless of role, will find themselves working with small groups (e.g., grade-level or subject area teams, curriculum committees). The specialist may be the leader of the group, and on other occasions a member of the group. In either case, an understanding of basic group dynamics and how to conduct a group meeting are critical for the group to work effectively. Aspects of group work are described below.

Planning

Planning includes setting goals for each meeting, preparing the agenda that assists in meeting these goals, and handling logistics for the meeting itself. It may be productive to spend the first few minutes of a meeting, especially the initial meeting of any group, on helping the group to become acquainted (or reacquainted) with each other. Group leaders may want members to introduce themselves, share some personal information, or discuss their views about working on the task to which they are assigned. The agenda should be structured so that items of priority are identified first; a specific amount of time can be designated for each item so that those at the bottom of the agenda are also addressed. Part of initial planning includes providing for the place in which the meeting will be held. If the meeting is a large one and information is being presented, a classroom setting with rows of desks may serve as the venue. But if group participation is desired, the room must be one in which participants can sit in a circle and see and hear each other. Often it helps if refreshments are provided, especially if the meeting is an after-school one (a common occurrence). All materials needed for the meeting should be at hand (e.g., handouts, flip charts). Planning also includes making decisions about how records are kept and disseminated. For some meetings, it might be important to keep minutes so that there is a permanent record of decisions made.

Establishing Rules for Group Behavior

The time spent in establishing rules for group behavior is well spent; otherwise, the group may flounder as it attempts to make decisions or handle uncomfortable situations in which individuals are at odds about a specific issue. If possible, such rules are better established at the beginning of the school year or when a group is being formed. Otherwise, a leader may have to work to redirect the process if the group is working in a dysfunctional matter; for example, only two of the six language arts teachers seem to do most of the talking, and in fact make the decisions in terms of scheduling and grouping; the other four leave the meeting "rolling their eyes" and basically feeling as though their voices are not being heard. Rules for the following may need to be addressed:

- What processes for decision making will be used (e.g., consensus, voting)?
- What roles are needed for effective group functioning (e.g., is there a need for a note taker or a facilitator)?
- How will conflict be addressed?
- How will the group make certain that all members have opportunities to be heard?

Although a working group tends to develop its own set of rules and behaviors, the leader plays an important role in helping the group decide on these and then to follow them.

Attending to Task and Relationship Aspects

The leader and all group members must work diligently to accomplish their goals or tasks. (Who has not heard grumbling about useless meetings in which items are discussed, rehashed, and then discussed again?) At the same time, the group members must be sensitive to the way in which the group is working so that all members participate, feel valued, and assume a sense of responsibility for group achievement. This is not always easy, and some meetings will be better than others. One of the most effective ways to build a sense of "esprit de corps" is to take time at the end of the session to talk about what went well and how the group might modify its behavior to improve its work.

Working with Disruptive Group Members

There may be individuals in some groups who are difficult to work with—they do not want to be in the group, they are not accustomed to working with groups, or they antagonize others because they are unwilling to listen to others' ideas. Perhaps individuals such as those described below (adapted from Parrott's book, *How to Handle Impossible People: High*

Maintenance Relationships, 1996) have been members of groups with which you have worked:

> The Critic—constantly complains about whatever is being discussed (e.g., "Why are we talking about changing our schedules again?").
> The Wet Blanket—negative and pessimistic about new ideas or suggestions (e.g., "That will never work!").
> The Control Freak—wants to direct and control the decisions that will be made; tends to talk a great deal and loudly; not inclined to listen to ideas of others; pushes for specific decision to be made.

There is no simple answer to working with such individuals. However, there are some techniques that may be effective in dealing with, say, George, who tends to be a critic. First, setting rules for appropriate group behavior as described above is key to changing or at least minimizing the effects of George's disruptive behavior. Second, within a group setting, the leader often can reduce disruptive or hostile behavior by giving George permission to express his frustrations or feelings. For some, having the opportunity to vent reduces or eliminates future negative behavior. Third, if all else fails, the leader may want to talk with George privately and describe the behavior about which he or she is concerned, asking, at the conclusion, whether there is anything the leader or the group can do to assist him in working more effectively with the other members. Finally, we need to remember that each of us can at times be a difficult group member, depending on the topic or our own emotional state at the time.

Planning Again!

A meeting should not end without taking the time to summarize what has been achieved and to make plans for the next meeting. Various members may be asked to take responsibility for handling one or more tasks before the next meeting. Often, it is helpful to send notes or minutes of the meeting to members, highlighting major decisions and reminding them of the tasks that need to be accomplished before the next meeting. And again, taking the time to reflect on what worked well during the meeting provides a starting point for the next meeting.

The ideas presented above are important for reading specialists who have major responsibility for developing school reading programs (see Chapter 8). Books that may be useful to those who frequently work with groups include Johnson and Johnson's (2003) *Joining Together: Group Theory and Group Skills,* Kaser and colleagues' *Leading Every Day: 124 Actions for Effective Leadership* (2002), or *Facilitator's Guide to Participatory Decision Making* (1996).

The Reading Specialist as Leader

Each reading specialist will handle leadership responsibilities in a slightly different way, depending on (1) job descriptions and opportunities, (2) the degree of fit between his or her personality and a leadership role, and (3) his or her leadership skills and abilities. A reading specialist who works with children for six periods a day will have less opportunity to assume leadership roles but can still serve as a leader as he or she works with individual teachers. The new reading specialist, with little experience, may not yet be ready to handle complex or large-scale leadership roles but can work with a mentor to gain experience with such tasks. All reading specialists need to have not only an awareness of their own leadership skills and strengths but an understanding of how to serve as an effective leader.

The vignette at the end of this chapter (pp. 83–86) describes the work of a reading specialist, Toni, who has many leadership responsibilities. In addition to serving as federal coordinator, Toni provides professional development for her team of reading teachers and for teachers in the building. This responsibility is handled in both formal and informal ways, from holding grade-level meetings to scheduling specific times for presentations or workshops. She indicates that the leadership role is the most difficult, but recognizes the importance of these responsibilities. When reading the vignette, think about why the leadership role may be the most demanding and most difficult.

Hersey and Blanchard (1977) provide a useful way of thinking about leadership in their discussion of situational leadership. They suggest classifying the actions of leaders into task actions (e.g., achieving the goal) or maintenance actions (e.g., moving the group along in the discussion or taking into consideration the feelings and competencies of group members). They purport that various combinations of leadership can be effective, depending on the makeup of the group: How motivated are members to accomplish this task? How knowledgeable are members? When group members do not have essential knowledge or skills, the leader must engage in high-task behaviors to keep the momentum flowing. Hersey and Blanchard suggest that in these instances, the leader may need to spend more time telling or transmitting information. The leader may also need to convince the members that they can accomplish the job (i.e., selling).

In groups where participants have a great deal of knowledge and are eager to work on the designated task, the leader can work in a different manner, serving as a participant in the group or even delegating responsibility. Imagine the following situation, for example. You are working with a group of experienced teachers who have different views and perspectives about the reading program they are currently using in their school. Their task is to identify criteria that they can use to select new material. All are eager to get new material, but there are some very strong opinions about what constitutes effective reading instruction and agreement is not imminent. Your role (most likely) is to help the group discuss the salient points in an effective manner while remaining sensitive to the different viewpoints and making certain that all members understand that their thoughts are valued. This group is eager to accomplish the task, and the members have much experiential knowledge. At the same time, they need a leader who can focus them on maintenance or relationship actions that help them to listen, respect different views, and learn from others.

One can also think about task and relationship behaviors when working with individual teachers. For example, if a reading specialist meets with a teacher who is concerned about the comprehension that he or she is providing for his or her third-grade students and asks for help in making instructional modifications or changes, it is obvious that this teacher is eager for help. Building a relationship will most likely not take much effort; rather the focus can be on the task of providing this teacher with effective ideas for teaching comprehension.

THINK ABOUT THIS

How comfortable would you be in your leadership role in the situation with experienced teachers whose task is to select new materials? What difficulties do you foresee in working with this group? What essential skills would you need for working with the third-grade teacher who is seeking information about teaching comprehension?

The following section describes ideas for ways in which the reading specialist can serve as a resource to others. This leadership role is an informal one that can be used by most reading specialists, regardless of experience or job description.

Serving as a Resource to Teachers

• *Inform teachers of new ideas and materials.* Such information does not need to be formally presented in a group meeting. Reading specialists can circulate key journal articles to interested teachers and administrators. They can also summarize articles in interesting ways and place them in faculty mailboxes. For example, after reading several articles about fluency, one reading specialist developed an attractive brochure presenting ideas for fluency instruction that could be sent to teachers (see Figure 4.1). When new material arrives at the school, reading specialists can inform teachers that such material is available and volunteer to "try out" the material with a selected group of students.

Sometimes it is helpful to talk about professional issues at lunch or before or after school. For example, the reading specialist might comment, "So, what do you think about the article in the paper questioning the effect of retention? How does that fit with the policy that we have in our school?"

• *Spread the word about effective teaching and teachers.* Given that reading specialists often observe effective teaching, they can also initiate conversations about what they have seen and encourage visits by other teachers. For example, if one of the second-grade teachers is especially effective in conducting writing workshops, the reading specialist, after seeking permission from that teacher, can suggest that another teacher observe in that classroom (with the reading specialist taking over the class of the visiting teacher).

• *Focus on the student.* In my view, most teachers want every child in their classroom to be a successful reader. Often teachers have tried many different strategies to help various children—sometimes with little success. Therefore, one key approach to serving as a resource to teachers is helping them implement strategies that may improve reading performance of one or more children. During a staff development project in which I served as a resource to teachers in one school, one of the tasks that I most enjoyed was helping a young teacher learn several effective strategies for improving the decoding abilities of her students. We reviewed assessment data and discussed several strategies, including Cunningham and Hall's (1994) Making Words technique. I then agreed to do a demonstration lesson of that procedure. I also gave the teacher a copy of Cunningham and Hall's book, *Making Words.* The teacher was very excited about the approach and invited me to observe her as she taught. The children were now learning a great deal—and she was excited about their success—and her own.

FLUENCY
The Missing Link
Strategies for Developing Fluency
by
Sandy Akers

Student–Adult Reading

- Adult orally reads story first.
- Student orally rereads story with adult assistance.
- Student orally rereads story as often as it takes to attain fluency.

Partner Reading

- All students listen to teacher read story orally.
- Each student "whisper" reads story to him- or herself. (Teacher assists where needed.)
- Partners reread sentences or paragraphs, switching parts.

Choral Reading

- Students select a short story or poem.
- Students practice reading in unison.
- Students perform their story or play for class.

Reader's Theatre

- Students practice lines from play over and over again until fluent reading is attained.
- Students take their play "on the road" to perform in other rooms.
- Students may add portable props.

Echo Reading

- An adult can read or you can use an audiotaped book.
- Student listens to small passage read by an adult or on tape.
- Student repeats passage using fluent reading and expression.

To learn more about fluency see:

Put Reading First. Washington, DC: Center for the Improvement of Early Reading Achievement (CIERA), 2001.
Rasinski, Timothy V. Speed does matter in reading. *The Reading Teacher*, October 2000, pp. 146–151.

FIGURE 4.1. Student brochure. Reprinted by permission of Sandra R. Akers.

- *Be available and follow through on your commitments.* Unless reading specialists are "seen" in the schools, there may be little chance of serving as a leader. It is easy to find tasks to attend to, such as paperwork or administrative duties, that take specialists away from the schools. When reading specialists take the time to stop in and visit teachers, post the days on which they will be at a specific school (if they travel), and volunteer to help teachers if they see an opening, they are acting as leaders. In our work with schools, we often find that much good work occurs informally or "on the fly." Teachers may stop the specialist in the hallway or the lunchroom to just ask a question that opens the door to more in-depth interactions at a later time. One literacy coach describes how her interaction with teachers increased when her office was moved from near the principal's office to near the students' bathroom (Bean & DeFord, n.d.).

Equally important is providing follow-through on every commitment made. Usually, teachers do not understand or appreciate cancellations, even when they appear to be unavoidable; for example, the principal may request that the reading specialist attend an important meeting. Certainly, there are times when the reading specialist may need to cancel or make changes in his or her schedule, but every effort must be made to assure the teacher that the commitment will be honored. The teachers should also be informed as soon as possible if there is to be a change in the schedule. Furthermore, the specialist should reschedule as soon as possible. Nothing destroys the credibility of the reading specialist more than the lack of follow-through. Otherwise, teachers may soon decide that there is little they can expect from the reading specialist and will close the door, literally and figuratively, to future interactions.

- *Be flexible.* Flexibility is an especially critical quality, because often creative and effective ideas emerge in the moment, as the reading specialist works with a specific teacher or teachers, and their implementation usually requires "on the spot" adjustments to planned work. These ideas may come from the reading specialist or the teacher. The most effective reading specialists quickly think of ways that they can facilitate the development and implementation of these ideas, rather than thinking of reasons why such ideas are impractical. In discussing leadership, Colin Powell said, "You don't know what you can get away with until you try" (Harari, 2002, p. 65). In other words, reading specialists are most effective when they look for ways to make things work.

Flexibility is also important in terms of working with individual teachers. For example, the reading specialist may be able to work as a coteacher in the classroom to implement guided reading with one teacher, because he or she is especially open to having another adult in the classroom. With another teacher, the reading specialist may only provide material and suggestions about guided reading, giving that individual an opportunity to think about the approach and how it might be implemented.

A Resource for Allied Professionals

The reading specialist can work collaboratively with other professionals in the building or district. These include the special education teachers, speech teachers, counselors, and psychologists, and may also include teachers of the arts, librarians, physical education instructors, as well as others. Reading specialists, special education teachers, speech teachers, and counselors may all be involved with the same students. Therefore, it is important that communication occur among *all* of these professionals. Although many schools have implemented special groups, such as instructional support teams in which key educators meet together to discuss specific children with special needs, there should also be informal conversations among these educators. Too often, children with special needs receive multiple and possibly conflicting intervention strategies because of the lack of communication among the educators involved with them. Educators can learn about the various approaches that may be used to improve reading performance from one another. For example, speech teachers are often well prepared to teach phonemic awareness to young children, and with the reading specialists' assistance, may be able to work with more teachers or students. Likewise, special educators may appreciate information about the various approaches to teaching reading that the reading specialist can share with them. Special educators, in turn, often have well-designed behavior management programs or instructional strategies that they can share with others.

In addition to working with educators connected with children who have special needs, involvement with others, such as art teachers, librarians, and so on, can promote improvement of reading for all students in the schools. I have observed music teachers whose programs help young children develop excellent phonemic awareness skills. The arts program can be used in the upper grades as a means of expanding and enhancing students' thematic learning in the various content areas. The librarian, of course, can be a source of information about book availability and work with teachers to promote student interest and motivation to read.

Interactions with school psychologists may also be an important part of the reading specialists' role, not only to obtain test information about students but to learn more about the child and to share information that may assist the psychologist in getting a more complete picture of a specific student. Often, the type of assessments that reading specialists administer help psychologists gain a more specific understanding of the child's instructional needs in relation to literacy. Hoffman and Jenkins (2002) conducted interviews with a group of reading specialists to learn more about their interactions with school psychologists. They found that these reading specialists had some collaborative experiences with the school psychologists, but that scheduling time for interactions was a problem. They also talked about the importance of establishing good personal relationships and knowing more about how to collaborate effectively.

A Resource for Administrators

Although many principals, especially those in the elementary school, have an in-depth understanding of reading instruction, some do not; given their multiple responsibilities, many do not have adequate time to devote to the leadership of the reading program. They may rely on the reading specialist in their school for specific information about how the school as a whole is doing (e.g., achievement scores in the areas of reading: decoding, comprehension, etc.). Principals may also need to be informed as to whether there is a need for additional staff development in the area of reading for specific teachers (e.g., content area teachers in the high school want to know more about how to use textbooks in their classes). In other words, reading specialists should inform the principal about what they are doing in the school, and solicit help from the principal in their efforts to improve classroom reading instruction. Reading specialists, in addition, should make themselves available to the principal so that they can respond to the principal's requests for support and information. Some principals schedule meetings with the specialist once a week; others prefer to receive written updates from the reading specialist on a regular basis. Because principals are busy with many different responsibilities, the reading specialist may need to initiate the interaction.

Summary

Reading specialists all have leadership responsibilities, but these differ depending on job opportunities, experience, and the technical skills of the specialist. Such skills include having the ability to (1) communicate with others, (2) work with teams, (3) achieve goals, (4) empower others, and (5) work in a respectful way with others. The leadership role for reading specialists is often one that requires leading by influence and that will differ, depending on the context in which one works. All reading specialists need to serve as a resource for teachers, administrators, and other professionals involved with struggling readers.

Reflections

1. Why is the leadership role of the reading specialist an important one? Why is it one of the most difficult tasks of the reading specialist?
2. Think about a group with which you have been involved recently. What was the style of the leader? How did the leader help the group to work effectively?

Activities

1. Interview a reading specialist to determine what leadership roles he or she assumes. Ask the specialist to identify what skills are needed to perform such tasks.
2. Attend a group meeting. Think about the leadership style of the leader. How did the group achieve its goals? In what ways did the group exhibit its ability to work together as a team?
3. Discuss the following scenario. What leadership style would be most effective, given the characteristics of the teacher?

   A new first-grade teacher has told you that she is having no difficulties teaching her students, is enjoying her experience, and does not need any specific help from you, the reading specialist. However, you have been in her classroom and have noticed some classroom practices that indicate that she has very little knowledge of how to teach phonics.

Toni: The Job of One Reading Specialist (a Brain on Overload)

Some questions to think about:

What lessons can be learned about the role of the reading specialist from this vignette?

What questions come to mind while reading this vignette?

What characteristics or behaviors make Toni an effective reading specialist?

It's Sunday night—time to get back into the "school mode." As I look at my Palm, I see another busy week ahead of me. (What meetings do I have this week? Meetings with classroom teachers? Parents? Administrators? What do I need to prepare for each meeting—agendas, handouts, subs to arrange, availability of meeting rooms, e-mails to participants? I need to check with teachers regarding the students about whom we are seriously concerned and inform the principal and the guidance counselor of at-risk students. How are my students doing? Have they been reading nightly? Do I need to call home?)

I am a reading specialist in a small suburban district with a student population of approximately 1,200 K–12 students; approximately 29% of the students qualify for free-and-reduced lunch. This year, my primary assignment is in the kindergarten through grade 3 building. I teach for approximately half of each day, and the other half is devoted to a wide range of activities. Another part of my job is that of Federal Programs Coordinator; I am responsible for writing and implementing the Title 1 and the Title 2A grants. In this position, I work with classroom teachers, parents, and administrators and oversee literacy aides who are employed by the district to support the language arts program. The reading staff is based in the Reading Room—a regular classroom with desks for me, another reading specialist, and three literacy aides—five females and lots of materials and resources all in the same room. It works for us, and the daily interaction is great. What questions and issues will arise today from aides, teachers, or administrators? I have to keep on top of my game to accurately provide answers—always new articles to read or new books to review—so much to learn and so little time!

I love my job; it presents opportunities, challenges, and rewards on a daily basis. What is it exactly that I do? As I think about my major responsibilities, they fall into three broad categories: instruction, assessment, and leadership. I describe each below.

Instruction

I spend a majority of my day involved in instruction, whether it be teaching students directly or working with teachers to provide appropriate instruction. My actual "teaching" duties change from year to year based on student need. This year I am working with small groups of at-risk first- and third-graders. I do predominately "pullout" service while our literacy aides work in the classroom and also see students in a pullout context. Since my students are the very high-risk group, I keep my groups small, from three to five students at a time for a 30- to 40-minute block of time daily. Instruction is very explicit with constant feedback to the students so that they know exactly what they are doing correctly and incorrectly immediately. I employ many of the strategies that I learned through my training for Reading Recovery. (Reading Recovery training was excellent; I learned so much that I use on a daily basis, even though I am no longer officially teaching "Reading Recovery.") One challenging task of the instructional aspect of my job is developing a schedule to meet with my students (all the teachers seem to want the same time of day—it takes some negotiating to come to a consensus regarding the schedule). Fortunately, the teachers value the support service provided so they are willing to work with me to develop a schedule that ensures the students will not miss important instruction while they are with me. Working with the students keeps me connected with the teachers and gives me multiple opportunities to talk to them about literacy instruction in the classroom.

I find myself asking lots of questions about the students with whom I work: Where are they weak? What skills have been taught in the classroom but not learned by these students? How can I back up and reteach these skills? Who's here today (attendance is a chronic issue with some of my students). Why are they not reading every evening at home? (I need to set up reading buddies here at school for some of them. I will have to call home also.)

Assessment

One of my responsibilities is that of overseeing reading assessments given to all students in the K–3 building in which I am housed. We use the Developmental Reading Assessment (DRA; Beaver, 2006), and one of my responsibilities is to teach all of the teachers how to administer it. Each year there are new members of the faculty to train and resident staff always have questions, so the training is ongoing. The majority of the teachers now know how to administer the DRA so we are now working on the analysis of data and instructional implications. I meet with teachers weekly, during a designated planning period, to contribute to the grade-level weekly planning of language arts instruction. This time is also used for review and analysis of data and the instructional implications of the data (e.g., How are we going to groups these students based on their assessment results? What can I do to support the differentiation of instruction based on student need?). The needs of all students are addressed weekly to ascertain whether the students are performing below grade level, at grade level, or above grade level in reading. (Looking at how all students perform across multiple grade levels is quite different from when I started in the field. Years ago, my focus was only on the at-risk students.) Teachers are becoming more and more attuned to student literacy needs as evidenced by the assessment results. Great teacher dialogue evolves from these weekly meetings.

The RTI model is used in our building, so ongoing assessment and progress monitoring are necessary for all of the at-risk students (e.g., What reading intervention is going to be most beneficial to each student? Is the one we are using effective? Why or why not? What is our next move?). Multiple assessments are used based on students' grade level and area of need. This process definitely keeps everyone thinking!

Leadership

Although assessment and instruction are important components of my job, the leadership component (which I find to be the most difficult) has the greatest impact on overall job effectiveness. Numerous leadership issues arise (particularly those that require interpersonal skills) in the process of dealing with various groups of people—literacy aides, classroom teachers, parents, administrators, and even school board members. Each participant in the education process plays a unique and important role in the development of lifelong learners. One piece of this process is professional development, which I provide to staff both informally and formally during staff development classes held at our district after school and during the summer months. (The teachers' room is a great place for short, informal conversations, but I've learned to be careful and not let the conversation get too lengthy and totally interrupt the time teachers have to "unwind.") Sometimes, a brief comment in the hall or a more defined time during a prep period is used to check on students, materials, or other reading-related issues. Parent interaction can be informal (e.g., a chat in the hall, a quick phone call, or note) or more formal during evening parent meetings.

Keeping administrators informed about reading-related issues and options is yet another responsibility. Administrators can help establish the environment necessary for change. Administrative support that I've received has been a major advantage. I continue to think about what I can suggest to them as we strive to improve and extend the reading program in the district. They have always been supportive and open as long as I have done my homework and bring them the information they need to make a decision. I'm really fortunate that I've had so much support. The leadership role is definitely the most challenging part of the job for me—dealing with so many audiences in effective and productive ways is tough.

What Can I Suggest to Others?

An important part of my job is staying current in the field. (This is necessary personally and professionally. How can I ask for change if I don't know what the possibilities for change are?) My district facilitates this aspect by sending me to conferences; some local, some not. The local resource center provides day "classes" in reading-related topics that I attend either by myself or with a team of teachers. I have been to the International Reading Association conference many times (Wow—what a way to get rejuvenated—just to talk to and hear so many individuals in the field of reading is so motivating!). I've also attended state reading conferences and federal programs conferences (I need to know what is going on in the state and locally!). Membership in professional organizations and reading professional journals and books also help me stay current.

(Wish I had more time to just sit and read; summer is a great time to catch up. I skim lots of material and mark articles that I want to go back to and read in depth.)

One thing I can say with no reservations: My job is *never* boring, never the same 2 days in a row—and it has infinite opportunities, challenges, and rewards. Nothing is as satisfying as watching a child evolve into a reader and watching teachers grow in their knowledge of literacy instruction. I love the field of reading and know that it is a complex skill that is crucial for children to acquire in order to function in the world. I have the best job in the world!

ANTONETTE SAUL, EdD
Reading Specialist and Federal Programs Coordinator
Allegheny Valley School District
Cheswick, Pennsylvania

5

Professional Development

Professional development is not about workshops ... it
is at its heart the development of habits of learning. ...
—FULLAN (2001, p. 253)

Michael Fullan has set forth an important notion about the professional development of teachers: Teachers must continue to be learners,
to be excited about learning more about being effective at the craft of
teaching. Professional development can be defined as efforts to improve
capabilities and performances of educators; yet professional development efforts that are standardized, based on transmission of information, and short term or irrelevant do little to help teachers improve
their practices. Although individuals may seek to improve their own
skills through reading, attending courses or workshops, or receiving
advanced degrees, much professional development occurs in schools
with groups of teachers. Such work can be extremely productive in that
larger numbers of teachers are reached, and they can be influenced by
their interactions with others in their own buildings. The effort can be
site specific and based on goals of the school or district.

Given the emphasis on high-quality literacy teaching in every classroom, reading specialists often have responsibilities related to professional development. They lead workshops to provide information about
effective literacy instruction or assessment; they lead grade-level or
departmental team meetings that help teachers think about instruction for a specific grade, academic subject, or component of literacy
(e.g., comprehension, phonics, study skills); and they coach, providing
resources, coplanning and coteaching, modeling, observing, and providing feedback to individual teachers about their literacy instruction.

In this chapter, I provide some background about what we know about effective professional development and provide specific ideas about how to conduct large- or small-group workshops. I also discuss standards for professional development and then describe two large-scale professional development projects to provide examples of intensive, long-term, systematic initiatives; one at the elementary and the other at the high school level. I conclude this chapter by describing various approaches to developing, leading, and evaluating various forms of professional development.

Revitalizing the Wasteland

Concerns about and interest in reading instruction, from national to local levels, have led to calls for improving teacher knowledge and performance in teaching literacy. Moreover, we now have evidence that teacher quality matters. For example, studies such as those conducted by Sanders and Horn (1994) and Sanders and Rivers (1996), which used value-added student achievement data, found that student achievement gains were much more influenced by a student's teacher than other factors such as class size and composition.

According to Snow and colleagues (1998), teachers need support and guidance throughout their careers in order to maintain and update their knowledge and instructional skills. As Louisa Moats puts it: *Teaching Reading IS Rocket Science* (1999). In that publication, the writers indicate that teachers must be experts in order to teach reading effectively. They must know a lot about their subject matter and the instructional strategies that will enable them to provide the best literacy experiences for their students.

Yet professional development, as it has been conducted in schools, has generally been considered the wasteland of education (Little, 1993). Teachers have been introduced to, and sometimes bombarded with, information about new projects or activities that happen to be in fashion at a specific time, often before there is research evidence to establish the innovation as effective. At times, initiatives have been placed in schools without attention to the implementation process. Fullan (1991) discussed the notion of an implementation dip, indicating that teachers may have initial difficulty using new ideas to which they have been introduced, and that without support and ongoing feedback, these new instructional approaches may not become part of the teachers' repertoire. Joyce and Showers (1995) called for creating change in schools using a professional development system that is "far more powerful and pervasive than the one that exists" (p. 5). The American Education Research Association (2005, p. 4) identified four critical elements of any professional development initiative:

- such professional development should focus on the subject matter being taught;
- learning opportunities should be aligned with real work experiences of the teachers;
- there should be adequate time with extended opportunities to learn and an emphasis on observing and analyzing students' understandings of the subject;
- and ongoing evaluation of the impact of such PD [professional development].

What Is Professional Development?

Guskey (2000) defines professional development as "those processes and activities designed to enhance the professional knowledge, skills, and attitudes of educators so that they might, in turn, improve the learning of students" (p. 16). This definition puts the focus on the end result of such initiatives: improving the learning of students. When professional development is considered in this light, it is much easier to think about how to structure it as part of the school day and how to evaluate it. Such a definition also reflects the belief that there are many different models of professional development, each with its advantages and shortcomings. Guskey identifies seven different models: training, observation/assessment, involvement in a development/improvement process, study groups, inquiry/action research, individually guided activities, and mentoring. Some of these models are more effective than others in specific contexts. Often a professional development plan is based on a combination of models. For example, in a professional development initiative that I codirected, teachers attended workshop sessions throughout the year and were asked to develop a focus or action research project, based on the needs of their students. Teachers also administered informal assessment tasks to determine the literacy strengths and needs of their students. Furthermore, they were observed implementing various strategies and given feedback about their instruction. In this project, coaches were responsible for helping the teacher understand the various strategies, and they assisted in implementation efforts.

In addition to various models of professional development, there are also different sources of professional development, from those offered by a state education department or a funding agency, to those initiated at a district level to those that are site or school based, sometimes with only a small number of teachers involved. States that received funding for Reading First were required to offer professional development for coaches, teachers, and principals. Districts often offer professional development for all schools in their district; for example, if the district decides it will use *Success for All* (Slavin et al., 1996) in all its schools, every faculty member will participate in the professional development efforts for that program. In this case, the initiative is one developed by "outside experts."

In other instances, district personnel may develop a literacy program based on standards that they themselves have developed or adopted and then provide the necessary staff development (perhaps using both internal and external experts). These initiatives, whether "homegrown" or based on a commercial program, have the advantage of focus, given that all teachers are provided with the staff development they need to use the specific approach.

Initiatives in which selected teachers volunteer to participate in a specific program benefit because participants are excited by what they have decided to do. On the other hand, such initiatives are likely to spawn several problems. The district or school may not completely understand what these teachers are doing and at times they do not provide the necessary support for these volunteers; there may be multiple initiatives in the district, and this may cause problems for teachers and for the school as a whole. In some cases volunteers are not certain of what they have agreed to do!

Individual teachers can attend various workshops or conferences and read journals or books that help them make changes in their instructional practices. These individuals, as described by Joyce and Showers (1995), are the "gourmet omnivores"; the 10% of teachers who are always seeking to improve. These teachers are always looking for ways to do a better job of teaching students. Still, they may have a difficult time using these newly learned approaches, which may be different from those recommended or required for use in the school, and the teachers may get little or no support for what they are doing.

THINK ABOUT THIS

What type of professional development have you participated in— school mandated, volunteer, group, or individual effort? Which has been most useful and why?

Improving Professional Development

Previous research on professional development indicates that participation in such efforts can change teachers' attitudes and practices and even improve student achievement (Desimone, Porter, Garet, Yoon, & Berman, 2002; National Institute of Child Health and Human Development, 2000; Sparks & Loucks-Horsley, 1990; Taylor, Pearson, & Rodriguez, 2005). In Taylor and colleagues' (2005) study of professional development in schools implementing a school change framework, they found that in schools that had high implementation, there was greater growth in students' reading achievement, and that there were greater effects when the results were examined after 2 years. The standards of the National Staff Development Council (2001) call for attention to content, context, and process issues. Those responsible for professional development must be certain that they have selected the appropriate content for teachers to learn for a particular context. In addition, they must develop and implement processes that recognize the nature of adult learning. The National Staff Development Council standards also call for building the capacity of teachers to use research-based teaching strategies that are appropriate for their students. A discussion of the standards specific to literacy follows.

Content

What do teachers need to know and be able to do? Reading specialists responsible for professional development have multiple resources that they can access to address this question. Figure 5.1 provides examples of resources that address reading instruction from birth through adulthood; these should be helpful to those responsible for planning professional development.

In most cases, the identified resources are based on research about literacy instruction; some of them use the evidence presented in the work of the National Institute of Child Health and Human Development (2000) and National Reading Research Commission (Snow et al., 1998).

Reading specialists involved in professional development efforts should, of course, consult the standards developed and often mandated by their state department of education or local districts. Often these district standards have been developed by the teachers in the district and align closely with state standards. For that reason, they provide important guidance for planning professional development for teachers in a specific school.

Early Learning

Learning to Read and Write: Developmentally Appropriate Practices for Young Children by the International Reading Association and the National Association for the Education of Young Children, 1998 (*www.reading.org/downloads/positions/ps102_NAEYC.pdf* or *www.naeyc.org/about/positions/pdf/PSREAD98.pdf.*

Starting Out Right: A Guide to Promoting Students' Reading Success edited by M. Susan Burns, Peg Griffin, and Catherine E. Snow. Washington, DC: National Academies Press, 1999.

Every Child Reading: A Professional Development Guide by the Learning First Alliance. Baltimore: Author, 2000.

Developing Early Literacy: Report of the National Early Literacy Panel. Washington, DC: National Institute for Literacy, 2008.

Elementary Focus

Several books based on the New Standards project are available from the National Center on Education and the Economy (*www.ncee.org*) and provide useful information:
- *New Standards Performance Standards*, 1997.
- *Reading and Writing Grade by Grade: Primary Literacy Standards for Kindergarten through Third Grade*, 2008.
- *Speaking and Listening for Preschool through Third Grade*, 2008.
- *From Spanish to English: Reading and Writing for English Language Learners*, 2003.
- *Using Rubrics to Improve Student Writing*, 2008.

Reading and Writing with Understanding: Comprehension in Fourth and Fifth Grades by Sally Hampton and Lauren B. Resnick. Newark, DE: International Reading Association, 2008.

Adolescence

Adolescent Literacy: A Position Statement by the International Reading Association (*www.reading.org/downloads/positions/ps1036_adolescent.pdf*).

Adolescent Literacy edited by Jacy Ippolito, Jennifer L. Steele, and Jennifer F. Sampson. Special issue of *Harvard Educational Review*, Spring 2008.

General

Standards for the English Language Arts by the National Council of Teachers of English and the International Reading Association (*www.ncte.org/library/NCTEFiles/Resources/Books/Sample/StandardsDoc.pdf* or *www.reading.org/downloads/publications/books/bk889.pdf*).

FIGURE 5.1. Selected professional development resources.

Context

The creation of a successful professional development plan must be based on the context in which it is to be presented. Several questions must be addressed:

> What are the experiences, skills, and abilities of the teachers who will implement the plan?
> Is the culture in the school one that is receptive and eager to change?
> What are teachers' attitudes about change?
> What are the characteristics and needs of the students in this context?
> What resources are available from the administration and the community?

In one school, faculty may be quite receptive to new ideas and ready to make changes in how they teach literacy. In other schools, more preliminary work may be needed before the actual program can be implemented. Often it is necessary for the staff development team to think about current practices and what may need to be eliminated before new practices can be instituted. One of the common complaints of teachers—and rightly so—is that they are always asked to add to what they are doing—in an already filled day!

Other legitimate issues include concerns about various practices that do not seem to fit together, that are incongruent with each other, or lack support or resources at the school level for a district-mandated practice policy. These issues need to be discussed by key personnel and teachers if the professional development effort is to be successful.

Processes

Process often gets short shrift as teachers receive what some call "flavor of the month" or "drive-by efforts." Successful efforts at professional development that generate teacher change have several process-related characteristics in common:

1. *Duration.* Effective programs are long-term or sustained endeavors. They may begin with a workshop in which teachers learn various strategies, but the program continues throughout the year, with opportunities for teacher practice, inquiry, and reflection.

2. *Opportunities for feedback.* Teachers have opportunities to talk about what they are implementing, what works, and questions/concerns

they have about implementation. The development plan includes a built-in mechanism to help teachers as they implement the new strategies: Individuals with expertise visit teachers and help them by demonstrating or observing practices and then taking the time to discuss aspects of the work. Such coaching is supportive rather than evaluative. (Coaching as a professional development tool is discussed in Chapters 6 and 7.)

   3. *Embedded into the classroom practices of teachers.* When the professional development effort is one that is closely related to what teachers do every day in teaching and assessing students, there is a much better chance that the initiative will succeed. One of the ways that this "fit" can be accomplished is to have teachers who have been able to implement a particular strategy effectively present their work to other teachers. Teachers appreciate hearing from those who have actively been able to "do it" in their classrooms, and they value seeing these teachers in action. Another approach is to work with teacher groups, studying carefully the work of their students and also the data from various assessment measures to generate discussion about what these sources of evidence mean for instructional practice.

   4. *Sense of recognition.* Teachers must be acknowledged for the work they do. There must be recognition of those who have "expertise"; for example, such teachers can demonstrate for others or assist others in implementation. My own work with professional development has led me to believe that when teachers feel a sense of accomplishment and empowerment, they contribute significantly to the success of the initiative. They make creative and specific suggestions for how the initiative can work more effectively, and they encourage other teachers to use the new strategies.

   In the section below, I describe two professional development efforts, one for primary teachers led by a team of faculty from several universities, and the other, a high school initiative funded by the State Department of Education and the Annenberg Foundation (the Pennsylvania High School Coaching Initiative). When reading about these initiatives, think about how the components of these efforts address the critical elements of effective professional development described previously.

LEADERS: A Professional Development Initiative

LEADERS (Literacy Educators Assessing and Developing Early Reading Success) was developed and funded by Eisenhower funds for a 3-year period. The initiative was intended to improve the teaching of K–3 teachers in schools where there was low student achievement and large numbers of high-poverty students (Bean, Swan, & Morris, 2003).

In this initiative, the leadership team was university based and volunteer teachers were recruited from various districts that were eligible for the program. One of the first decisions to make was what it was we wanted students to know and be able to do, regardless of the school they attended. We needed to make certain that what we presented was appropriate despite the use of different basals and different curricular efforts in the various districts. In the first year, *Every Child a Reader: Applying Reading Research in the Classroom* (Center for the Improvement of Early Reading Achievement, 1998) was used as a text for teachers. Later, each teacher was given a copy of *Put Reading First* (Armbruster & Osborn, 2001), a book that summarized the findings of the National Reading Panel Report for teachers. We believed that the focus should include (1) efforts to increase knowledge and understanding of teachers (i.e., what did they need to know about teaching reading?), and (2) opportunities to learn various strategies or approaches that have been found to be effective in teaching reading. The belief was that regardless of the different basals or anthologies used in schools, teachers overall would find the knowledge and accompanying strategies to be useful in their classrooms.

In order to adapt to the various contexts in which we worked, a site liaison or coach was assigned to each school. This individual had to meet with the principal or superintendent and with teachers to make the necessary modifications for that school. For example, one school district was subject to a districtwide initiative, and teachers were required to use specific approaches mandated by that district (e.g., a word-building strategy to help students learn phonics; Beck & Hamilton, 1996). We were able to help teachers understand how to use that approach effectively and also share with them specific management strategies that would make their implementation easier. In one school, teachers were asked to "level" their books. The coach for that school worked with teachers at the site to assist them in the actual work of identifying levels for each of the books. In most cases, we were able to adjust or add to our work to meet the needs of a specific school. In one instance, we did experience difficulty because the classroom management system promoted by the district was antithetical to what we were promoting.

The strengths of this professional development initiative lay in the processes we used. The coach (previously mentioned) went to the school on a regular basis to support and reinforce the teachers' work by providing demonstrations, observing, and giving feedback, and assisting in the work being done by the teacher (e.g., helping with the administration of the assessment battery to students in each classroom). Working with individual students provided coaches with insights about the teacher's students and helped them develop relationships with students as well as the teacher. The work with students and the demonstration lessons also helped coaches to establish credibility. Each coach functioned some- what differently (depending on the site). I not only observed, demon- strated, and assisted with testing, I also took teachers to visit another school, attended several parent meetings in the evening, and met with the principals and superintendent to discuss the relationship of LEAD- ERS with other initiatives in the district. One of my colleagues joined a study group of teachers at a school, and they continued to meet on a regular basis.

Another critical aspect of the project was the assessment tool, LAB (Literacy Assessment Battery). We believed that if teachers would use data not only from their observations but also from these informal mea- sures, they would begin to make instructional decisions that would ben- efit students. Each coach spent time talking with teachers about test results, examining student work, comparing students' work samples, and then discussing what instructional decisions needed to be made.

A third dimension of the project was the "focus" or "action research" project. This project was to be based on the results of the LAB. Teachers were asked to decide where they wanted to focus their energies, given the profiles of their students. Teachers were required to develop a poster for an end-of-the-year celebration that included examples of the activities they were implementing, displays of student progress, and a statement of what they themselves had learned. Several teachers in one district, for example, recognized the need to improve the writing performance of their students and embarked upon a year-long writing project. They expressed their excitement when they saw their students' enthusiasm for writing in journals and participating in the writing workshop—and when they saw the progress of their students at the end of the year!

A fourth aspect of LEADERS was the opportunity for networking. Teachers indicated that they valued opportunities to talk with others who taught at the same grade level or in other schools or districts. As in most schools, there is very little or no opportunity for teachers to talk with each other during the school day.

As mentioned above, our major focus was enhancing student per- formance. In what ways did LEADERS affect students' literacy growth? Evaluation efforts from LAB indicated that students made significant progress in each of the assessed components of reading (Bean, Swan, & Morris, 2003). We were also required to assess the growth of teachers on a teacher knowledge test and, again, there was significant growth on this instrument. Teacher satisfaction was also high, as measured by various questionnaires and reports given in focus group meetings. Some of the comments made in the focus group sessions include the following:

> "LEADERS has made the biggest difference in my teaching life. It has worked on empowering teachers—and I thank you for that. I now know how to teach reading. I didn't *really* know what I could do when kids weren't successful with the basal."
>
> "I'm really excited about the assessments. Now I can see what my students need—and work on it."
>
> "I love the coach—it's like having a personal trainer—I'll really miss him next year!"

LEADERS is an example of a professional development initiative developed by external facilitators and implemented as one project within several schools. In that sense, it had varied effects on each school, depending on the number of teachers from each school who attended and the congruence of this initiative with others going on in the schools. The outcomes of LEADERS were many: Teachers did much more than expected; they began to think about themselves as professionals, writing for mini-grants, collaborating with others, and thinking about how they might attend and then present at various professional meetings. Some pursued additional graduate study and are now in leadership positions in their school districts. A few have become literacy coaches!

Pennsylvania High School Coaching Initiative

The goal of this statewide initiative, supported by the Pennsylvania Department of Education and the Annenberg Foundation, was to improve student learning by improving the teaching of literacy across content areas in high-need high schools. The design of the Pennsylvania High School Coaching Initiative (PAHSCI) included three major components. First, instructional coaches (math and reading) were employed to help teachers work one-on-one with teachers in their classrooms and also to lead group activities with teams of faculty. Second, specific professional development was provided for the selected high schools to give the necessary support to administrators, coaches, and teachers. Finally, the Penn Literacy Network (PLN) Framework was identified as the model for promoting literacy across the content areas. This framework is based on four interrelated "lenses" of literacy: literacy is meaning-centered, it is social, language based, and human (Brown et al., p. 7) and identifies a number of literacy-based strategies appropriate for use in the content areas (e.g., jigsaw, self-questioning, mental imaging, etc.). Coaches, school leaders, and teachers attended a variety of professional development sessions conducted by the PLN; in fact, teachers could receive college credits for attending these courses. Coaches then were available in the school to help teachers implement what they were learning from these workshops. In addition, the project provided mentor teams for the coaches and for school leadership to assist with problem solving and reflective practice. Network meetings were available for coaches to provide them with additional support as they worked with teachers in the schools. Research for Action (Brown et al., 2007), which conducted an evaluation of PAHSCI, found that teachers across subject areas were working with coaches and using the strategies of the PLN. Moreover, when teachers used the strategies, students were participating more actively in their classrooms. The evaluators concluded that the initiative provided teachers with "a common language and a set of principles for planning and reflecting on instruction" (p. 42). For more information about this initiative, read the article by Bean and Eisenberg (2009) in *Literacy Instruction for Adolescents: Research-Based Practices.*

THINK ABOUT THIS

Think about the two initiatives described above. In what ways are the content, context, and process variables addressed? How are these initiatives similar? Different? What do you see as the strengths of each of them? What problems or difficulties might be faced by the providers if the initiative were implemented in your school?

Guidelines for Developing, Leading, Implementing, and Evaluating an Effective Professional Development Program

1. *Know the goals and needs of your audience.* As indicated previously, an understanding of the context is essential. If the reading specialist is conducting a program in his or her own school, such knowledge is easier to come by than if the program is to be developed for another school or district. This information might be obtained by interviewing administrators or teachers, visiting the school, or observing in the classrooms. Lyons and Pinnell (2001) provide an excellent list of characteristics to look for in the school culture (see Figure 5.2).

2. *Hold sessions in environments that are conducive to learning.* In the LEADERS initiative, we designed the room in which we held sessions to

 1. As you enter the building, what do you see?
 2. Is there a welcoming atmosphere?
 3. Is the building as a whole clean and attractive?
 4. Is the school office a welcoming place where people are acknowledged and helped?
 5. Are the classrooms, cafeteria, office, and library clean and attractive?
 6. Do staff members speak respectfully to students and do students talk in respectful tones to one another?
 7. What is happening in the yard or playground? Are students playing? Are teachers interacting with students?
 8. Are the students and their community a visible part of the school? Is student work displayed and valued in the corridors, office, library, and other gathering places?
 9. How available are books? Can students find books to read in places besides the library?
10. Is the principal accessible? Does the principal interact in a friendly way with students, staff members, and visitors?
11. Do people in the school talk with one another? What do they talk about? Do they talk about their work?
12. Are professional development books and materials available?
13. Do teachers have a place where they can meet and work together? Is it attractive and welcoming?
14. When asked about the school, what do people say? Are their comments positive?
15. When asked about the students in the school, what do people say? Are their comments positive?
16. When asked about the parents and the community, what do people say? Are their comments positive?

FIGURE 5.2. What to look for in the school culture. From Lyons and Pinnell (2001, p. 78). Copyright 2001 by Heinemann. Reprinted by permission.

look like the classroom that we expected teachers to have: There were learning centers, reading and writing areas, and examples of student work on the walls and bulletin boards. The room was equipped with tables so that there was opportunity for group work and discussion. The environment was a comfortable one that enabled participants to interact as a community of learners. (Every so often, we had to work in a classroom with individual desks set in rows, and the difference in the interaction and attitude of participants was remarkable!)

It is also important to think about the physical needs of the participants. Plan for breaks and refreshments, as needed. My initial work with professional development was done with a colleague who always said, "You have to feed your group!" Although we chuckled about that statement, it is true that teachers who come to a Saturday workshop or who need to attend a professional development meeting after school really need—and enjoy—light refreshments. It not only meets an actual physical need but also provides an opportunity for social bonding.

3. *Be aware of the learning styles and needs of adults.* Teachers, as adult learners, bring to the learning experience a variety of experiences, skills, and knowledge that influence how new ideas are received and the degree to which they acquire and implement new skills. They bring with them their multiple roles and responsibilities not only as teachers but also as parents, homemakers, and so on. They bring the many experiences they have had in life and work, as well as their feelings or emotions associated with past learning experiences. Teachers participate in professional development for monetary incentives on occasion but more often because they hope to gain concrete and practical ideas that will enhance the learning outcomes of their students (Guskey, 1986). Indeed, Guskey reported evidence that positive change in "learning outcomes of students generally precedes and may be a prerequisite to significant change in the beliefs and attitudes of most teachers" (1986, p. 7). Change is gradual for most teachers and requires a well-developed, long-term effort. Guskey (p. 9) also discussed several characteristics of effective staff development efforts: (1) The new program or approach should be presented in a clear, explicit, and concrete manner; (2) personal concerns of teachers must be addressed; and (3) the person presenting the program should be credible, articulate, and able to describe how the practice can be used by teachers. Even then, some teachers may leave the meeting not convinced that the new ideas will work for them; at best, they will try them!

Some suggestions for making effective presentations to adults are listed in Figure 5.3. These suggestions come from my own experience and from *How to Run Seminars and Workshops* (Jolles, 2001), a book that I have found helpful.

4. *Use a variety of activities and approaches, especially those that require active participation on the part of those attending.* People learn best by "doing," and therefore, professional development sessions should provide opportunities for individuals to think about and discuss various aspects of literacy. Approaches that have been successful include the following:

• *Study groups.* When teachers are involved in an activity that is especially meaningful to them, they become more engaged in the process and are generally more willing to apply what they are learning to

1. Create an atmosphere conducive to adult learning; it should be relaxed, yet businesslike. Seating should be conducive to discussion and interaction. Breaks and refreshments should be planned.

2. Stimulate and maintain interest. Use visuals to reinforce learning; tell stories; ask questions of the group or use small-group activities.

3. Involve participants to engender interest and increase retention. In addition to small-group activities and questioning, the learner can ask participants to perform some task.

4. Set your goals and inform participants (i.e., What do you expect them to know or do when the session is over?).

5. Show enthusiasm and use your voice effectively.

6. Plan your session so that you know how much time you will give to each segment.

7. Create a strong beginning and ending. This is where you capture the attention of the group and what the group will remember when they leave!

FIGURE 5.2. Making Effective Presentations

their classroom practices. Participation in a study group puts teachers in charge of their own learning, providing them with materials that they can read, reflect, write about, and discuss with others. Groups may be formal ones established by the school district, or they may function informally, with a group of teachers deciding what they will read, and when and how often they will meet. Often there is a designated leader for each meeting who facilitates the discussion by thinking of questions and activities that may be appropriate for the material to be discussed. A resource that may be helpful is the brief on leading study groups published on the website of the Literacy Coaching Clearinghouse (*www.literacycoachingonline.org*). Walpole and Beauchat (2008) in this brief highlight several important points: Work with participants as a colearner, provide for choice and voice, and facilitate opportunities that enable members to make personal connections. For example, hold discussions about how ideas being discussed might be implemented in classrooms, and the challenges that teachers might face, or the resources that they might need.

Thibodeau (2008), a literacy specialist, writes about the study group that she led with a volunteer group of high school content teachers who taught a number of different subjects (e.g., English, geometry, algebra, etc.). The group met for an introductory meeting in the summer and then held meetings once a month for 2 hours after school for a year. As she states, the group learned "with and from one another" (p. 56); moreover, the teachers made changes in their instructional practices and felt that their students benefited from the literacy strategies being taught in the classrooms.

- *Analyzing student work.* In LEADERS, teachers brought samples of their students' work and discussed them with others who taught at the same grade level but in different schools. This activity always generated much discussion and reflection, with teachers able to think about how well their students were doing in comparison to those in other classrooms. More importantly, teachers discussed which strategies and activities were helpful in promoting successful performance.

- *Analyzing student assignments.* Often, this activity can complement the analysis of student work. Teachers who teach a similar subject at one grade level (e.g., English literature) can share the assignments that they ask students to complete to meet the same standard or objective. Teachers may be surprised when they see the differences in expectations across classrooms. Matsumura's text *Creating High-Quality Classroom Assignments* (2006) provides helpful ideas for those wishing to delve more deeply into this approach to professional development.

- *Use of videos (classroom practices).* There is no doubt that "seeing is believing." Although we often modeled new strategies for teachers in LEADERS, they always appreciated seeing teachers demonstrate specific strategies with their students. In the beginning, we used tapes that had been developed for other purposes; as we continued with LEADERS, we were able to show tapes that had been made by teachers participating in the project. In one high school participating in PAHSCI, individual teachers agreed to have their lessons taped and then to participate in a group discussion with other teachers, discussing the ways in which the lessons exemplified active engagement of students (the focus of the professional development initiative in this school). Certainly, this was a group of teachers who enjoyed working with each other and were not threatened by making their teaching public!

- *Use of technology.* Technology can be used in many different ways to enhance professional development efforts. It can be used to facilitate communication, to obtain valuable information, or to serve as the primary provider of professional development. For example, in the LEADERS project, we developed a website that participants could access and a private listserve that teachers could use to communicate with others. Also, the Internet has provided teachers with opportunities to locate resources to learn more about various aspects of literacy. They can obtain professional resources or practical ideas, including lesson plans or activities. Several examples of valuable websites include:

International Reading Association; Read, Write, Think: *www.readwritethink.org*
Reading Rockets: *www.readingrockets.org*

America Reads; Resources: *www.ed.gov/inits/americareads/resources.html*

National Council for Teachers of English: *www.ncte.org*

Florida Center for Reading Research: *www.fcrr.org*

Technology can also serve as the provider of professional development. In Pennsylvania, teachers and coaches in Reading First participated in a series of online courses on effective primary reading instruction; coaches could also take courses on coaching (*www.learningscience.org*). Florida also offered a series of online experiences for teachers in grades pre-K–12 (Zygouris-Coe, Yao, Tao, Hahs-Vaughn, & Baumbach, 2004). In the Classrooms of the Future initiative in Pennsylvania, whose goals are to improve the ways in which teachers at the secondary level use technology, coaches in the initiative participated in webinars, blogs, and forums to enhance their knowledge and to communicate with others. One of the exciting aspects of this large-scale project was that coaches could hold regional meetings in different locations and still present the same information to all participants by using technology. Such efforts, using technology, should provide opportunities for more differentiated, teacher-centered, and self-directed models of teacher learning.

• *Action research.* When teachers are given opportunities to raise and answer questions they have about their students' learning, they become the ultimate professional. They implement best practices and then assess their effectiveness. In LEADERS, we created a simple framework based on four questions for helping teachers think about their projects:

What do your students need to become better readers or writers?

What activities or strategies are you going to use to help students succeed?

What was the outcome? What effect did your intervention have on students?

What have you learned about yourself and your teaching?

Teachers summarized what they knew by writing a brief summary and developing a poster that illustrated their responses to each of the questions. Teacher research generates ongoing learning and may facilitate change in classroom practice. Teachers interested in such activities need to be encouraged and supported in their efforts. They can discuss their work with other teachers in faculty meetings, they may write a short column for the school or community newspaper, they can collaborate with others to investigate a specific issue, or as in LEADERS, they may develop posters that display evidence of their work and its effect on classroom performance. For those interested in reading more about teacher research, the book by Cochran-Smith and Lytle (1993) is an excellent resource.

• *Reflection.* Give teachers opportunities to discuss and reflect upon what they have done in their classrooms. They may keep logs or they can be given opportunities to talk informally with their peers about their experiences. One of the greatest opportunities for reflection is after teaching a lesson (discussed further in Chapter 7).

5. *Provide opportunities for teachers to receive feedback about implementation in the classroom.* In LEADERS, whenever coaches observed teachers, they met with them to discuss the results of the observation (discussed further in Chapter 7).

6. *Provide for evaluation of the professional development initiative.* Both formative and summative approaches to professional development are essential. *Formative,* or ongoing, evaluation provides opportunities for modification, adaptation, or change. *Summative* evaluation, which addresses impact and results, enables the developer to determine the effect of the professional development effort on individuals and on the system as a whole. Guskey (2000) identified five levels of evaluation: participants' reactions, participants' learning, organizational support and change, participants' use of new knowledge and skills, and student learning outcomes.

In LEADERS, we used the following techniques for addressing each of the levels:

Level 1. Participants' reactions	Questionnaires at end of each workshop Midyear focus group
Level 2. Participants' learning	Teacher content test (pre–post)
Level 3. Organizational support and change	Interviews/questionnaires with principals and teachers
Level 4. Participants' use of new knowledge	Classroom observations
Level 5. Student learning outcomes	Pre–post tests (LEADERS assessment battery)

In Figure 5.4, we provide a rating scale that can be used to assess the professional development initiatives in a specific school or district (Bean & Morewood, 2007).

Summary

In this chapter, I discussed the importance of professional development, describing various models and the standards of the National Staff Development Council that can be used in developing and evaluating such initiatives. Two professional development initiatives were described to provide specific illustrations of intensive, systematic efforts to improve student learning. Guidelines for developing, leading, implementing, and evaluating an effective professional development program were then presented.

Reflections

Discuss with your classmates professional development in which you have participated. What activities did you find to be most useful? What, in your view, was least useful?

Activities

1. Interview an administrator at your school about the professional development plan for teachers in the school, especially as it relates to literacy instruction. Think about whether that plan addresses content, context, and process standards, as developed by the National Staff Development Council. (Use Figure 5.4 to guide your discussion.)
2. Prepare a professional development session for your classmates (or for the teachers in your school), in which you introduce them to one new idea or strategy. Use information from the guidelines in this chapter to develop that presentation. Ask the participants to evaluate the session, using a short questionnaire. Then self-evaluate your performance, reflecting on the ideas presented in this chapter.

Rating Scale

3	High implementation
2	Partial implementation
1	Not an established part of the comprehensive professional development program or plan.

Content

Score	Description
	School has coherent set of literacy goals and standards across grade levels that can be used as a framework to guide professional development. (Standards for literacy performance at each grade level have been identified, e.g., what should students know and be able to do?
	Curriculum and instructional practices are evidence based.
	Curriculum and instructional practices set high expectations for all students.
	Curriculum and instructional practices to be emphasized relate to needs of students as determined by multiple sources of data.
	Opportunities enable teachers to gain in-depth understanding of the theory and research underlying practices (why something is important).

____/15 Total

Collaboration and Sense of Community in the School

Score	Description
	Teachers have decision making role in how they learn what is necessary to achieve goals set by the school.
	Teachers in school are given opportunities to work together, interact, network, learn from one another (e.g., grade-level meetings, study groups, etc.) in a collegial manner.
	There is a focus on the value of parents and their role as members of the community.
	Teachers are recognized for the work that they do.
	Teachers have opportunities to serve as leaders in planning and implementing professional development activities.

____/15 Total

(cont.)

FIGURE 5.4. Professional development for promoting school change in literacy. From Bean and Morewood (2007, pp. 381–382).

Duration and Amount of Time

Score	Description
	Professional development programs are on-going (over time) and give teachers opportunities to develop in depth understanding of the content to be learned.
	Teachers have ample contact hours related to the PD topic.

____/6 Total

Active Learning

Score	Description
	School makes use of new technologies in helping teachers achieve their professional goals.
	Teachers use information from their classrooms and students in their professional development work, e.g., they use data, review student work samples, do lesson study.
	Activities are differentiated according to teacher needs and styles of learning.
	Teachers have opportunities to participate in inquiry-based activities that necessitate critical thinking, application, and reflection.
	Teachers have opportunities to practice what they are learning with their peers or in small groups.

____/15 Total

Application and feedback Opportunities

Score	Description
	Teachers have opportunities to apply what they are learning in their classrooms.
	Teachers interact with their peers about their experiences in a risk-free environment and reflect on what they are doing.
	Feedback is geared towards supporting and guiding teacher practices (it is not evaluative).
	Teachers are recognized for what they know and do.
	Teachers have opportunities to self-evaluate and reflect on their work (e.g., video, etc.)

____/15 Total

FIGURE 5.4. *(cont.)*

6

Coaching
Improving Classroom and School Literacy Instruction

Literacy coaching is "very hot."
—CASSIDY AND CASSIDY (2009, p. 8)

In this chapter and the following one, I discuss literacy coaching as an important aspect of the role of the reading specialist. As stated above, literacy coaching, during the past 10 years, has been identified as one of the key approaches to improving teacher practices and ultimately, student learning. Notice the emphasis on coach*ing*; not coach*es*. Many individuals within a school may have coaching responsibilities: teachers who work with student teachers or paraprofessionals and the principal who visits teachers to provide support and guidance rather than to evaluate their performance. And yes, even the reading specialist whose primary role is instruction. In some schools, however, reading specialists have been asked to change the way in which they work, moving from primarily an instructional role to a coaching role, perhaps without having the necessary preparation to handle coaching responsibilities successfully—at least not without much "on-the-job-training." We know much more now than we did 8 years ago about coaching, and given that knowledge, there are two chapters on coaching in this edition, rather than one. Moreover, those reading specialists who coach or want to know more about coaching will find information in the other chapters equally important, especially discussions about assessment, professional development, and leadership.

In this chapter, I begin by discussing the rationale for coaching; this is followed by a description of an interactive framework of coaching; I also describe the qualifications that I believe literacy coaches need if they are to be successful. In the final section, I discuss findings from several coaching initiatives—K–12—to help readers gain an understanding of the various ways in which coaching can be implemented in schools. This chapter ends with a list of possible activities that coaches can use to work with teachers. In Chapter 7, I describe in more depth the various activities in which coaches might engage in their work with individual teachers and provide examples of what is meant by each of the activities.

Why Coaching?

One criticism of professional development programs is the lack of ongoing support for implementation efforts. Without such support, teachers may have difficulty implementing the strategies or approaches to which they have been introduced and choose to revert to familiar or comfortable procedures. For this reason many schools have begun employing literacy coaches when they adopt new approaches and desire to improve teacher practices and student learning. Furthermore, in various federal and state legislation (e.g., Reading First and Striving Readers), there has been support or even a requirement that implementation efforts include a coach in the schools.

The term "literacy coach" is quite appropriate in many ways— especially if we think of the definition of a coach as one with expertise who provides the guidance or feedback that enables someone else to become more proficient. Even as we think of the great football coaches— Vince Lombardi (Green Bay Packers), Chuck Noll (Pittsburgh Steelers), and Ara Parsegian (Notre Dame)—we think of individuals who were not only able to teach in the traditional sense but were able to inspire and motivate their players to do their very best and to live up to their potential. In Nater and Gallimore's book (2006) about John Wooden, the legendary basketball coach at the University of California, Los Angeles (UCLA), they detail the teaching methods that made him a great coach and teacher: "teacher respect, motivation, self-improvement, deep subject knowledge, preparation, and transferring information" (p. xiv). According to these authors, Wooden thought of himself "first and foremost as a teacher" (p. xiii).

THINK ABOUT THIS

The title of the Nater and Gallimore book (2006) is *You Haven't Taught Until They Have Learned: John Wooden's Teaching Principles and Practices*. What do you think this title means? Do you agree with it? Do you think it relates in any way to literacy coaching, and if so, how?

So it is with literacy coaches: Their job is to work with teachers in their schools and to help them do their very best to facilitate student achievement. Teachers may be novices, needing a great deal of feedback or guidance, or they may be more experienced, having taught for many years. The experienced teachers may benefit from feedback about new approaches, and they may need some reinforcement, reassurance, recognition, or even some motivation that promotes ongoing learning.

Educators in the field do not always define the word "coach" in a similar fashion. To some, literacy coaches are teachers who coach children, enabling them to do better. Others see them as teachers with expertise in reading (often, reading specialists) who have multiple responsibilities, from working with paraprofessionals or community agencies to working with teachers in the role described above—primarily responsible for providing support and guidance, so that classroom instruction for students is effective.

The coaching role can vary, therefore, depending not only on the job requirements of the coach or reading specialist but on the "readiness" of the teachers. For example, reading specialists can serve as a resource to teachers by providing materials or suggestions for working with struggling readers; they can attend or lead study group meetings, conduct professional development workshops, or just sit and listen to teachers who want to reflect on ways that they can improve instructional practices.

What Is Coaching?

Although I focus on *literacy* coaching in this book, in some schools, coaches have a broader or different role. For example, there are instructional and curriculum coaches who are responsible for working with teachers in many subject areas. There are also technology, math, and science coaches who are responsible for supporting teachers' work in those areas. Indeed, much of what is discussed in this book has relevance to those broader or different coaching roles; however, given the purpose and audience of this book, I focus on "literacy" coaching. Various authors have defined coaching in slightly different ways. For example, read the two definitions below, and think about whether these authors view coaching in a similar or different manner.

THINK ABOUT THIS

What are the views of the following authors about the goals of coaching and its focus? What do you think each position requires in terms of qualifications?

... an experienced teacher who has a strong knowledge base in reading and experience providing effective reading instruction to students, especially struggling readers. In addition ... has been trained to work effectively with peer colleagues to help them improve their students' reading outcomes. ... (Hasbrouck & Denton, 2005, p. 1)

The role of the coach is the same in every domain ... develop a relationship with me, develop expertise so that you would know how to help me, plan for my success, communicate your confidence in me and my potential, help me find the very best in myself, and in the end, step out of the way so that I could claim the change as my own. (Burkins, 2007, p. 5)

You probably noted in Hasbrouck and Denton's definition that there is an emphasis on student learning, specifically reading achievement, and a focus on the need for a strong reading background for the coach. In Burkins's definition, there is more of a focus on the importance of teacher learning and growth, and on the teacher as the source of ideas for coaching. Both definitions provide important insights into coaching—and to the variations that exist in its definition. In other words, the nature of coaching is complex. Given that, I propose an interactive framework of instructional coaching that may help those interested in coaching—coaches, teachers, administrators, researchers, and those who prepare reading specialists—to think about the factors that may affect how coaching is implemented in a given school.

An Interactive Framework of Instructional Coaching

As shown in Figure 6.1, there are three specific elements—the model, the context, and the coach—that affect how coaching will be defined, implemented, and evaluated within a given school. These elements overlap and interact with each other and each is affected by the other. I discuss each of these below.

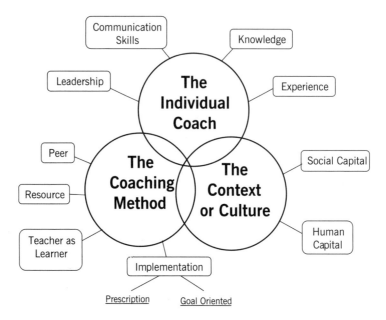

FIGURE 6.1. An interactive framework of literacy coaching.

The Model of Coaching

Although others (McKenna & Walpole, 2008; Toll, 2004) have proposed various models of coaching, from those that are more structured or prescriptive to those that, as Toll (2004) states, "provide a fresh alternative" (p. 13), I identify below five general models of coaching that may be implemented within a school.

Peer Coaching

In this model, colleagues work with each other to provide feedback and support. This model, proposed by Joyce and Showers (2002) was one of the original approaches to coaching, and emphasized the fact that both coach and teacher were of equal status. In a given school, the language arts teachers in a middle school might decide to implement literature discussion groups, and after attending a workshop and reading resource materials, observe each other as they facilitate such discussions. Actually, Joyce and Showers in 2002 revised their procedures for peer coaching by first of all, omitting feedback as a coaching component. Too often, feedback given by peers became evaluative or supervisory in nature rather than supportive, and therefore incongruent with the concept of peer coaching. Also, Joyce and Showers redefined the meaning of coach. According to them, "the one teaching is the 'coach' and the one observing is the 'coached'" (p. 89). In other words, the coach models for the other teacher who then is expected to just talk briefly about what he or she has observed and then apply the learning in instructional practice.

Resource Model

This model is one in which there is much flexibility on the part of the reading specialist. In addition to working with students, this specialist has the freedom to work with teachers in many different ways. I once served in such a role (Bean & Wilson, 1981) and had many opportunities to work with novice teachers who wanted my assistance in how to organize their reading groups, teach phonics or comprehension, and so on, or differentiate instruction. I also worked with teachers who had concerns about their struggling students and wanted some additional ideas about how to help them succeed. And, I was privileged to work with several high school teachers who wanted to incorporate literacy into their content teaching. I also worked with a high school reading specialist. Together, we started a program in which high school struggling readers tutored elementary students who were having difficulties learning to read. The key notion of this role is that the reading specialist or coach generally responds to requests from teachers or administrators, although there are always opportunities to initiate activities and to be proactive.

Focus on Teacher as Learner

In this model, the goal of coaching is to support teachers in achieving their own goals and to facilitate teacher learning. Toll's (2006, p. 13) "fresh alternative" model and Costa and Garmston's (2002) Cognitive Coaching model emphasize the importance of listening to teachers to get an in-depth understanding of their concerns, interests, and needs. This focus on teacher as learner respects the individual goals of teachers, highlights the importance of reflective practice, and provides for personalized or individualized coaching. The goal of this model is to enhance teachers' ability to self-manage, self-monitor, and self-modify (Costa & Garmston, 2002, p. 21).

Implementation Model

I divide this model into two categories: prescriptive and goal oriented. In my view, these two models are the ones seen most frequently in schools during the past 10 years. They are a reflection of the accountability and standards movement that stresses the importance of student achievement or performance. Both highlight the importance of implementing particular approaches or programs appropriately; however, there are differences between the two models.

PRESCRIPTIVE

In this model, there is little opportunity for teacher choice in strategies, materials, or approaches. The program selected requires teachers to follow certain procedures—at times, scripted—and the coach's role is to make certain that teachers can and do use those approaches in their classrooms. Often this is called "fidelity to implementation."

GOAL ORIENTED

In this model, there is more opportunity for choice although there are specific goals that have been identified by the school and/or a literacy framework that has been adopted. For example, in Pennsylvania, schools that are part of the Pennsylvania High School Coaching Initiative (PAHSCI) have agreed to implement a specific literacy plan, the Penn Literacy Network (PLN) Framework in content areas. At the same time, teachers can be selective in terms of which aspects of the framework they want to emphasize in their classrooms (e.g., active engagement strategies, self-questioning, etc.), and coaches can support teachers in achieving *their* individual goals.

The model selected affects how one coaches—from whom the coach will work with to how the coach works with an individual. For example, in an implementation model that is prescriptive, the coach will most likely decide whether teachers are implementing "correctly" and will work with those teachers who are not doing so. In a school in which I have worked, the principal stated empathetically to the coach, "I want you to focus on working with two teachers who are experiencing difficulty—a new teacher and one who seems to have problems with implementing the curriculum." In a resource model, the coach will have much more flexibility, most often relying on requests of individual teachers. And in a teacher-as-learner model, the coach will develop a personalized coaching plan for teachers with whom they work. What is intriguing to consider are the different views that teachers may have of coaching, depending on the model.

The Context of the School

Common wisdom as well as research emphasize the relationship between the climate and culture of the school and student learning. Reeves (2005) explains that the keys to improved achievement are the "professional practices of teachers and leaders" (p. 374). He identifies nine important factors, several of which relate to the culture that exists in the schools: teacher collaboration, valuing and using the talents of every adult in the system, and cross-disciplinary integration.

There are two important constructs that underlie the context or culture of the school: one is human capital and the other, social capital. Leana and Pil (2006) discuss two types of social capital: internal and external. Internal social capital relates to the interactions and relationships among teachers, administrators, and others that promote a common and shared vision within a school setting. Positive internal social capital includes the following: sense of responsibility for all students, belief that all students in a school can learn, high expectations, and sense of common goals for students. Leana and Pil, in their study of schools in a large urban school district, found significant relationships between what they defined as internal "social capital" in schools and improved student achievement.

External social capital relates to the links between the school setting and its community. In this case, teachers and administrators work collaboratively with parents and with various agencies to promote student learning. This is exemplified by efforts to not only inform parents, but to seek information and support from them. I discuss this in Chapter 10.

Human capital relates to the human resources that exist in the schools: the teachers, their educational experiences and various talents; and the additional personnel who can support instructional differentiation (e.g., reading specialists, librarians, literacy coaches, speech and language therapists, school psychologists, special educators, etc.). We know the importance of a stable staff, one in which teachers stay for long periods of time, and where literacy coaches can build on the work of the previous year and not have to work with a large number of new teachers. The principal is also an important human resource; his or her understanding of and support for the literacy coach's role are important to the success of the coach. The principal also has a key role in building a sense of community by reinforcing and supporting the work of teachers.

The kind of work coaches can do and the outcomes they can achieve are often related to the context or culture of the school in which they work; that is, the norms or ways things get done! Too often, these norms are unspoken and difficult to discern. Listed below are some topics that can create difficulty *or* be a source of support for coaches.

- Work issues related to contract agreements
- Teacher experiences and/or beliefs about students, learning, and teaching
- Leadership issues
- Number of professional development initiatives, some of which may not align with others in the schools
- Clarity of and support for the coaching role by administrators and by teachers

There are other topics, of course, and each organization has its own set. In the previous chapter, Figure 5.2 lists questions that help you think about the culture of a school. Described below are two situations that highlight how culture can positively or negatively affect the work of the coach. What is your response to each of these scenarios?

THINK ABOUT THIS

1. In Brown Middle School, the principal and teachers met together to discuss the test scores in the various content areas, including social studies, science, and reading. The content area teachers were concerned about the test scores and indicated a need to learn more about how to help students with the literacy demands of their discipline. After much discussion, the principal and teachers decided that it would be advantageous to change the position of Ms. Smith, the reading specialist, from one in which she worked with students only to one that provided her with time to also work with teachers. The principal agreed to modify the teaching schedule for the reading specialist and also to provide common planning time for teachers of a specific discipline. Ms. Smith, who had worked in the school as an English teacher and then as a reading specialist had the credibility and respect that enabled her to work collaboratively with teachers in the school.

2. In Green Elementary School, the principal had written a grant
    to support the work of a literacy coach, with an emphasis on an
    approach to reading instruction different from that used by the
    teachers. The teachers were surprised when the principal met with
    them and introduced the coach, who had not worked in the district,
    but had been a reading specialist for a number of years in a neigh-
    boring district. The principal explained that the coach's responsibil-
    ity was to "help them improve their teaching of reading." Although
    the literacy coach met with grade-level teachers on a regular basis,
    much of what she was asking them to do was contradictory to what
    their current reading series promoted. Teachers became frustrated
    with trying to incorporate two different approaches to reading
    instruction in their classrooms and the literacy coach was even
    more frustrated because the district reading program, according to
    the district supervisor, was the approach that teachers needed to
    use.

    Where were the differences in the conditions in the schools in
    terms of their readiness for coaching? Talk with others about those
    conditions—and about the factors that would promote a successful
    coaching initiative. What could be changed that would promote a bet-
    ter coaching initiative in Green Elementary School?

The Individual Coach

The International Reading Association (2004), in its position statement on coaching, has indicated that the qualified coach is one who has
teaching experience at the grade level at which he or she coaches, has
experience in working with adults, excellent interpersonal and leadership skills, and has reading specialist certification. In their brief "Qualifications for Literacy Coaches: Achieving the Gold Standard," Frost and
Bean (2006) agree with the qualifications identified by the International Reading Association, but go on to explain that too often such
well-qualified individuals are not available, and that school districts
must choose the best possible candidate and provide the experiences
and staff development to support that individual. Such on-the-job training is not the best approach to use but at times it is a reality and these
inexperienced coaches may need to begin slowly, learning the content
and process of coaching while they are actually working with and building relationships with teachers. A helpful approach to on-the-job training is to have new coaches join a network of coaches so that they can
learn from the experiences of others.

At the same time, even the best-qualified coaches must recognize that their beliefs, styles of teaching, and personalities influence how they work with and perceive others. Kise, in her book, *Differentiated Coaching: A Framework for Helping Teachers Change* (2006), explains that all of us have our own preferences for organizing our lives and approaching our work. So, one coach may be extremely well organized, and in his or her previous classroom teaching experience, set stock by the way in which he or she managed the classroom, believing that students need the structure of routines in order to learn effectively. It may be difficult then for this coach to walk into the classroom of a teacher, who although known as an excellent teacher, has a much more laissez-faire approach to classroom organization. What is critical is that coaches understand their preferences and those of the teacher—and recognize and value the differences. After a presentation that I gave on coaching, two coaches came up to me, chuckling. They worked together in the same elementary school and it was clear that they enjoyed their work. As one of them told me, "I'm like a bulldog; I never give up—I'm tenacious." The other coach said, "and I'm like a big, old Labrador retriever, nurturing and supporting teachers." They went on to tell me that it was obvious that teachers in the school seemed to have a preference for one or the other, and this was fine with them. In other words, they knew their own strengths and their tendencies, and recognized the same in teachers in the school. Not all schools, however, can offer choice of coaches to teachers, but it is important that coaches understand that their personal style, communication skills, and so on, have an impact on those they coach and that they will be able to work more easily with some rather than others.

Characteristics of Effective Coaches

The literature on leadership and supervision, as well as my own research in the schools, highlights four important qualifications of literacy coaches:

1. *Know your stuff.* As one principal put it, it is a given that literacy coaches have excellent, up-to-date knowledge of literacy instruction and assessment and the research that undergirds that knowledge. Coaches need this knowledge in order to analyze the lessons they see and identify the relevant aspects of instruction for discussion with the teacher. Those who have a deep understanding of their field are able to "see" things that novices or those with less understanding may not see. An analogy might be a golf instructor who quickly sees that the student is bending his or

her arms (not good), not keeping the lower body stable and balanced, or making some other mistake. Likewise, the literacy coach can readily observe, for example, (1) when a teacher moves so quickly through a lesson that students are experiencing difficulty understanding what is being taught, or (2) where the teacher might have stopped to check for understanding or provided additional examples of a specific concept or skill as a means of giving additional scaffolding to students. Clearly, reading specialists must be learners themselves, reading the current literature and research and attending conferences and workshops. Certainly, reading specialists must maintain their own professional libraries and join professional organizations so that they remain knowledgeable in their field (see Chapter 12 for more about the reading specialist as a lifelong learner).

2. *Experience.* Literacy coaches are more effective if they have had successful experiences as teachers. Although longevity is not an issue, literacy coaches should have the experience that makes them creditable with classroom teachers and enables them to feel empathy for the teachers' many responsibilities. Some can transcend the need for experience, but in the long run, reading specialists benefit from having worked with classrooms of students with their diverse needs and interests.

3. *Ability to work with adults.* When we talk with coaches about how prepared they were to fulfill their roles, many of them tell us that they felt comfortable with the content (literacy instruction and assessment), but less comfortable with knowing how to work with adults. An understanding of adult learning is essential. Such learning includes the realization that adults come with previous experiences and beliefs that influence new learning, they want their learning to be meaningful to them, they require multiple exposures to help them see the value of the new initiative or idea, and they have busy lives and don't want to waste their time.

4. *Effective interpersonal and leadership skills.* To function successfully as a coach who has responsibility for observing and giving feedback to teachers, the reading specialist must have excellent interpersonal and communication skills. Coaches must be good listeners, be able to empathize with the teachers, and provide balanced feedback that reinforces excellent teaching behavior and provides ideas for improvement. They must also be able to develop a trusting relationship with the teachers whom they coach, so that their feedback is valued. Essentially, coaches must be able to get their messages across to their colleagues; that is, the teachers in the classrooms. (See Chapter 4 for more information about interpersonal and leadership skills.)

Identified below are some principles that should be taken into consideration when one is involved in coaching activities.

1. *Share your plans and ideas with teachers.* Teachers should understand what coaching means and what it does not mean, why they are involved, and how it will benefit their students. Teachers need to understand that the coaching process is not an evaluative one, but rather one that strives to help them be more effective. To the degree possible, teachers should be invited to participate because they will be more receptive to the process.

2. *Obtain teacher input.* Take time to hear and respond to teachers' concerns. Furthermore, by addressing teachers' needs, coaching will be much more effective.

3. *Provide necessary support.* Once the coaching process begins, it is important to provide the resources that teachers need if they are going to make changes in their classroom instruction. In other words, if a coach identifies a specific need (e.g., additional training or supplemental material), such support should be provided.

4. *Take time to develop the trust needed to be an effective coach.* Begin with those who are eager and willing to participate. By working with teachers who are receptive, coaches themselves will be more relaxed and can use these initial cycles as opportunities to practice their "coaching" and communication skills. One builds trust by maintaining confidentiality. Coaches who talk about what they have seen in classrooms will not be seen as individuals whose responsibility is one of providing support. Teachers will be less likely to respond in a positive manner to them.

Some resources that may be helpful to those involved in such coaching are *Cognitive Coaching* (Costa & Garmston, 2002) and *How to Implement a Peer Coaching Program* (Robbins, 1991).

Summary of the Interactive Framework of Instructional Coaching

What I hope to illustrate is that coaching does not occur in a vacuum. Successful coaching requires a context in which the conditions are conducive to coaching, a coach who has the skills and abilities to work within that environment, and an understanding of the model of coaching being implemented. When individuals talk about schools in which coaching does not seem to be effective, it is important to think about each one of these dimensions: Is the school one in which there is support, understanding of, and even enthusiasm for coaching? Does the coach have the skills, knowledge, and abilities that enable him or her to work within that context? Is the model of coaching understood and is it appropriate for the teachers in that school?

Activities of Coaching

There are many different coaching activities that can be used to support and guide instructional efforts in schools (see Figure 6.2 for a list). Note that these activities are divided broadly into group and individual activities. Coaches may also assist teachers by providing direct service to students; that is, assessing students who may have been absent or helping teachers with ongoing progress monitoring, or teaching a group of students for a predetermined amount of time, but the focus in this chapter and in Chapter 7 is on coaching activities.

In 2004, I categorized the various coaching activities according to levels of intensity or risk (Bean, 2004); this list can also be found in the International Reading Association (2004) position statement on the Role and Qualifications of the Reading Coach in the United States.

Group Activities
- Developing, locating, or sharing resources with teachers (written or oral)
- Meetings with grade-level or subject area teams to discuss assessment, instruction, curriculum, analyzing student work, teacher assignments, and so on
- Committee work (developing curriculum, preparing materials)
- Leading or participating in study groups to discuss specific materials read by the group
- Leading or participating in more traditional types of professional development workshops
- Participating in more formal lesson study (Stigler & Herbert, 1999) with groups of teachers
- Assisting teachers with online professional development

Individual Activities
- COTF (Coaching-on-the-Fly)—impromptu meeting with a teacher to discuss topic of importance to that teacher (a specific student, test scores, etc.)
- Coplanning lessons
- Conversations with individual teachers
- Modeling
- Coteaching
- Observing and providing feedback
- Combination—coaches may combine modeling, coteaching, and observing while working with teachers in the classroom. (Coach is generally in the classroom for a block of time.)

FIGURE 6.2. Coaching activities.

In other words, some activities are more informal and create less anxiety for teacher and coach (e.g., an informal discussion about a specific student experiencing difficulty), while others may be of greater risk or intensity (e.g., observing and providing feedback about the teacher's instruction).

THINK ABOUT THIS

In looking at the activities identified in Figure 6.2, which of those would you feel most comfortable doing? Least comfortable? Which do you think would be most threatening to teachers?

In Chapter 7, I discuss coaching activities that are focused on working with individual teachers. Group activities are discussed in Chapters 4 and 5. What is important to remember is that although reading specialists who serve as coaches may not be involved in all of the activities described in Figure 6.2, all reading specialists will, at different times, need the knowledge, skills, and abilities that enable them to undertake most of these activities, although not as frequently as someone designated as a literacy coach.

Summary

In this chapter, I discussed the "what and why" of literacy coaching. This was followed with the presentation of an interactive framework of literacy coaching that consists of three important components: the individual coach, the context, and the coaching model. After discussing characteristics of effective coaches, I identified some principles of coaching. I concluded by discussing the many different activities that coaches may use as a means of working with teachers and others in their schools.

Reflections

1. Think about a school with which you are familiar and its readiness for coaching (as described in the interactive framework of coaching. What are the conditions that would make coaching easy or difficult?

2. How comfortable would you be in a coaching role? What experiences, knowledge, and skills do you possess that would make you an effective coach? What do you think you need to do to improve?

Activities

1. Select a book on coaching and read to identify how the author(s) define coaching. Does the definition align with any of the models of coaching described in this chapter?
2. Develop with a group some interview questions that could be asked of a literacy coach. Relate those questions to the interactive framework of coaching.
3. Shadow or follow a literacy coach for a day and then be prepared to discuss what you saw. What coaching activities did you observe?

7

What Coaches Do
to Improve Instruction
Working with Individual Teachers

In this chapter, I begin by discussing ways that reading specialists, new to coaching, can develop the relationships necessary for them to be successful in their work. This is followed by sections that highlight the work that coaches do with individual teachers: modeling, coteaching, and observing. I also discuss two other approaches to coaching—on-the-fly and combination coaching, two activities that coaches use in their work with teachers (Bean et al., 2008). As mentioned in previous chapters, coaches can work with teachers in grade-level groups, disciplinary teams, or interest groups, and they can also conduct more formal professional development sessions to support teacher learning (these aspects of coaching are discussed in Chapters 4, 5, and 6). Coaching activities require conversing with teachers as a means of sharing and elaborating on insights; therefore the information in Chapter 4 on communication skills is especially relevant to those who coach.

The Reading Specialist as Coach: Getting Started

In a recent study of coaches in Reading First schools in Pennsylvania (Bean et al., 2008), we found that some schools employed coaches who were new to the school while others selected coaches who had been teachers in that school. Interestingly, both sets of coaches saw advantages and disadvantages to this selection process. Coaches new to a school felt that they came to the position without any previous bias about the school and its staff; teachers likewise had no prior experiences with the coach on which to base judgment. On the other hand, these coaches recognized that they had to work quickly and effectively to gain an understanding of the culture of the school, to learn more about teachers and their knowledge and beliefs, as well as to learn more about the students attending these schools. In other words, they had no sense of any "landmines." Most coaches who were hired from within felt as though they had the credibility and respect necessary to do the job and in addition, understood the cultural dynamics in the school. A few, however, recognized that there might be resentment since they were now leaving the teacher ranks or because they had competed for the position with another colleague. They also understood that their prior experiences at the school could be helpful in some ways, but detrimental in others. What all coaches new to the position recognized was that they had to begin *quickly* establishing themselves in this role, and at the same time, move *slowly* enough that they could develop a sense of trust between teachers and themselves.

Katy, in the vignette at the end of this chapter, talks about her thoughts and fears as she prepared to take a new position as a coach in a combined elementary/middle school. Coaches with whom I have worked have identified the following key ideas for getting started:

1. *Make yourself accessible.* A new coach needs to be seen, walking the halls, or stopping by classrooms to talk with teachers. All coaches and especially those new to the school should post their schedule and identify their availability; such a schedule can also provide space for teachers to "sign up" for a conversation, request resources, and so on. Certainly, all teachers should have an e-mail address and telephone number for contacting the coach. As mentioned in a previous chapter, even the location of the office is important. Coaches who keep their office doors open, who have instructional materials available that teachers can borrow, and who are willing to participate in professional conversations will have an easier time developing that important sense of trust.

2. *Initiate activities and seek responsibilities.* New coaches have at times indicated that they aren't sure what to do or how to start getting involved. In the beginning weeks of school, several approaches might be useful. New coaches can write an introductory letter describing their background and then identify some of the ways in which they might work with teachers. Or a new coach can develop a reading room, perhaps in the coach's office, that includes various professional and instructional materials and then invite teachers to visit the room (coffee or chocolate candy might be available also) and to borrow the materials. Another coach might schedule informal conversations with each teacher, suggesting that such a conversation will help the coach develop a more in-

depth understanding of the students in each classroom, their abilities and needs, and how the coach might help teachers address those needs. Figure 7.1 describes some ideas for this conversation and suggests possible questions that the coach might ask the teacher. Some coaches have also asked teachers if they might teach a mini-lesson in their classrooms to get to know the students (since the coach will be in the classroom at different times during the year). And, of course, coaches at the beginning of the year can help teachers as they attempt to conduct the initial assessments that are often required in schools.

3. *Build a sense of trust.* As mentioned in Chapter 6, some activities of coaches are seen as more threatening (i.e., observing and giving feedback) than others. To help teachers understand that coaching is meant to be supportive and nonevaluative, it is critical to develop a sense of trust. So, starting the position by serving as a resource is most likely a good idea; the activities mentioned above are ones that help develop trust between teacher and coach. But so too, is maintaining *confidentiality.* In almost all cases, what coaches see and hear when they talk with teachers or visit their classrooms must remain between teacher and coach, although there may be a few instances when a situation affects the well-being of a child or children, and in that case, confidentiality

---

Schedule a time to meet with each teacher individually in a comfortable situation and when it is convenient for the teacher to talk. Below is a suggested framework for the conversation.

1. **Breaking the ice.** Share with the teacher some information about yourself— your goals as a coach, your background (if new to the school). Talk with the teacher about his or her background, interests. Sometimes, there are pictures of grandchildren, vacation trips, or pets that can spark a short conversation.

2. **Setting a goal.** Establish the reason why you are holding these conversations: Get to know the teacher's goals for the students; a little more about the students in the classroom and their strengths and needs.

3. **Suggested questions:**
   a. What are your goals for your students this year? (think about broad goals of the reading program).
   b. What are the skills and abilities of students in terms of achieving the goals? How can I help you learn more about your students?
   c. What strategies/approaches seem to work for you and help you achieve your goals?
   d. What resources would be helpful to you?
   e. In what ways can I be helpful?

FIGURE 7.1. Questions for an initial conversation with teachers.

does not apply. Likewise, coaches will hear things from administrators that are not to be shared with teachers.

4. *Start with the willing.* Although coaches most often work with all teachers in a school, I suggest that, if possible, they begin by working with volunteers; that is, those teachers who seem to want or request coaching support. By working with volunteers, coaches can hone their own skills in a supportive environment. Moreover, the word often spreads … "coaching was very helpful!" Although starting with eager and willing teachers can be helpful, coaches should not stop there. In order to effect school change, they must continue to seek opportunities to work with all teachers in the school, although they will not work with all teachers in the same way nor to the same extent. Below, I elaborate on various coaching activities.

THINK ABOUT THIS

Which of the ideas above do you think are most useful for a new coach? Are there others that might work well?

Demonstrating or Modeling

One of the most important means of coaching is demonstrating or modeling specific behaviors or strategies. As mentioned previously, Fullan (1991) described the "implementation dip" that often occurs in our schools. Specifically, he discusses the fact that even after teachers have attended workshops or presentations about effective programs or approaches, their successful implementation of what they learned remains an issue. So, if the goal is to have a teacher learn to use a specific strategy, such as Beck and McKeown's "Text-Talk" (2001), the coach may need to model that approach while the teacher observes. In the LEADERS project, described in Chapter 5, participating teachers indicated that demonstration lessons were extremely helpful to them. When they saw another individual using a specific approach or strategy, especially in their classrooms with their students, these teachers felt as though they had a much better understanding of how to implement that strategy. Some guidelines for doing such demonstration lessons follow:

1. Plan with teachers so that they have some role in the lesson, assisting children or conducting a small part of the lesson. This active involvement creates much more interest and understanding on the part of the teacher—as well as commitment. One effective coach always gave

the teacher a role in the modeled lesson; for example, "I would like you to monitor the work of Jimmy and Chelsea while I teach. Generally they have difficulty following directions. Perhaps if you sat next to them, it would be helpful." Other coaches frame questions with teachers prior to the modeled lesson that will be used to discuss what happened in the lesson (i.e., student responses and reactions).

2. Discuss the lesson with the teacher as soon as possible after teaching it. Reflect with the teacher on the effectiveness of the lesson. Did I achieve my goals, and if not, why? What went well? What could have gone better? Be certain to address those questions that created the need for modeling in the first place! Be honest in sharing with the teacher unexpected aspects of the lesson (e.g., handling of a behavior problem). Few lessons are perfect and teachers will feel more comfortable working with a coach when they see that the coach also can have difficulty with a disruptive student or elicit little response from students, despite earnest efforts to stimulate interaction. Be sure to give teachers the opportunity to ask questions, reflect, and make comments as well.

3. Address next steps. Make certain that there is some follow-up to the modeled lesson. Such follow-up could include observing the teacher presenting the same type of lesson that was modeled. This is a critical step that helps to ensure that the teacher has actually benefited from the demonstration lesson. At the same time, there may be teachers who are uncomfortable with this step and the coach may need to do some coteaching that creates more of a sense of a partnership or co-ownership of the lesson. Likewise, the coach may also coplan a similar lesson with the teacher, but not observe until the teacher has had an opportunity to teach such a lesson several times. Notice that there is more than one way to follow-up with a modeled lesson; often the coach needs to follow the lead of the teacher (i.e., what makes sense for him or her?).

Coplanning

As mentioned previously, coaches need to understand where the teacher is in terms of readiness for coaching. Some teachers may welcome the coach if he or she is willing to help the teacher plan one lesson, several lessons that focus on developing a specific strategy or skill, or a unit of work. For example, the coach and teacher may want to work on lessons that help students understand how to participate in structured discussions to enhance comprehension. Coplanning may include lessons that introduce students to key ideas about participating in a discussion and the various roles that they can assume (e.g., leading, facilitating, etc.); other lessons may include looking at the materials of instruction and deciding what key questions to ask and where the best "stops" are for asking key questions. What is important is that the coach and teacher schedule follow-up meetings where they discuss reactions to and reflections about the lessons. Such coplanning can often precede coach observations.

Observations

One of the most effective coaching approaches to professional development is observing the work of teachers and providing feedback. It is there that the coach can actually intercede, provide reinforcement, alter various behaviors, or augment the teaching approaches of those observed. Observations, however, are too often synonymous with evaluation, because too often that has been their primary purpose. In the coaching model described below, the focus is on facilitating the teacher's growth and the coach is seen as a resource. Indeed, using this coaching model in an evaluative manner distorts its value and hinders the coach from developing the trust and openness necessary for success. Figure 7.2 outlines a model for coaching similar to the models proposed by Costa and Garmston (1994) and Glickman (1990). The four steps include planning, observing, analyzing/reflecting, and conferring. In

Step 1. Planning

Talk with the teacher, using the following questions: What are the goals for the lesson? What does the teacher hope to gain from the experience? In what ways should data be collected?

Step 2. Observing

Observe in the classroom, focusing on the aspects that have been jointly agreed upon in the planning meeting.

Step 3. Analyzing/reflecting

Both coach and teacher think about the lesson that has been observed. The coach analyzes data from observation and identifies topics/issues for discussion. The teacher generates questions and ideas for discussion.

Step 4. Conferring

Coach and teacher meet to discuss the lesson, using data obtained in steps 2 and 3. The goal of this step is to obtain a commitment from the teacher as to what aspects will be applied in future lessons.

FIGURE 7.2. Coaching cycle.

the following sections, each of the four steps is described, with examples from several coaching "cycles."

Planning

Planning is an important first step. Walking into the classroom without a focus is similar to traveling in an unfamiliar city without a map and trying to get from one location to another—there are many different directions to take and many different means of transportation. Likewise, with observation. The planning conference enables the coach and the teacher to discuss important issues:

> What are the goals of the lesson?
> What does the teacher hope to gain from the observation?
> What is the best means of obtaining the information needed to address the teacher's goals?
> What are the procedures to be followed? (For example, Where should the coach sit? How long should the coach stay?)

The planning session provides an opportunity for building trust and promoting reflection. It also enables the coach to gain information about the class, the lesson, and the teacher. For example, this may be the first lesson that the teacher has taught using a particular strategy, or perhaps there is a student with special needs who just arrived 2 days ago. One planning meeting between a second-grade teacher and a coach went as follows:

> Sally, a second-grade teacher, was trying an approach new to her: teaching a mini-lesson on writing, specifically informational writing. She wanted Teresa, the coach, to provide her with some feedback about her lesson. Sally and Teresa agreed that Teresa would observe, noting the procedures that Sally used in teaching the lesson. They agreed that Teresa needed to attend to the behavior of the students to determine whether they understood and were involved in the lesson. Teresa indicated that she would "script" the lesson, trying to record exactly what Sally and the students were doing at significant points in the lesson. Sally reminded Teresa that she would be working with the entire class and that her class was not familiar with informational writing. This would be a lesson introducing a sequential framework to the class. They agreed on a time and place for the observation.

Once the coach has established a working relationship with the teacher and has observed, the planning step of the next cycle is often embedded in the follow-up conversation. Teresa says to Sally:

"Overall, your students seemed to be able to arrange the sentence strips correctly; they really understood the sequence of making a peanut butter sandwich. What do you think the next steps might be; how can you move your students along?" Teresa asks the teacher to generate some ideas. The coach then asks, "Sally, you also raised some concern about Juan and Maria, two ELL students who seemed to be somewhat puzzled. I agree, they seemed to have some difficulty following your directions. I wonder whether it would be good to work with them in a smaller group so that they get more opportunity for support and scaffolding. What do you think?" The coach and teacher might agree that the teacher could teach another sequencing lesson, but only with a small group of students (perhaps while the other students are working in their learning centers). Or perhaps the teacher and coach might see the benefit of the coach teaching a similar lesson with these two students and a few others to get a better idea of what they do and do not understand.

The planning session can be quite short, and even occur on the fly as you are conversing with the teacher in the hallway or at lunch. Its greatest benefits are two: it establishes a common goal for coach and teacher and it focuses the observation!

Carrying Out the Observation

Many excellent texts provide a great deal of information on approaches to observation: Glickman (1990), Costa and Garmston (1994), and Lyons and Pinnell (2001), to cite a few. There are also many different data collection tools, including audio and video recordings, frequency counts of various behaviors, checklists, and complete scripting of teacher verbal behaviors. Some of these techniques are very comprehensive and time consuming; others, less so. In this text I describe several approaches that can be useful for the observations that literacy coaches typically make, given their major foci on instructional strategies, effective classroom management, and classroom environments that best enhance students' literacy achievement, including one for use in observing content area instruction. Described below are three important aspects of classroom instruction that can be observed.

Classroom Environment

There is clear evidence that effective teachers design their classrooms in ways to promote literacy. For example, many children's books are available and easily accessible—not hidden away where students cannot get to them. Student work is prominently displayed; in fact, there is more student work than commercial posters and charts. The presence of small-group work or learning centers indicates teachers' respect and appreciation for productive social interaction among small groups of students focused on an educational endeavor. Posted literacy standards further help students understand what is expected of them. Although some readers may think these descriptions of classroom environment apply only to the elementary schools, this is not true. Teachers at the upper levels—in all classrooms—have a responsibility to design an environment that creates excitement about learning and provides a place that is conducive to student learning. They too can organize their classrooms to facilitate small-group and individual work. According to some of our coaches, when they are beginning their work with teachers, a focus on the environment seems to be less threatening and helps them establish a sense of trust with their colleagues. Questions such as the following can be quite useful:

> How have you organized the room so that students can obtain resources they need and places to work independently?
> What learning supports can you provide on the walls (e.g., vocabulary aids, study hints)?
> In what way can you recognize student work in the environment?

THINK ABOUT THIS

What do you think are the key features for an effective learning environment at the preschool, elementary, middle school, or secondary levels (especially in the various academic subjects)? You might want to interview teachers at each of these levels to solicit their impressions.

Classroom Management

Taylor, Pressley, and Pearson (2002) indicated that the management systems of effective teachers are so subtle that one is not aware that such a system exists. In other words, students know the routines and the teacher's behavioral expectations. Regardless of the type of grouping for instruction—individual, partner, small group, or whole class—students move from task to task without chaos or confusion. There is a sense of community and a positive tone in the classroom, as the teacher provides reinforcement and reassurance to guide the work of students. Students are respectful of the teacher and each other. In one first-grade classroom in which I observed, the teacher never raised her voice; she was conferring with individual students while pairs of students worked together at the chalkboard. As I marveled at this well-orchestrated com-

munity of learners, she commented, "Too often, these children are sub-
jected to yelling and screaming at home; they seem to appreciate the
quiet of this classroom."

Although some literacy coaches have indicated that their responsibilities do not include helping teachers with classroom management,
the bottom line is that instruction and classroom management are
closely intertwined. Unless teachers have mastered this aspect of teaching, little time can be spent on effective instruction; too much time is
spent on redirecting student behavior. Or, perhaps by working with the
teacher to provide appropriate classroom instruction that excites students, there can be improvement in classroom behavior. In other words,
active engagement and excitement about learning can lead to more
effective student behavior.

Instruction

Since their role is to assist teachers in mastering new or different strategies being promoted in the school, one of the major areas that literacy
coaches must address is that of instruction. It is here that the coaches
use their knowledge and understanding of reading instruction to determine whether the teachers are implementing strategies in an efficient
and effective manner. In addition, literacy coaches can assist teachers
by attending to two other aspects of teaching: (1) responding to student
errors, and (2) maintaining active involvement of students.

RESPONDING TO STUDENT ERRORS

As teachers, we often solicit responses from students to determine their
understanding as well as to maintain attention. What happens when a
student responds with an incorrect answer? Does the teacher quickly call
on another student, or is there "scaffolding" that enables the student to
answer correctly? Is scaffolding done quickly and effectively so that the
attention of the class is maintained? Recently, I watched a first-grade
teacher as she listened to students reading a selection. She quickly and
efficiently helped students when they made errors in oral reading. In
some cases, she told the student the word; in other cases, she asked them
to try to sound it out (e.g., "Take off the ending … think of that word
family at the end"); and in other situations, she mentioned that the student should think about what makes sense. All of this was done so effectively that all those in the group remained attentive to the story being
read. This is critical also at upper levels, where students who respond
incorrectly may never voluntarily respond again if their comments are
not treated with respect. At the upper levels especially, teachers must

develop classrooms that are "low risk"; that is, students know that divergent thinking is encouraged and that their opinions and thoughts are treated with respect.

Although teachers may implement a strategy or approach in an appropriate manner, difficulties with student attention still may arise. This difficulty is especially likely to occur when teachers are working with the entire class, and the lesson does not address the individual needs of students. It is critical that the coach work with the teacher so that active involvement can be maintained. When the inattention of students becomes obvious, teachers need to be encouraged to think of ways to stimulate mental and physical alertness. Adjusting lesson content, small-group or partner work, the use of manipulatives, and active participation can be discussed in the post-observation conference.

Conducting Observations

As mentioned previously, there are many different frameworks or systems that can be used for collecting data during observations. The one described below requires the coach to describe what is happening—not to interpret or make judgments *about* what is happening. Using paper and pen or with a laptop computer, the coach records exactly what is going on in the classroom. The end product provides the coach with "data" that can be shared with the classroom teacher; for example, "Here's what the students were doing when. ... " Specific steps are summarized in Figure 7.3.

When entering the classroom, it is best to remain as unobtrusive as possible, finding a spot to sit and observe without interrupting the flow of the lesson. There are times, however, when the teacher will choose to introduce the coach/specialist; if so, smiling, greeting the students, and then finding a place to sit and watch are recommended. There are also occasions when the teacher attempts to have the coach interact with the students and the lesson. In those instances, the coach may choose to join in and actually help teach the lesson. The teacher can learn a great deal by having the coach work with him or her, and because the coach's goal is to be helpful to the teacher, this modification may be just what is needed at this time. Depending on the coach's job responsibilities, he or she may also return to observe the teacher doing the lesson unaided! In that case, the teacher should be told that in the next lesson, the coach/reading specialist will observe and not participate.

1. Upon entering the room, spend several minutes doing an environmental sweep and collecting information about number of students, literacy environment in the room, and seating arrangements. You may want to draw a picture of the classroom.

2. Using blank sheets of paper, divide the sheet into two sections with a line down the middle, with Teacher in the left section and Students in the right section.

3. Begin identifying what is occurring in the classroom. If there is classroom discourse (i.e., the teacher is interacting with the students), try to jot down key phrases or words that the teacher and the students are saying. You may also want to identify whether specific students are responding. Remember to note whatever is especially relevant to the focus or goal identified in the planning session. For example, if the teacher wants the coach to attend to levels of questions, then recording the specific questions is important. If the teacher wants the coach to observe whether students are actively involved, then the coach would need to attend to that dimension of instruction. At the same time, observing what is happening overall may be the key to identifying why students are not actively involved.

4. When the teacher is serving more as a facilitator, the coach can focus on what students are doing, or not doing, as well as what the teacher is doing.

Example of a script:

Teacher	Students
Walking around helping students, answering questions.	*Students are all writing in their journals.*
Helps child by asking him to read what he had written in journal.	*One student has head down and is not writing. (OC: task too difficult?)*

5. Every 5 minutes, draw a line under what you have written so that you have some indication of how long various activities have lasted and when they occurred. Sometimes, you may want to draw a line when an activity changes; for example, the teacher has finished reading a story and is now beginning to ask questions about the selection.

6. Mark "OC" (observer's comment) when there are events in the lesson about which you want to talk with the teacher or have questions. For example, mark "OC" next to the note, "Student refused to do work" and note query, "Can't do?"

7. Every 5 minutes or so (when it seems appropriate), it is wise to stop writing and just look around the classroom. It is easy to become so immersed in the writing that you miss some of the nonverbal and physical interactions.

FIGURE 7.3. Observation system for data collection.

It does take time to learn to observe using this approach. However, with practice it becomes a very effective means of collecting the information needed to interact effectively with teachers. See Appendix A for a form for using this approach.

Other Observation Systems

In this section, I describe three other observation forms that may be useful to coaches. The observation form in Figure 7.4 was used in the collection of data for an evaluation project in which we observed classroom literacy instruction in grades K–8 (Bean, Eichelberger, Turner, & Tellez, 2002). This form was influenced by the work of Taylor and Pearson (2002); several of the categories and specific behaviors from their School Change Classroom Observation Scheme have been adapted for use. The form can also be useful for thinking about the various dimensions to be observed (e.g., instruction, materials, classroom management, etc.).

The observation protocol in Figure 7.5 is adapted from a protocol used to observe Reading First classrooms (K–3); the adapted version can be used to observe reading instruction across the elementary grades. It provides observers with specific descriptors of what they might expect to see when observing reading instruction and also a scale that could be used to determine the extent to which specific indicators are present in the classroom or seen during the observation period. Appendix B describes an observation protocol that can be used for observing in content areas in upper elementary, middle, or high schools. This protocol provides information about the literacy activities of students and how the teacher facilitates learning, as well as information about grouping and materials used.

The observation protocols described previously are ones that can be used when observing different types of lessons. However, observers who are going into classrooms to see how well teachers are implementing a specific skill or strategy (e.g., Text-Talk by Beck & McKeown, 2001) may choose to develop an observation protocol that addresses steps of that strategy or skill. Or, if a school has a literacy framework that emphasizes certain strategies, then the literacy coach may choose to develop an observational protocol that focuses on those strategies. For example, Thibodeau (2008), a literacy coach, worked with several secondary content area teachers and taught them specific literacy strategies that could be used before, during, and after reading text selections. In that case, an observation protocol could be developed that addresses dimensions of those strategies.

Name: _____ Grade: ____ School: _____ Subject: _____

Instruction
Evidence of:
_____ student engagement
_____ clarity of explanations/directions
(helping students understand)
_____ modeling/coaching/scaffolding
_____ flexible grouping

Specific strategies observed:

Comments:

Classroom Management
Evidence that the teacher:
_____ uses positive reinforcement
_____ exhibits positive-feeling tone
_____ establishes clear expectations for behavior
_____ establishes routines that students understand

Comments:

Literate Environment
Evidence of:
_____ student work around the room
_____ classroom libraries
_____ places for small-group work (reading center,
learning centers, etc.)
_____ print-rich
_____ standards/expectations for students

Grouping
whole class
small group
pairs
individual
other

Materials
text
student writing
board/chart
worksheet
games
other

Teacher Interaction
tell/give information
modeling
recitation
discussion
coaching/scaffolding
listening/watching
reading aloud
check work (monitoring)
other

Student Response
reading
reading turn-taking
talking
listening
writing
manipulating

Code: 0 = not at all evident; 1 = evident sometimes;
         2 = evident most of the time; 3 = evident throughout

Comments:

Time Period	1	2	3	4	5	6
Students on task						
75% or more students on task						
50–75% students on task						
Less than 50% students on task						

FIGURE 7.4. Classroom Observation Form.

Teacher: _____ Grade Level: _____

Date: _____ Time Begin: _____ End: _____

Students Present: _____ Lesson Focus: _____

Materials: (Check all that apply)

☐ Textbook	Group: (Check all	Adults: (Check all that apply)
☐ Board/Chart	that apply)	☐ Teacher ☐ Student Teacher
☐ Computer	☐ Whole Class	☐ Reading Specialist ☐ Teacher Intern
☐ Worksheet	☐ Small Group	☐ Reading Coach ☐ Other_____
☐ Student Work	☐ Pairs	☐ Instructional Aide
☐ Other	☐ Individual	

Protocol to be used as a guide. Scale to be completed after the observation has been completed.

Scale:	Great Extent	Some Extent	Minimal Extent	Not Observed
	(4)	(3)	(2)	(1)
Classroom Environment: Print Rich				
Classroom Library Is Accessible *Students are able to gain easy access to the library in the classroom. Books are eye-level.*	☐	☐	☐	☐
Library Has Wide Variety of Books/Genres *Library includes informational, pleasure, poetry, language play, reference materials, etc.*	☐	☐	☐	☐
Reading and/or Writing Strategies Are Displayed *Strategies posted are informative tools designed to promote classroom learning.*	☐	☐	☐	☐
Reading Spaces Are Inviting	☐ yes	☐ no		
Learning Centers Are Evident	☐ yes	☐ no		
Student Work on Display Inside/Outside	☐ yes	☐ no		

Scale:	Great Extent	Some Extent	Minimal Extent	Not Observed
	(4)	(3)	(2)	(1)
Classroom Management/Climate				
Maintains Positive Learning Environment *Interactions are respectful and supportive. Tone and atmosphere are encouraging.*	☐	☐	☐	☐

FIGURE 7.5. From Bean, Fulmer, and Zigmond (2009).

	Great Extent (4)	Some Extent (3)	Minimal Extent (2)	Not Observed (1)
Encourages High Level of Student Participation *Teacher facilitates active engagement of students during lesson.*	☐	☐	☐	☐
Maintains Effective Behavioral Routines *Clear expectations are established by teacher and internalized by students. Minimum time is spent in transitions.*	☐	☐	☐	☐
Maintains Robust Literacy Routines *Teacher facilitates strong literacy routines that are recognized and understood by students.*	☐	☐	☐	☐
Preserves Student On-Task Behavior *Teacher consistently facilitates student engagement during reading instruction.*	☐	☐	☐	☐

Scale:	Great Extent	Some Extent	Minimal Extent	Not Observed
	(4)	(3)	(2)	(1)
Instructional Practices				
Introduces/Reviews Concepts/Skills Clearly *Teacher develops concept or skill plainly and accurately. The concept or skill introduced is evident.*	☐	☐	☐	☐
Differentiates Literacy Instruction *Teacher appears to use individual student literacy performance in planning instruction. Literacy learning is structured for small groups or individual students.*	☐	☐	☐	☐
Facilitates Text Comprehension *Teacher helps students to make connections to targeted concepts; activates student background knowledge; engages students in high-level thinking activities; encourages students to make predictions; summarizes, retells, or makes use of graphic organizers to organize their thinking.*	☐	☐	☐	☐
Engages in Coaching/Scaffolding *Teacher provides corrective feedback by prompting the student in an effort to encourage the student to arrive at the correct answer independently.*	☐	☐	☐	☐

FIGURE 7.5. *(cont.)*

Highlights Significance of Reading Process *Teacher emphasizes the reading and writing process and the use of strategies; "A good reader sees the parts of words to help her decode. A good reader/writer does . . .*	☐	☐	☐	☐
Models Skills/Strategies Teacher demonstrates a particular skill or strategy to students.	☐	☐	☐	☐
Provides Guided Practice Teacher supports students in practicing targeted skill or concept. Teacher provides opportunities to practice literacy learning.	☐	☐	☐	☐
Provides/Monitors Independent Practice Teacher has students practice targeted concept/ skill individually and monitors by giving feedback when needed.	☐	☐	☐	☐
Provides Application Activities Teacher has students apply targeted concept to new learning for problem solving and independent learning. Students take responsibility for their own literacy learning.	☐	☐	☐	☐

Gradual Release of Responsibility Model (GRRM) (Pearson & Gallagher, 1983).

FIGURE 7.5. *(cont.)*

Analyzing/Reflecting

Each step of the coaching cycle is an important one; however, the step of analyzing/reflecting is critical, for without it, there is little chance of making an impact on teacher performance. Reflection is not only the purview of the coach but also of the teacher. Before meeting for a postconference, both literacy coach and teacher must think about what occurred in the lesson, and especially in what ways the questions raised in the preconference or planning stage can be addressed. The literacy coach may ask the teacher to jot down a few ideas, or such a question may be raised in the conference itself. The coach should take time before the conference to analyze what has been observed.

It is here, in the analysis phase, that the coach can make good use of the notes or scripts that were written during the observation. These notes provide excellent information that can be shared with the teacher during the conference. What levels of questions did the teacher ask? What steps did he or she follow in teaching the strategy? How many students (and who) were not involved during the lesson? Going back through the notes and thinking about answers to the following questions enable the coach to plan a strategy for the postconference to be held with the teacher:

What are the key points to raise? (What factors are most important in terms of possible impact on student learning?)

How do I want to start the conference? (Do I start with identification of some strengths? Can I ask the teacher to discuss his or her views?)

What changes would best improve the instruction going on in that classroom? (Are the changes doable? What support would be needed by the teacher to implement the changes?)

What approach might be best in working with this teacher?

Conferring with the Teacher

The postconference should occur as close in time to the actual observation as possible, not only to allay the teacher's concerns, but also because recall and memory of what occurred is much better. However, the analysis and reflection step is important and should not be eliminated. I find it helpful to talk briefly with teachers immediately after an observation, thanking them for the opportunity to work with them and making a positive comment about some aspect of the lesson (e.g., the classroom environment, one student's performance, etc.).

One goal of the conference is to promote teacher reflection to the highest degree possible, focusing on teacher and student behaviors (Who was doing what?), comparing actual and desired behaviors, or considering reasons why these occurred or did not occur.

One of the most important goals of the postconference is the generation of future plans: What can the teacher take back from the conference that will facilitate instruction in the classroom? Another goal is to assess the effects of the coaching experience: In what ways was the experience helpful—and what comes next?

Coaches need to be cognizant of the individual strengths, experiences, and learning styles of teachers. Using this knowledge, coaches can work with teachers in one of three ways: as a mirror, as a collaborator, or as an expert (Robbins, 1991).

Coach as Mirror

In this instance, the teacher is self-reflective and quickly assumes a leadership role in the conference. The coach then serves to confirm and validate what the teacher articulates. These types of conferences generally move along quite easily, because the teacher sees whether he or she has achieved the lesson goals, why or why not, and suggests possible solutions to any problems. The coach then serves as a mirror by reflecting back to the teacher specific examples that indicate support for what the teacher is saying. In the example below, the coach is working with an experienced kindergarten teacher who analyzes her own behavior and sets future goals for herself.

> KINDERGARTEN TEACHER: I lost the group after about 15 minutes. They were really with me until I started asking various questions about the main character. I don't think they lost interest in the story; I think they were sitting too long. I wonder if I might have asked several of them to ...
>
> COACH: Yes, I think you're right. After about the third question, when you were trying ...

Coach as Collaborator

In this case, the literacy coach and teacher work together to determine the strengths and possible weaknesses of the lessons. They are both struggling to identify what was especially effective and what may have been done better.

> SEVENTH-GRADE SOCIAL STUDIES TEACHER: It seems to me that there has to be a better way to get more students involved in the discussion. It seems as though the same students are always raising their hands, while the others wait for them to reply.
>
> COACH: Let's talk about this. Remember that chapter about holding effective discussions in the classroom in Kylene Beers's book, *When Kids Can't Read: What Teachers Can Do* (2003)? Let's think about the recommendations she makes. One suggestion was that students talk to each other before ...
>
> TEACHER: Oh, yes! I remember; that's a great idea. Another thought I had was to ask students to generate questions for other students. Let's talk about how I might do that.
>
> COACH: Terrific idea; I think your students would really enjoy the challenge of that.

Coach as Expert

In some instances, especially with novice teachers or teachers who are attempting a new approach for the first time, the coach may need to serve as expert: as the individual who can provide information that helps teachers understand whether they are implementing various strategies or approaches effectively.

> FIFTH-GRADE TEACHER: So, when I was trying the K-W-L, I wasn't sure what I should do after students identified all they knew about turtles. Exactly how should I move to the *W* step?
>
> COACH: I think you did a great job! You had the students review what they knew, and then you commented: "Wow, we know a lot, but it appears that there is still much more to learn. For example, I wondered what the differences were between land turtles and sea turtles? What are some things you are wondering about?" You can help to jump-start the students by modeling for them.

Giving Feedback

The feedback that coaches provide to teachers about their instructional practices may require teachers to consider some changes in what or how they teach. If the teacher and coach together can identify those areas or behaviors in which change is desired (i.e., coach as mirror or coach as collaborator), then the feedback session is generally a productive and positive one. On the other hand, there are times when the coach has to be more direct in working with a teacher. Always, the desire is to provide feedback that is constructive and workable. Nevertheless, some teachers may react defensively and be unable to accept or benefit from feedback, unless it is provided in a carefully balanced manner. Several suggestions for giving feedback follow:

1. *Be specific.* Telling the teacher that the lesson was good, fine, or interesting is not constructive—it does not provide information the teacher can use to improve classroom practices. Instead the coach must be as specific as possible. For example, if the coach wants to reinforce the many ways the teacher has made the environment student-friendly, he or she can describe specifically what he or she saw (e.g., many different kinds of books in places where students could readily access them; student work posted on the walls; a chart that read "You Made My Day," with students' names on it). Likewise, if the coach has concerns about an instructional aspect of the lesson (e.g., the teacher called only on the few students whose hands were up), the coach can show the teacher the data from the observation that shows who was called on and who wasn't.

Or, if teacher questioning was only at a literal level, even though the emphasis was on inferential thinking, the coach can share the data with the teacher and they can analyze the level of questions used together.

2. *Behave in ways that reduce defensive behavior.* It is natural for all of us to defend what we have done in response to what we perceive as criticism. Coaches can reduce defensive behavior in several ways. First, they can focus on describing what they observed rather than making a judgment about it and, to the degree possible, create a problem-solving situation (e.g., "I noticed that students were less attentive in the discussion part of the lesson than while reading the story. Let's talk about that. What do you think caused their inattention?"). Such an approach promotes collaboration and reduces the tendency for the coach to be perceived as the only one who has the answers. Second, coaches can acknowledge the fact that the teacher has unique experiences and knowledge that will contribute to the solution of the problem. Teachers know the goals they are trying to achieve and the personalities of the students with whom they work. They can therefore contribute to the solutions or suggestions in ways the coach cannot. For example, "Tell me about your goals for the lesson, and let's talk about what you did to reach those goals."

3. *Provide balanced feedback.* Make certain that the teacher clearly understands the issue or item under discussion and how to resolve it. For example, if the teacher is providing opportunities for students to develop fluency but the students are reading books that are too difficult for them to read without making many errors, the coach needs to make certain that the teacher understands that fluency practice is important and valued but that, in order for it to be productive, the material needs to be at an instructional or independent level. Feedback can be divided into a two-step process, as follows:

> a. *Discuss the merits of what the teacher is doing* (e.g., the merits of providing fluency practice for students).
>
> > "We know that in order to be effective readers, students need to have opportunities to practice reading. The use of partner reading is certainly an effective strategy, and so is repeated reading. It was great to see that happening in your classroom."
>
> b. *Identify the concern or area that needs changing.*
>
> > "One of the ways that you can increase the effectiveness of the fluency practice you are providing is by chang-

ing the difficulty level of the material that students are using. What materials do you have available that might be appropriate? Or, let's see what is available in the resource room."

Notice that, in the example above, the coach was not critical of the teacher but instead relayed information on how the teacher could increase the effect of an important strategy that he or she had attempted in the classroom. Balanced feedback should include specific information as to what is effective and what can be improved. The teacher and coach both should explore ideas for how to address the concern.

4. *Focus the feedback on one or two important possibilities.* In other words, "less is more." What is most important to consider and how doable is it? Is it something that the teacher can do somewhat easily and achieve success?

5. *Celebrate the successes of the teacher.* This suggestion is closely aligned with balanced feedback, but it deserves to be mentioned again. Although the coach is there to help guide improvement, there are most likely aspects of the lesson that deserve some celebration (e.g., the teacher has student work displayed and many different reading materials available for students, the students are attentive and on task, etc.). All of us need positive reinforcement and the coach should acknowledge what has been especially effective in the classroom.

6. *Most important, support the teacher in self-reflection efforts.* Even though this suggestion is last, it may be the most important. The old adage, "give a man a fish and he eats for a day; teach a man to fish and he eats for a lifetime," is appropriate here. To the extent that the teacher can identify, address, and think about the lesson—its successes and how to improve it—the most likely it is that there will be follow through in future practices. Such reflective behavior can be facilitated when the coach is a good listener and able to scaffold and build on the thoughts of the teacher (see Chapter 4).

Coaching can be a valuable approach to improving the literacy instruction in a school. It can also be a growth experience for both the coach and the teacher. However, given that schools have not generally focused on these types of supportive observations, it takes time to build an atmosphere of trust and receptivity to this approach. In talking with an individual responsible for working with new teachers, I asked her what she thought were the most important components of effective coaching. She shared these comments:

1. *Confidentiality.* What is seen by the coach and said by the teacher always stays between them. Nothing should ever be repeated, criticized, or made fun of in the teachers' lounge, principal's office, or at a school function.

2. *Nonthreatening demeanor.* The coach is present as a colleague, not an evaluator. Bring to the conscious level all of the good things that are happening in the class and offer suggestions about other possible methods of presenting the information. The coach is not there to make a teacher feel incompetent!

3. *Focus.* It is always advantageous to have a mutually agreed-upon target to focus the observation. When the conference occurs, the coach is ready with multiple suggestions and questions designed to make the teacher think and grow professionally (personal communication, 2001).

One of the most difficult tasks for coaches is providing this feedback to teachers because often they have been the peers of their colleagues or they recognize that they have no evaluative responsibility. Moreover, for many of us, confrontation or conflict is difficult. Learning to be a critical friend takes time and has to occur in a culture where teachers feel comfortable and value making their teaching public.

The Reality of the School

In the work that my colleagues and I have done with coaches (Bean et al., 2008), we have learned that although many coaches would value the opportunity to work in a systematic way with teachers (e.g., going through the formal observation cycle, from planning through postdiscussion), school schedules, multiple demands on the coach, as well as differing needs of teachers, create the need for other forms of coaching beyond those discussed previously. One is what I call "on-the-fly" or opportunistic coaching; that is, coaches make themselves accessible so that they can respond to the needs and requests of teachers. The other is "combination coaching" in which teachers and coaches work together in a somewhat seamless fashion, moving from modeling to coteaching to observing; for example, within a specific time period. Coaches may also want to do walk-throughs either by themselves or with some other school personnel (e.g., administrator, school curriculum director, special educator). Each of these is discussed below.

On-the-Fly Coaching

In a study of coaches in Reading First in Pennsylvania (Bean et al., 2008), we found that frequently coaches spent short amounts of time conversing with teachers, specialists, librarians, and principals in the hallways, between classes, at lunch, or before or after school. Such conversations actually led to important work with these school personnel and below I provide some examples of what is meant by on-the-fly coaching.

Fred, the coach, was stopped by Harry, a third-grade teacher, as they waited for their students to get off the bus in the morning. He wondered why the district was asking teachers to administer another assessment test, besides the one that was given every 6 weeks. What would be gained by giving this assessment? Fred and Harry spent about 5 minutes talking about the new measure and how it was different from the one that was currently being administered. Fred also told Harry that he would be happy to stop by and show him the informal measure and, if Harry wanted, to model the administration of it with several of his students.

Fred also walked with the librarian on their way to the staff development meeting that was to be held after school. The librarian was working with the sixth-grade science teacher on a unit about planets. She wanted to know what she could read that would help her understand this new emphasis on "informational text" and what she might do in her library classes that would be useful to the students in that science class. Fred indicated that he would stop by the next day with an article about informational text that she might find useful. He also told the librarian that he would be happy to spend some time discussing this with her during her planning period, if she was interested.

What is clear is that these meetings are opportunities for more in-depth coaching and that coaches need to take advantage of these quick, spontaneous conversations that can come up throughout the day.

Combination Coaching

In our work with Reading First coaches (Zigmond & Bean, 2008), we found that some coaches stayed in the classrooms of teachers for an extended period, working with them for an entire reading block of 90 minutes. During this time, they modeled, cotaught, and even observed. Then later that day, or the next day, they discussed their work and planned for the next teaching segment. We saw this sort of coaching especially when teachers were new to the school or to teaching a specific grade level. Reading coaches tended to spend extensive amounts of time helping these novice teachers learn more about how to provide or differentiate instruction.

Walk-Throughs

During the past few years, leaders in schools have begun to make frequent, short visits to classrooms to get a better picture of what is occurring across the school. Often these walk-throughs are done by several individuals (e.g., a principal and curriculum developer, two teachers, etc.). I heard someone describe a single observation as a snapshot or photograph, walk-throughs as a photograph album. Certainly, this description illustrates the advantages of such a coaching approach. If coaches walk through all the classrooms at a grade level (e.g., at least once a week), they will get a sense of the similarities and differences across the classrooms in instruction, environment, and management, which may help coaches as they work with teachers in grade-level meetings. They will get a sense of how a classroom functions over a number of visits. Also, another advantage is that teachers and students become comfortable with the coach in the classroom, especially if the walk-through is an informal, friendly event. If the coach is making a walk-through alone, the following suggestions may be helpful:

1. Try to get an overall sense of what the classroom looks like (the environment).
2. Listen carefully to the teacher to get a sense of what teaching is going on; what instructional strategies are being used.
3. Also, some coaches like to focus on the students, which can be very informative. Take time to stop by the desks of a few children: Do they understand what they are to do? Are they completing a task as expected? Sometimes, I like to ask students to explain to me what they are to do and why they think it is important for them to complete this task.

Most often, a simple "thank you" or a wave is sufficient when leaving the room, especially if coaches have informed teachers that they will be doing these walk-throughs on a regular basis. However, I have found that teachers appreciate it if the coach leaves a quick note (Post-It Notes are terrific) that reinforces something that occurred during the visit (e.g., the kids seemed to really be enjoying the story today).

Summary

This chapter discussed the importance of coaching as an approach to providing professional development for teachers. Ideas for getting started as a coach were identified followed by specific suggestions for modeling and coteaching. Observing in the classroom as a means of improving classroom teaching practices was emphasized. Steps comprising a coaching cycle for observing were identified, as were protocols for data collection and techniques for providing feedback to teachers. Finally, three variations on coaching procedures; on-the-fly, combination, and walk-throughs were described.

Reflections

1. Given your experiences, how comfortable would you be observing in a classroom and providing feedback to teachers? What skills do you think you need to develop more fully?
2. Think about the coaching cycle. What would be the most difficult steps for you to implement? Why?

Activities

1. Go through a coaching cycle with a colleague. Think about the following after you have completed the cycle. What did you learn from the planning conference that affected the way in which you observed? In your analysis of the observation, what points did you identify as important to discuss with the colleague? In what ways did you provide feedback to the teacher? How successful do you think you were in conducting this coaching cycle? What would you do differently?
2. Try providing balanced feedback. Work with a colleague or a member of your class. Here are two scenarios to try. Remember, (1) clarify what has occurred, (2) provide specific feedback about the merits of a situation or behavior, and (3) discuss ways to address any concern.

   Scenario 1. Carlos observed Frank, a sixth-grade social studies teacher, as he used an anticipation guide to introduce a new unit on the Civil War. He gave the class a sheet on which there were a number of facts about the war and asked them to indicate whether they agreed or disagreed with the facts. Immediately, hands were raised; students grumbled that they could not read certain words or that they did not know what to do. Frank told them to put the sheet in their desks and to open their books to the first page of the chapter.

   Scenario 2. Henrietta arrived to observe Greta, a third-grade teacher, who had indicated that she was trying to use flexible grouping in her classroom, but that students were not able to work independently. She wanted help from Henrietta because, at this point, as she stated, "These kids can't work independently." Now Greta was conducting guided reading with a group of six students. On the board was a list indicating what the other students should be doing: reading books silently, working on the computer, or doing worksheets. And some were actually doing those things. However, four or five students were wandering around, talking to others. Two had their heads on the desk and appeared to be sleeping. Every 2 minutes or so, Greta would look around, away from the group with whom she was working, and remind students firmly, "You know what you should be doing. Let's get to it!"

Katy: A Coach in an Urban Elementary/Middle School

Some questions to think about:

What lessons can be learned abut the coaching role of the reading specialist from this vignette?

What questions come to mind from reading this vignette?

What key characteristics or behaviors make Katy an effective reading specialist and coach?

Although I have always worked in urban schools, the level at which I have worked has differed. I have been a kindergarten teacher and also a coach in an elementary school. But 3 years ago, when I applied for the coaching position that I have now, I knew it would be challenging. I was new to the building, so I did not know the teachers and the principal had a reputation for being very demanding. The school was going from a K–5 to a K–8 configuration and I would have to work between two buildings that are about a mile apart (K–4 in one building and 5–8 in the other).

I was nervous for most of that summer. As I mentioned previously, most of my teaching experiences were in kindergarten and primary grades, so I had serious reservations about my ability to be effective with older students and upper elementary and middle school teachers. I received assurance from many people that I would be "fine." I didn't want to be fine, however. I wanted to be better than fine. I wanted to be effective.

As a child, before I left the house every morning on my way to elementary and high school, my father always said, "Remember your name is Carroll." That meant so many different things, but most important it meant that I was supposed to be the best at whatever I set out to do that day. I kept hearing that mantra in my head as I prepared for my new position that summer and it made me wonder how I was going to succeed working with so many teachers on so many levels and with children who really scared me!

As I worked through my fears that summer and throughout that school year, I realized that no matter what level you coach, there are fundamental principles that if followed, can lead to success. The two most important principles for me are using data to drive instruction and developing reflective practitioners.

Assessment and Instruction

I would never want to reduce children to simple numbers. I know there is so much more to each individual child than a DIBELS [Dynamic Indicators of Basic Early Literary Skills], unit, and/or state assessment score. Those scores, however, give us a place to start. I began many conversations with teachers by asking them to bring different sets of data to meetings. It was a safe way for us to get to know each other. The numbers were concrete and they seemed to put us all on a level playing field.

If I asked teachers to bring a teacher-made assessment, it led to conversations about whether what we asked students to do on the assessment was really helping us gather the information we wanted. After completing Error Pattern Analysis with the DIBELS, we had very deep conversations about the instructional practices teachers needed to incorporate into their routines and schedules to better meet the needs of their students. Teachers began to bring their own questions to our meetings or they would pull me aside in the hallway to ask data-related questions. All of these group and one-on-one conversations inevitably led to discussions about individual children—their strengths, weaknesses, and what we could do as a team to better educate that child.

When we got to the point of discussing our teaching practices as they related to individual children, I knew we had reached a higher level with our work. What began as conversations about numbers and groups of children had now shifted to teacher practice. Teachers began to open up and share what they do in their classrooms and to be very honest about what worked and what was not working. They were able to acknowledge when they were effective and what they did to be most effective. They admitted when they had not planned or did not know about a teaching practice.

One meeting with grade 6–8 teachers stands out. We were able to articulate the fact that some of us are "reading teachers," some are "literature teachers," and some are both. That might sound small, but it was actually huge! It gave us the chance to discuss the differences when teaching children to learn to read versus reading to learn. It helped one teacher truly understand, for the first time, why she was having so much trouble with some of her students. She had come from high school to teach middle school and had never learned how to really teach someone to read. Now that she was faced with students who could not do the work in her class because they could not read, she had two choices: continue to fail the children because of their deficiencies, or be willing to be vulnerable in front of her colleagues and learn new strategies in order to better teach her struggling students. Thankfully, she chose the latter. It turned into a learning experience for all involved. It helped us reflect on our own practices when we worked with children. We studied best practices, we shared our learning and our ideas, I modeled, teachers tried things in their classrooms, and we always reported back to the group.

What I Have Learned

The process of coaching is not always smooth. Teachers don't always understand my role—some still see me as a supply clerk—my job description has changed many times over the past 3 years and, at times, I am asked to do things that have absolutely nothing to do with coaching. The lack of smoothness, however, is what makes the job so exciting. When I first considered the job many years ago, a mentor told me that if I took it, I would no longer have children as my students. My students would now be the teachers with whom I work. It took me a long time to accept this. Now that I have, however, I get the same joy when I see a teacher understand a new concept, and when they try something in the classroom and it goes well. I have the same sense of pride when a teacher tries something in the classroom and it fails, but they see the learning that comes from the failure. I get the same excitement when I facilitate and observe groups of teachers having professional banter around different teaching and learning ideas. I am able to see so many changes in them. They are less defensive, more willing to share ideas, and are more open to the suggestions of others. When I reflect on those meetings, I know that my work with teachers has been better than fine, I have truly been effective.

KATY CARROLL, EdD
Literacy Coach
Lincoln School
Pittsburgh, PA

8

Developing a School Reading Program

The more things change, the more they remain the same.
—ALPHONSE KARR (1849, *www.thinkexist.com*)

The goal of this chapter is to provide information and cultivate awareness about the role of reading specialists in developing and sustaining an effective reading program in the entire school or district. In previous chapters, the importance of working with individuals or small groups as a means of promoting change at the classroom level was discussed. Although such efforts are important, even for large-scale program improvement, it is also essential that reading specialists be informed about their potential roles in facilitating/promoting total school or district change. This chapter begins with those issues or problems that often prevent the development of effective reading programs in schools. In the following sections, guidelines for effective change are offered, beginning with a discussion of curriculum and curriculum development; then suggestions for material selection and usage are presented. I also discuss technology and its value in helping students become critical readers. A concluding section addresses the importance of familiarity with the various requirements of state and federal educational agencies. Schools must adhere to requirements imposed by legislation and address the accountability demanded by these agencies. Often, it is a reading specialist who is responsible for leading the efforts to write district standards, develop the plan for Title 1 programs, or write a proposal to receive additional funding to meet the needs of struggling readers.

Problems of Effecting Large-Scale Change

In order to enhance the possibility of success, educators involved in efforts to develop schoolwide reading programs need to be aware of the barriers or issues that create difficulties in school improvement or reform efforts. Fullan (1991), Fullan and Hargreaves (1996), Hall and Hord (1987), and others have written about barriers to educational change. Fullan and Hargreaves identified six basic problems, each of which can be related to school reading program development: overload, isolation, "groupthink," untapped competence (and neglected incompetence), narrowness in teachers' roles, and poor solutions or failed reform (p. 2). Each of these, as they relate to literacy instruction, is discussed below.

Overload

Teachers are required to do much in today's schools. Not only are they responsible for teaching various subjects or skills, they are also asked to handle students with special needs or serious discipline problems. Some work in schools where there are large numbers of students from poverty backgrounds, which are generally associated with other problems such as lack of positive literacy experiences and poor attendance. Teachers may be asked to learn about and implement many initiatives or programs, some of which are not compatible with each other. Sometimes these initiatives are driven by the funding that is available to school districts, with requirements in the funding regulations. For example, in one district, a school had obtained funding to implement a program based on a form of individually prescribed instruction. At the same time, the district was attempting to implement a form of classroom management that recommended whole-class instruction, with provision for individual differences through multilevel tasks. Teachers were confused and legitimately frustrated in the face of administrative refusal to deal with their concerns; administrators contended that there was no problem in a marriage of the two initiatives. If this was not enough to cause problems, one of the schools embarked on a writing initiative that required teachers to attend professional development sessions *in addition* to the ones they were attending for the first two initiatives!

Isolation

A sentiment I hear expressed frequently is, "It doesn't matter what I hear in school meetings; I just shut my door and do what I believe is best."

Often, these statements are made with every good intention by teachers who have seen initiatives come—and go! In the past, schools tended to be organized around an isolationist perspective, with each teacher assuming major responsibility for the 25 or more students in his or her classroom. At the present time, classroom teachers are being asked to work with other teachers and with support specialists to make decisions about how to provide the best possible instruction for students; such decisions require collaboration among grade-level or subject area teachers. Teachers are being asked to produce, share, and review data, both objective and subjective, that help them design appropriate instruction. Initiatives such as RTI and in-class support from reading specialists require teachers to work together in new ways.

There is evidence that such collaboration is important in building a school vision and in creating an environment in which teachers believe that they have an important role in helping students succeed. In fact, results of studies (Hord, 2004; Leana & Pils, 2006) indicate that there is a strong relationship between achievement and the extent to which schools exhibit a strong sense of community or a collaborative commitment to effective instruction for all students. Such a new way of thinking about teaching may be difficult for some teachers who must now share information about their teaching and their students with other personnel in the school. Often these teachers need support and staff development experiences that will help them to participate successfully in such programs. As an example, teachers must be willing to discuss with the reading specialist assigned to support classroom instruction, ways that students might be grouped, a schedule that would work for both teacher and specialist, the management strategies that are employed, as well as specific ideas for instruction. They must be able to plan, teach, and evaluate what they do on an ongoing basis.

Groupthink

As mentioned above, in today's schools, a great deal of emphasis is placed on developing communities or networks of learners; for example, highlighting the importance of collegiality and collaboration in promoting school change. Although such efforts can be powerful forces for change, there are some downsides to them. Fullan and Hargreaves (1996) indicated the importance of continuing to support individual creativity and diversity while, at the same time, enhancing the ability of individuals to work together for change. Once a group establishes a norm, it is often difficult for the creative thinker to be heard. Such an individual may be thought of as reluctant or resistant to change. At the same time, this individual may be able to bring new and fresh insights to a specific issue.

Untapped Competence (and Neglected Incompetence)

Each and every educator in the school has the potential to contribute to an effective school reading program and assume a leadership role in creating school change. When school administrations function in ways that limit the extent to which all teachers can participate in the change process, they ignore the competence and knowledge of their teachers. Interacting with teachers provides information about activities that work or do not work, instructional strategies that have been modified so that they are more effective for younger or older students, and management techniques that create an atmosphere in which learning can take place. We need to capture the talent that exists in schools, not only to develop effective reading programs, but also to give teachers the sense of pride and ownership that enhances individual classroom instruction. At the same time, we must be bold enough to challenge those few who are incompetent or who refuse to work with students in ways that promote learning.

Narrowness in Teachers' Roles

There is a call for teachers to serve as leaders in the schools in new and different ways. No longer do teachers have to leave the classroom to have leadership responsibilities. As schools change, teachers and reading specialists can serve as leaders in curriculum and professional development efforts, in spearheading efforts to select materials or change reporting procedures, and so on. When teachers are offered and accept major responsibility and the power to make decisions, the commitment to follow through on implementation is greatly strengthened. Researchers (e.g., Hord, 2004; Newmann & Wehlage, 1995; Scribner & Reyes, 1999) discuss the positive relationship between school achievement and schools functioning as professional communities in which teachers have a voice in decision making—where they too have leadership responsibilities.

Poor Solutions or Failed Reform

The lack of success of many school reform efforts in literacy can be attributed to a variety of reasons: ineffective, overly circumscribed solutions (e.g., a belief that one particular approach or program will create the changes in school performance); lackluster or poor implementation (e.g., the selection of effective approaches or programs, but little effort given to helping teachers learn how to implement the program in their classrooms); or lack of sustainability (e.g., too many new initiatives, with little time to learn one well). At times, schools do not stay with an initiative long enough to make a difference. In the evaluation of Reading First in Pennsylvania, Zigmond and I (2008) found that after 5 years, almost 80% of our schools had shown increases in percent of students reading at proficiency and a reduction in percent of students at risk. But for some of the schools, it took 5 years to reach this goal. Moreover, in some schools, the problems are so complex that reform must address many different problems beyond instructional ones (e.g., student absenteeism or mobility, weak leadership, teacher turnover).

What Should We Do?

Schools that have "beat the odds"—that is, they have done better than expected, given the demographics of the school population—provide some direction (and much inspiration) for us in our efforts to make large-scale changes in our schools. According to Taylor and colleagues (2002), "research on effective teachers and schools is surprisingly convergent" (p. 371). These schools employ teachers who have excellent classroom management skills and provide excellent literacy instruction, often involving small-group instruction for students. A sense of collaboration characterizes these schools as teachers work closely with reading specialists and other personnel, as well as with the parents of the students.

Alvermann (2002) noted:

> Effective literacy instruction for adolescents must take into account a host of factors, including students' perceptions of their competencies as readers and writers, their level of motivation and background knowledge, and their interests. To be effective, such instruction must be embedded in the regular curriculum and make use of multiple forms of texts read for multiple purposes in a variety of learning situations. (p. 203)

Alvermann's remarks are critical ones for reading specialists in middle or secondary schools. She calls for teachers, including reading specialists, to demonstrate sensitivity to the needs and interests of their adolescent students. Moreover, reading specialists are encouraged to work closely with content teachers to embed literacy into the content curriculum.

We *can* improve literacy instruction in our schools. Reading specialists have an important role in this endeavor, not only in working with individual teachers but with groups of teachers. Information presented in Chapters 4, 5, 6, and 7, provide important guidelines for such work. This chapter focuses on the school curriculum and how reading specialists in leadership roles can contribute to the development of the literacy curriculum.

Curriculum Development

Guidelines useful in thinking about a framework for a school reading program are discussed below (Bean, 2008, pp. 13–18):

1. *Base goals and standards for reading on theory and research.* We hear much today about scientifically based reading research, and although there are areas of disagreement, there is much that we *do* know about reading instruction, especially beginning reading instruction. Reading specialists must be familiar with current information about reading instruction and assessment. Earlier syntheses of research such as the National Reading Panel Report (National Institute of Child Health and Human Development, 2000), Snow and colleagues' book *Preventing Reading Difficulties in Young Children* (1998), and the synthesis of studies in the *Handbook of Reading Research* (Kamil, Mosenthal, Pearson, & Barr, 2000) can be helpful resources. More recent work, such as August and Shanahan's (2006) edited volume on second language learners, can also provide important information. What is essential is that reading specialists keep abreast of the research and its implications for instruction. Professional journals, reviews, and reports from governmental agencies and foundations can all provide useful information. Also, school personnel must know the requirements of their specific states regarding reading instruction, and, if they are eligible for federal funding, they must be aware of the requirements of legislation for specific grants. Guidelines, standards, and requirements all provide a basis for discussion and for curriculum development or modification.

What is key is that the school have in mind a sequential and comprehensive plan that identifies all the components essential in a strong literacy program, pre-K–12. Such a plan will enable teachers to gain a better understanding of articulation from grade level to grade level (vertical articulation) and to help them think about what needs to be taught and how at specific grade levels (horizontal articulation). Bean (2008) presents such a plan (see Figure 8.1), and distinguishes between those skills that need to be taught early and well, what Paris (2005)

Pre-K	K	1	2	3	4	5	6	7	8	9	10	11	12

Motivation (Independent Reading)

Writing

Comprehension of Text

Meaning Vocabulary

Oral Language/Concept Development

Concepts of Print

Phonemic Awareness

Phonics

Fluency of Words and Text

Other Decoding Skills: Structural Analysis, Latin Roots, Greek Combining Forms

FIGURE 8.1. Components of a pre-K–12 reading program. From Bean (2008, p. 16). Copyright 2008 by Teachers College Press. Reprinted by permission.

calls constrained skills, and those components that must be addressed throughout the school years; that is, motivation, writing, comprehension, meaning vocabulary, oral language and concept development. Reading specialists may have responsibility for developing reading programs at the middle or secondary levels, as well as the elementary level; therefore, below, I discuss in more depth some critical issues related to these upper levels of schooling.

The reading program at the middle and high school levels. Across the country, there is an awareness that special attention must be given to the secondary schools, especially high schools. Too many students are dropping out (Biancarosa & Snow, 2004), are struggling readers (National Assessment of Educational Progress, 2005; National Center for Education Statistics, 2003), or don't have the high-level reading skills that enable them to compete successfully at the college level or in our global economy. Many schools are addressing this issue, at least in part, by providing all teachers in the school with a better understanding of "disciplinary" literacy. So, at the secondary level, reading specialists not only have the task of developing or designing programs for students who are having difficulty with reading, but they must work closely with content area teachers to design approaches that help students process content specific information. In other words, teachers must help students understand the ways in which experts in each academic area communicate; they must learn to read and write like historians, scientists, or mathematicians (Moje, 2008; Shanahan & Shanahan, 2008).

So, just as at the elementary level, there must be provision in the secondary levels for differentiation of instruction. Programs at the secondary level may include a pullout program for some students, with programs such as Reading Apprenticeship (Schoenbach, Greenleaf, Cyiko, & Hurwitz, 1999), Read 180 (Scholastic, 2002), and so on, taught by a reading teacher or reading specialist. The program may also include special study skills classes that help students understand effective study strategies, including how to take tests. But to meet the needs of all students, the program must also address reading and writing in the content areas. The Standards for Middle and Secondary School Coaches (IRA, 2006) can be useful to coaches because in addition to identifying general leadership standards, the document identifies standards for each of four academic disciplines: English, science, social studies, and math.

Some important resources at the secondary level include *Reading Next: A Vision for Action and Research in Middle and High School Literacy* (Biancarosa & Snow, 2004), and *Creating a Culture of Literacy: A Guide for Middle and High School Principals* (National Association of Secondary School Principals, 2005). In the article by Elizabeth Moje (2008) mentioned above, she raises issues important for those involved in secondary literacy reform: content teachers' knowledge of their own discipline, ways that teachers can encourage students to interact with their content area texts, role of technology and new media on students' learning, and school structures that would facilitate this sort of instruction. She concludes as follows: "The integration of literacy instruction in the secondary schools is a complex change process that will require collaboration, communication, and a commitment to major conceptual, structural, and culture changes" (p. 105).

THINK ABOUT THIS

What are the issues that your school or a school with which you are familiar face about a vision for literacy at the secondary level? What are your thoughts about disciplinary literacy and what it means for reading specialists involved in a secondary reading program?

2. *Select materials that facilitate accomplishment of school goals.* Schools should identify their curricular goals before selecting materials; however, too often the reverse is true! Too often, the materials in the school reading program become the curriculum. Certainly, the materials must reflect the beliefs and goals identified by school personnel, but a strict adherence to the identified materials may lead to a narrow program in which there is little adjustment for the needs of the specific students in the school. In other words, the content and quality of materials selected should reflect the needs and interests of students in the school, as well as the forms of diversity that exist in society (i.e., race, ethnicity, gender, cultural, linguistic, economic, etc.). Providing such material in schools is important both for increasing student skills and the motivation to read. Although the need for a wide variety of materials in schools exists at all levels, it is especially critical that adolescents be provided with materials to which they can relate. Brozo and Gaskins (2009), in a chapter that focuses on adolescent boys, presents five principles of engagement that are relevant for readers of all ages:

- Create conditions in classrooms that promote self-efficacy, a belief in one's own capacity to achieve;
- Promote interest in new reading;
- Connect out-of-school with inside-school literacies;
- Make sure there is an abundance of interesting texts available;
- Provide for choice and options. (pp. 172–180)

The importance of motivation, choice, and culturally relevant material in engaging student reading is well described in texts such as *Teaching Reading to Black African American Males: Closing the Achievement Gap* (Tatum, 2005), *Effective Literacy Instruction for Adolescents* (Alvermann, 2001), *Engaging Adolescents in Reading* (Guthrie, 2008), or *Engaging Young Readers: Promoting Achievement and Motivation, Solving Problems in the Teaching of Literacy* (Baker, Dreher, & Guthrie, 2000). Later in this chapter I discuss a process for selection because, often, the reading specialist is involved in such decision making.

3. *Organize the curriculum framework so that it is usable.* Too often, curriculum plans sit on shelves or in teacher's desks, consulted only infrequently. Those involved in curriculum development must be certain to formulate plans that are coherent yet simple to use. It is essential that such plans provide a sequence of literacy instruction for K–12. With such a framework, teachers can gain a sense of "where in the curriculum various understandings, skills, and attitudes are addressed" (Bean, 2002, p. 6).

4. *Relate teacher beliefs and knowledge about reading instruction to research.* Reading specialists who work with teachers must not only gain a sense of what those teachers believe and know about reading instruction, they also must provide opportunities for teacher reflection and discussion about their beliefs. Teachers bring their own experiences, knowledge, and beliefs to the teaching of reading; they interpret research findings through different lenses. I am reminded of a teacher from a secondary background assigned to teach third grade. Although the work in her graduate courses and experiences in primary classrooms convinced her that students did need to learn phonics, her belief was that such lessons needed to be embedded within a meaningful context, and she experienced much difficulty with the core reading program in which such instruction was not present. She was also frustrated when listening to other teachers talk about their lessons, which seemd to provide little opportunity for students to read and write. Unless the reading specialist was aware of this individual's beliefs and knew how to help her work collaboratively with others in a group to state her position, problems could arise when she began to participate in curriculum development meetings.

THINK ABOUT THIS

Think about the individual teacher, described above, who works with primary teachers who believe in a strong decoding program. What problems might arise? How could the beliefs and strengths of this individual be tapped in a way that improves reading instruction? Is it possible that there are some misunderstandings that exist and that an open discussion would be helpful?

To develop a common understanding and terminology, teachers may be asked to read current articles about reading instruction that provide a springboard for discussion. These readings can also provide teachers with up-to-date information that will enable them to think more deeply about what they do in their classrooms and how it relates to what research indicates is best practice.

Process for Change

According to Good (1973) in the *Dictionary of Education*, curriculum development is "a task of supervision directed towards designing or redesigning the guidelines for instruction, includes development of specifications indicating what is to be taught, by whom, when, where, and in what sequence or pattern" (p. 158). When schools decide to change the literacy program, most do so by selecting a representative group of constituents (e.g., teachers, parents, administrators), who will be involved in this important effort. Such a process recognizes the importance of grassroots involvement in curricular and instructional decision making. The reading specialist may be assigned to serve as a member of such a team or often, to lead the effort. There are several important stages in curriculum development work. Described below are the initial stages that are important prerequisites to the actual development of curriculum (and to the later issues of implementation and evaluation).

Stage 1

What is the current situation in the school? Before the current curriculum is changed, it is essential to have a clear picture of what is occurring in the school and the level of the current knowledge about reading instruction. To gather this information requires consulting teachers about what they believe are the strengths and weaknesses of their current approaches. In addition, test data can be used to supply additional information about the effectiveness of the school's programs. Teachers may be interviewed, asked to complete questionnaires, or to participate in meetings to discuss their views about the reading program in their school.

One of the approaches to curriculum development is that of having teachers map the curriculum they are currently using. Jacobs (1997) described mapping as an activity that "enables teachers to show student work as it actually happens in the classroom and in relation to state or district standards" (p. 8). She lists seven steps in the mapping process. In the first step, teachers actually create a map of the three major elements of their curriculum—(1) content in terms of essential concepts and topics, (2) processes and skills, and (3) products and performances for assessment—using an agreed-upon form approved by the district. Jacobs suggested that teachers use the calendar as a basic guide for compiling the form, recording what they actually do in their classrooms. The remaining steps in her procedure consist of efforts to share what is being taught at the various grade levels and across grade levels and to make decisions about what needs to be reviewed and revised. This effort can certainly constitute a long-range professional development project for teachers. Teachers are often surprised by the repetition that occurs across grades or the fact that some things are not taught at all!

This mapping procedure can be used by reading specialists as a means of developing teachers' awareness of what is taught at each grade level; it can also generate topics for discussion that can be extremely helpful in developing the literacy curriculum and making modifications in instructional practices. Figure 8.2 provides a partial example

Month	Skills/strategies	Content used	Assessment
September	Review of consonants (initial and ending) Introduce short vowels Finding main idea	Basal stories 1–4	Worksheets Unit test Fluency checks
October	Short vowels Summarizing	Basal stories 5–8 Selected trade book	Worksheets Pseudo words Journal responses to each chapter in book

FIGURE 8.2. Map of second-grade reading instruction (partial).

of one such form. The leader of the curriculum development effort, in collaboration with others, must decide how to approach the actual change process:

Will all teachers be involved or a representative few?
If not all are involved, how can others be consulted and informed?
What is the time line for the process?
What are the goals and outcomes of the effort?

Stage 2

What can we learn from research and theory? Information from books and journal articles should be shared with teachers; study groups can be formed in which teachers can discuss what they are learning. Also, outside experts may be consulted so that all have a sense of current knowledge and theory about reading instruction. Often, districts invite an expert to address all teachers or a representative committee; this event should be followed by opportunities for discussion and debate about the issues presented. At this point, as well as in later stages, teachers' beliefs, attitudes, and ideas must be taken into consideration and opportunities for discussion about differences provided.

Stage 3

What constitutes a coherent, usable curriculum plan? Armed with knowledge of the curriculum used in the school and a solid understanding of the current research about literacy instruction, the group or groups responsible for curriculum development can begin to struggle with the content and format of the plan, investigating what structure can best be used by the classroom teachers. This stage offers a wonderful opportunity for teachers across the grades (K–12) to begin to communicate with each other so that the developed plan contains an articulated, sequential identification of skills, strategies, understandings, and knowledge. During this stage, drafts of plans should be shared with those not working on this effort and requests for feedback included.

Au, Raphael, and Mooney (2008) describe one process, the Standards-Based Change Process (SBC), for guiding change in a school. The SBC Process is organized around four major concepts: "establishing a philosophy and vision of the excellent reader; (2) establishing grade-level end-of-year goals stated both in teachers' professional language and in student-friendly language; (3) collecting, evaluating, and representing assessment evidence of where students are in relation to end-of-year goals; and (4) improving instruction on the basis of this assessment evidence" (p. 74). Teachers are asked to identify central beliefs about teaching, learning, and literacy, and a vision of what students can accomplish at a specific grade level, and then a shared vision of what excellent readers can do when they leave that elementary school. This process is one that requires time for discussion and interaction among the faculty at the school and is undertaken before teachers begin to work on the curriculum. A process like this requires administrative support, time for teachers to engage in discussions, and a recognition that such curricular development will take time. In the long run, however, it is a source of professional development for teachers and builds a sense of ownership among teachers. Such a process also provides for a building of a coherent, sequential, and comprehensive curriculum.

Stage 4

How should the plan be shared with others? What implementation strategies are necessary? Too often, it is the implementation stage that falls short of the goal. Those who have worked on the development of the plan are committed to it—and perhaps use it. Others, if they do not understand the plan and how it works, may just ignore it or implement it halfheartedly. If teachers have been involved during the entire process, they are more likely to accept and use the plan. Therefore, it is important to keep all teachers apprised during each stage and to seek their input.

Stage 5

How will the plan be evaluated and modified, if necessary? Curriculum development, its implementation and modification, should be ongoing; it is a recursive process. Thus, there is a need to develop a mechanism to obtain input from teachers about what works and what doesn't work. Such input can come from grade-level or subject area meetings, or from the work of a curriculum committee. Evaluation can include reactions of teachers, actual observation of what is occurring in classrooms, and a study of various assessment measures used to document student learning. At higher levels, especially middle and secondary, input from students can also inform the evaluation process. As mentioned in Chapter 5, Guskey's (2000) five levels of evaluation could be helpful in thinking about how to evaluate a school's reading program.

Selection of Materials

Teachers frequently make decisions about classroom instruction based on the anthologies or basals that they are using in their classroom. In fact, researchers (e.g., Fawson & Reutzel, 2000; Hoffman et al., 1998) have reported that such materials are still the most significant component of literacy instruction. And, given that specific materials, once selected, become a driving force for at least 5 or more years, careful attention must be given to selecting materials so that they fit with the objectives, goals, and standards that have been formulated by the district. Too often the materials selected become the curriculum guide or plan for the district.

Guidelines for Selecting a Basal or Core Program

Once the district has decided that it is going to adopt a specific series as a means of providing a core reading program, literacy personnel need to think about both content and process issues. Both are important.

Process

The process to be used is extremely important because it often involves more than professional issues. Publishers are eager to obtain adoptions; school districts need to be certain that they abide by the same guidelines or rules for all materials being considered.

What selection procedure should be used?
Will all teachers, or a representative group, serve on the committee?
What are the rules?

If publishers are invited to present their "wares," how much time do
they get and what can they "give" or provide to teachers?

Will the district decide upon piloting the materials (a common
practice)?

A careful consideration of the process reduces the possibility that
the outcome will be met by accusations of unfairness or bias in materials
selection. Most districts try to select a committee that includes a representative group of teachers and administrators. All grade levels in which
materials will be used should be represented; so should all schools in
a district. At the same time, it would be wise to include parents; they
provide a unique perspective as well as generate the community support
needed to approve the final decision. Students may also be included
on the committee, especially if the materials to be selected apply to the
upper levels.

Content

The following guidelines can be useful in thinking about which basal or
anthology to select:

1. *Review the philosophy.* Before proceeding with a review of materials, spend time reviewing or developing the philosophy or goals of
the district especially as they relate to the teaching of reading or literacy instruction. In that way, materials can be selected that match the
goals of the school, thereby reducing the possibility that the scope and
sequence of the basal will become the curriculum of the school.

2. *Conduct a needs assessment of teachers in the district.* A short questionnaire or brief talks with all teachers can generate a list of priorities. Often, teachers have specific concerns about current materials and
their inability to meet the needs of the children. Time spent obtaining
ideas about what the group thinks is important and usually means there
will be less dissension later.

3. *Plan for a research update.* Make certain that the committee knows
what is current in the field. An expert can be invited to make a presentation; the group can be given materials to read. Both should be followed
by group discussion. A resolution of the International Reading Association Board, titled "Buyer Be Wary" (2002a), discusses the need for those
involved in selecting materials to be especially cautious in their delib-
erations. This document encourages program reviewers to look closely
at the publishers' claims in relation to program effectiveness.

4. *Decide upon the "ideal."* What should the final material look like?
What should it include? By designing a checklist, or modifying an existing

one, the group can more efficiently review materials. Various checklists are available, such as those developed by Lapp, Fisher, and Flood (2008) and Simmons and Kame'enui (2002). Most of the checklists include a review of content, the teachers' manual, the scope and sequence of skills, the supplemental material (including workbooks), and assessment procedures. Although it might be helpful to start with a published checklist, teachers should review the checklist and modify it so that the criteria are those that address the vision and goals of the school.

5. *Review materials.* The committee can quickly screen and discard those basals that do not meet the identified criteria. Then an in-depth review must be made of those that appear to be acceptable. The committee can break into smaller groups to review specific texts and present findings to the entire group, or everyone in the group may review all texts. They may consult reviews done by others (i.e., What Works Clearinghouse; *http://ies.ed.gov/ncee/wwc.*)The group may decide to track the teaching of a specific strategy or skill through the grades, to determine how the strategy is taught at each level. For example, committee members could focus on how students are taught to summarize from the early grades through grade 8.

Teachers, of course, are interested in the readability of the text. Although readability formulas can be used, such estimates are subjective and should be used cautiously. Schumm and Mangrum (1991) have developed a strategy, known as FLIP (framework for fostering textbook thinking) that helps those in middle grades conduct an evaluation of text difficulty.

6. *Make a final decision.* In addition to using information from in-depth reviews, the committee may talk with teachers in other districts who are using the materials to get their perspectives. At this stage, the committee should come to a consensus, or if necessary, vote to make a decision about the text to be selected. It is, of course, much better if the group can agree on the "best" basal, but this may not be possible. If no clear-cut decision emerges, more time may need to be spent in analyzing the available materials.

Materials to Help Students Achieve the Goals Established by the School

Although I focus on the core or basal program above, the same criteria apply to the materials used for supplemental or intensive instruction. Schools have the responsibility of teaching all students and providing for them; therefore, consideration must be given to how to meet the needs of gifted students, special education students, ELLs, and so on. Those leading material selection efforts should be able to justify why they are using specific supplemental materials, how they support or enhance the core program, who should use them, and why. Careful attention must be given to how the various materials "fit together."

Technology in the Reading Program

Teachers in today's schools need to be competent users of technology, employing it as a tool to enhance the literacy program in their classrooms. Indeed, technology is fast becoming an integral part of every classroom. According to Parsad and Jones (2005), 95% of U.S. classrooms (K–12) have Internet connections. And the "new literacies" that include digital and media technologies (Leu et al., 2004, 2005; Warschauer, 2006) are becoming more and more commonplace. At the same time, teachers do not always feel prepared or comfortable using these new approaches to learning. They need many skills to use electronic technology effectively: locating resources about literacy on the Internet; communicating with others using technology; entering, accessing, and interpreting data about students and their accomplishments; becoming knowledgeable about the various software programs that can be used to deliver instruction to students; and integrating technology as part of instructional delivery. Barone and Wright (2008–2009) describe a fourth-grade classroom in which the teacher uses laptops to complement and extend traditional literacy instruction and support differentiated instruction. In Pennsylvania, the Classrooms for the Future project (*www.edportal.ed.state.pa.us*) for high schools, provides both the technology resources and coaches to help high school teachers become more familiar with the technology and to use it in their instruction. In other words, the new literacies can provide new and more complex learning opportunities for students; technology in the classroom has become much more than adding software packages to the reading program.

At the same time, given the availability of such software, it is important to have criteria for the selection of such programs. McVee and Dickson (2002) developed a rubric as a guide for reviewing software for programs designed for use in K–3 classrooms. The rubric identifies the following questions as ones that can be used for reviewing software:

1. What observations can we make about overall media presentation?
2. How easy is the software to navigate?
3. Does the software change over time? With each use? With prolonged interactions? Multiple uses?
4. Which types of assessments are built into the program? How important or useful are these for users and teachers?

5. How closely do activities fit classroom needs? Are they interesting? Educational? Fun?
6. How would we rate the overall value of the software? Would this be a good investment for my classroom?
7. How compatible is this software with an emergent literacy approach that integrates reading, writing, listening, and speaking? (p. 639)

These questions can be adapted for use at upper grade levels. Also, one resource that can be used by schools to heighten awareness of what is needed in the area of technology is the National Educational Technology Standards for Students (International Society for Technology in Education, 2007), which identifies standards at all levels for both preservice teachers and pre-K–12 students.

Knowledge and Understanding of State and Federal Requirements

Every district, regardless of student demographics, location, or size, has requirements that it must meet to comply with state legislation on curriculum, assessment, and instruction matters. Most states have developed standards that students must meet; therefore, schools must use those standards in developing their literacy curriculum. Furthermore, any district eligible for Title 1 services must, of course, develop a plan that addresses the requirements in state and federal legislation; issues such as eligibility, accountability, models for instruction, inclusion of parent involvement programs, and so on may all need to be described in the district plan. Moreover, there may be potential funding programs at the state or federal levels that require district personnel to write a proposal that enables them to receive that funding. Generally, schools assign teams to write those plans and often that team includes reading specialists or others knowledgeable about literacy instruction.

Such opportunities offer the possibility of receiving increased funding for improving reading instruction; at the same time, they require that schools write proposals that meet certain requirements and expectations. Often, reading specialists along with other school district personnel are responsible for writing those proposals. If so, writers must (1) become knowledgeable about the requirements of the legislation, (2) write a coherent plan that addresses the requirements, and (3) work with others so that the contents of the plan are consistent with what is required, and at the same time, reflect the goals, practices, and beliefs of the district and its educators. Often, school district personnel must seek partners, such as universities or evaluation centers, to work with them on programmatic or evaluation issues. For example, in writing a grant to address early childhood needs, school personnel may ask literacy personnel at a local university to work with them in providing professional development support for teachers in the school. (Chapter 11 provides information that may be helpful to reading specialists who have direct responsibility for writing proposals to receive state or federal funding.) In the following sections, the role of reading specialists in relation to various state and federal initiatives is discussed. As part of this discussion, there is a section that describes the No Child Left Behind (NCLB; U.S. Department of Education, 2009b) legislation; I also discuss briefly the impact that Reading First (U.S. Department of Education, 2002a) as part of the NCLB legislation, had on reading instruction in schools obtaining that funding..

Impact of Federal or State Initiatives on the Role of Reading Specialists

Reading specialists in all schools must keep up-to-date about various governmental regulations and legislation. State or federal government agencies send information to school officials and sometimes invite one or more educators from a district to attend informational meetings in which specific initiatives are discussed. Conferences held by the state, local educational support agencies, or professional groups typically offer sessions in which such legislation is described. Information can also be obtained from the state or federal websites on which various legislative actions are described or summarized. The website of the International Reading Association (*www.reading.org*) also provides useful information. The information below about the NCLB legislation comes from the federal government's website (*www.nclb.gov/next/overview/index.html*).

No Child Left Behind

The NCLB law, according to the website, represents the most sweeping changes to the Elementary and Secondary Education Act (ESEA) since it was enacted in 1965. The legislation has an impact on education in grades K–12 and is based on four basic principles: strong accountability, local control and flexibility, an increased role for parents, and scientifically based reading research. As part of this legislation, Title 1 received the largest funding increase in its history, with annual expenditures totaling more than $10 billion (Borman, 2002–2003). At the present time, NCLB is up for reauthorization, and will most likely be changed. Many groups, including the International Reading Association (2008–2009, pp. 1, 4–5), have developed recommendations that they hope will influence policy. This policy document calls for a continuation of the emphasis on accountability; however, it criticizes the use of single-assessment measures and the use of assessment to label and punish schools. Rather it calls for assessment to be used as a means of informing and improving instruction. The policy document also calls for investments in teacher preparation and professional development of teachers as a means of meeting the needs of all students.

THINK ABOUT THIS

What are your thoughts and feelings about No Child Left Behind? What do you think are its benefits? Its shortcomings? What changes would you like to see in No Child Left Behind?

At the present time, as part of the accountability effort, each state must develop a set of standards for what children should know and be able to do in various areas, including reading. Then all students must be tested, in grades 3–8, using assessment measures that are aligned with the standards. The law also requires districts to administer at least one reading and writing measure at grades 9–12. Schools are expected to make adequate yearly progress (AYP). Results are disaggregated to determine the growth of various groups, including those who are economically disadvantaged, those from racial or ethnic minority groups, those with learning disabilities, and those with limited English proficiency. If progress is inadequate, schools are held accountable—that is, low-scoring schools are penalized. NCLB (U.S. Department of Education, 2002b) affects all public schools in this country, K–12; therefore, reading specialists at all levels need to be familiar with it and the implications it has for students and their teachers.

Reading First Revisited

In the first edition of this text, I discussed Reading First (U.S. Department of Education, 2002a), its content, and the process required to apply for funding. At this time, Reading First is in its final year, and its future is uncertain. Given the impact of Reading First on reading instruction in the primary grades and the fact that Reading First in many ways was based on an RTI model, I summarize some of what we learned from Reading First, with the expectation that this information can be helpful to reading specialists involved in new and different initiatives established by their states, the federal government, or their district. Reading

First not only influenced how reading was taught in K–3 in many schools across the country, but it supported the hiring of thousands of literacy coaches, whose responsibilities included providing job-embedded professional development for the teachers in Reading First schools. Reading First provides an example of how legislation and policy decisions influence how reading is taught in schools.

In this large-scale, highly funded, and prescriptive program, enacted as part of the NCLB legislation, education dollars were distributed to states with approved proposals. The goal of the program was to improve reading instruction for K–3 students and ensure that children learned to read well by the end of grade 3. Reading First funds were designated for districts in which there were large numbers of students living in poverty and in which there was low achievement. State applications were reviewed by an expert panel; once approved, eligible districts were invited to submit their plans for review at the state level. Plans were required to specify how districts would address the following areas:

- Develop a reading program that was based on scientifically sound reading research and that would teach all students to read at or above grade level no later than the end of grade 3.
- District procedures used for providing professional development and other support to K–3 teachers (and special education teachers K–12), so that they can teach students to read more effectively.
- The assessment measures—outcome, screening, diagnostic, and classroom based—allocated to determine students' strengths and needs and to make decisions about how to modify instruction for those students who were having difficulties.
- The materials proposed to implement the essential components of reading instruction.
- The procedures proposed to strengthen coordination among schools, early literacy programs, and family literacy programs.

The legislation defined scientifically based reading research as "research that applies rigorous, systematic, and objective procedures to obtain valid knowledge relevant to reading development, reading instruction, and reading difficulties" (No Child Left Behind Act of 2001, Sec. 1208). The International Reading Association's position statement, "What Is Evidence-Based Reading Research" (2002b), provides a clear definition and a number of resources for those interested in learning more about this topic. In that statement, scientifically based research is defined as follows:

Objective. Data obtained in the research would be identified and interpreted in a similar manner by any reader.

Valid. The data represent tasks that are relevant to reading; that is, what children need to accomplish to be successful readers.

Reliable. Data will be the same regardless of who collects them or when they are collected.

Systematic. There is a rigorous research design (in the Reading First legislation, this meant either experimentation or observation).

Refereed. The research has appeared in a peer-reviewed journal, which indicates that it has been approved for publication by other researchers or scholars.

Research that provides the strongest designs for demonstrating effectiveness are those that are experimental—that is, those in which results from a specific practice or approach are compared to a control group, with random assignment to the groups. Quasi-experimental designs are often used in education because of the difficulty or inappropriateness of random assignment. In this case, random assignment is not used, but various statistical procedures are used to control for any selected preexisting differences in the groups. Experts also agree that there must be a convergence of information from a number of studies before any single finding is accepted as conclusive.

Another aspect of the focus on scientifically based research was that districts were being asked to select and use materials or reading programs based on such research. Doing so is a difficult task because few studies of large reading programs can be defined as scientifically based. Often, districts justified the use of specific materials by analyzing the research that undergirds the instructional processes for specific reading elements within those programs. For example, a school district would analyze a large basal program to determine whether it presents phonics instruction in a manner found to be effective through scientifically based research. Specifically, is phonics taught in a systematic and explicit manner (National Institute of Child Health and Human Development, 2000)? As mentioned previously in this chapter, various checklists are available that can be used to review such comprehensive reading materials. Also, assessment outcomes were an important part of Reading First; students and their performance had to be monitored on a regular basis, and there had to be provision for diagnostic assessment if students were not progressing as expected.

Every state participated in Reading First and over 5,000 schools across the country were identified as Reading First schools. In the national study of Reading First, Gamse, Jacob, Horst, Boulay, and Unlu

(2008) found that there were differences in classroom reading instruction between Reading First and non-Reading First schools; moreover, teachers in Reading First schools received more professional development than teachers in non-Reading First schools. However, there has been much disappointment and controversy about the finding that there was no significant difference in reading comprehension achievement between Reading First and non-Reading First schools. At the same time, survey results of school personnel (Center for Educational Policy, 2007) and state evaluation reports have reported that Reading First has made a difference. What is reflected in this story of Reading First is the fact that it has had a major influence on many schools across our country, not only in the schools that received funding to implement such programs, but in others, which quickly moved to adopt progress monitoring and screening tools, and to implement the scientifically based reading instruction promoted in Reading First legislation.

Summary

In this chapter, problems associated with creating change in schools were discussed to provide a backdrop to the issue of developing a school reading program. Guidelines for developing a school reading program were presented and processes for creating change elaborated, highlighting the importance of involving as many teachers as possible in the curriculum development process. This was followed by a discussion of materials selection that emphasizes the need for establishing criteria with which to analyze the materials. There was also a discussion about the importance of technology and the resources that enhance knowledge of this aspect of a reading program. Finally, there was a section that described basic elements of No Child Left Behind and provided a summary of what was learned from the Reading First legislation.

Reflections

1. Think about the problems associated with large-scale change described earlier in this chapter as they relate to a school with which you are familiar. Does the school you are thinking about have any of those problems? Others?
2. Meet with several colleagues to talk about your vision of what an excellent reader (at the end of a specific grade) can do. Discuss your views with each other. How similar are they? Different?

Activities

1. If you are a classroom teacher, try to map your reading curriculum for the entire year. Use that map to think about whether the curriculum helps you accomplish the goals that you think are important for your students.
2. Use the criteria from one of the suggested frameworks to evaluate a set of basal materials. Compare your evaluation with a colleague's.

9

Assessment of Classroom and School Reading Programs

You have not taught until they have learned.
—NATER AND GALLIMORE (2006, p. 103)

Swen Nater tells John Wooden, one of the greatest basketball coaches of all time, of his disappointment that, although he taught his team to rebound, they "just don't learn" (p. 103). Wooden replied with the profound statement printed above!

Assessment helps us determine the difference between *teaching* and *learning*. The term "assessment" generates much emotion in today's schools. There are those who believe that the emphasis on assessment is an important means of improving instruction; others believe that we put too much emphasis on assessment, thereby narrowing the curriculum and reducing teacher creativity. In reality, assessment is an important aspect of the total school reading program and one that must be planned and implemented as carefully as the curriculum and instructional plans for the schools. Kapinus (2008) says it well: "The goal of all assessment is to support effective teaching and learning" (p. 145).

Reading specialists may have many experiences in their coursework with assessment, but often the emphasis is on assessment of an individual child or a small group of students. In this chapter, the focus is on assessment directly related to improving reading instruction within a classroom or in a school. In today's schools, the assessment demands of NCLB (U.S. Department of Education, 2002a) have created the need for reading specialists to be well versed in how to use assessment results to help teachers plan instruction that will meet the needs of their students and, in addition, to be knowledgeable about how to work with

178

teachers and administrators to interpret and use schoolwide results as a means of improving student learning. This chapter begins by identifying four different types of assessment measures and then goes on to discuss principles of assessment. This is followed by a discussion of the limitations of standardized tests.

What and Why?

The terms "assessment" and "tests" are often confused. Assessment is the task of gathering data on which to base evaluative or judgment-oriented decisions. Such data are multidimensional, encompassing more than just standardized tests. They can range from observations, checklists, and interviews to informal tasks and performance measures, such as writing a retell or responding to a selection. Assessment, indeed, can be closely aligned with instruction. Even as they are teaching lessons, teachers often modify or adapt what they are doing, based on their informal assessment of whether students are "getting it."

Assessment measures are necessary for a number of reasons, and they are relevant to many different audiences. Four types of assessment, why they are useful and some of their limitations, are described below.

Outcome Measures

Certainly, the school administration and the community (including parents and taxpayers) are interested in whether their schools are performing satisfactorily. In this case, assessment measures serve as an *outcome* or accountability tool. Frequently, norm-referenced tests that compare students from a specific district or school with others like them are used. Most often these measures are administered to groups of students and use some sort of multiple-choice format. Information from these measures can be helpful to the school in determining in which areas their program is strong (e.g., students do well in reading vocabulary) and in which areas they might need to improve (e.g., comprehension scores are weak). Results are also helpful in determining whether specific groups of students (e.g., ELLs, special education students) are experiencing difficulty in learning. These measures, however, are not very helpful to teachers for planning daily lessons for the students in their classrooms. In a study conducted by Buly and Valencia (2002), in which they did additional testing of 108 fifth-grade students who had failed the state reading test given at the end of fourth grade, they found several distinctive and multifaceted patterns of reading abilities that were not discernable in students' performance on the state measure. They made the point that the state measure was not very useful for making instructional decisions. Yet, these assessments are often known as "high-stakes" measures because they are used to make major decisions; for example, student promotion or retention, availability of school funding, or labeling of schools as successful or failing (Afferbach, 2004). Such measures have also been criticized because, given the focus on accountability, some schools have focused on "teaching to the test" by narrowing their curriculum to emphasize only those skills that appear on the test; yet too often, these tests are limited in their ability to assess complex and high-level reading tasks. It is important, then, to be cautious about how these measures are used, given their limitations.

THINK ABOUT THIS

In what ways are outcome measures used in the schools with which you are familiar? To what extent do the results influence the curriculum in the school—and judgments about the success of the school in educating its students? Do you agree with the concerns raised above about the limitations of these tests?

Initial Screening Instruments

Measures that serve as *initial screening* tools that assist teachers in quickly determining whether some students are in need of more assistance or more in-depth assessment are also available. These measures are meant to be administered quickly and they provide a general picture of whether a student may or may not be proficient with a specific reading task. One of these initial screening measures is the DIBELS, which provides information about students' decoding skills, fluency, and retelling skills. According to the authors (Good & Kaminski, 2002), the DIBELS provides a quick screening that enables the teachers to know whether there is a need for more in-depth assessment and possible intervention. They consider this quick screening to be efficient and compare it to taking a temperature to determine if an individual has a fever. Many commercial reading programs also provide their own screening measures that can be used by teachers and reading specialists at the beginning of the year or before various instructional units to provide baseline information about students and to make decisions about which children may need additional support. At the secondary level, reading specialists may choose to administer a cloze procedure test as a screening measure to determine the readability of a specific textbook as well as the abilities of students in a specific content class to read that text. Although these initial screening instruments may be useful, those who administer them must remember that they are "screening" instruments and no more. Certainly the DIBELS has had its share of criticism (e.g., Goodman, 2006; Kloo, 2006), although some of this criticism may actually be the result of misinterpretations about what the instrument is really capable of providing. Schools that teach the tasks of the DIBELS, instead of using results to guide instruction, are misusing the information provided by the test. This is an excellent example of the importance of reading specialists being knowledgeable about assessment tools and how to interpret and use the results.

Diagnostic Assessments

Diagnostic assessments assist teachers in making decisions about instruction and in pinpointing possible areas to address if a student is experiencing difficulty. If a child has difficulties on a screening measure, the diagnostic measure will provide the in-depth information needed to plan instruction. For example, if a child does poorly on an initial screening of decoding, the teacher or reading specialist may want to administer a more detailed phonics inventory to get a better picture of what the student can and cannot do. Reading specialists often use an informal reading inventory to get an in-depth picture of how well students read materials of different genre at various levels.

Progress Monitoring

Progress monitoring measures are administered at specific times during the year to help determine whether students have made improvement over time. At times, an alternative form of an initial screening measure is given. But in addition, such measures might include changes in recognition of sight words, fluency checks, or writing. These measures can be helpful tools for teachers, who can then decide whether there is a need for additional support, a change in instructional practice, or a need for a diagnostic assessment to obtain more information about a child's performance. Another form of progress monitoring is that of using evidence such as student work samples or checklists completed by the teacher several times a year to assess whether students are improving in their ability to perform various tasks (see Figure 9.1 for an example of a checklist used when observing the oral reading of primary grade students). These informal and authentic progress monitoring measures can be extremely helpful because they are closely related to the instructional practices at a specific grade level (e.g., teachers decide to rate writing samples of fifth-graders three times a year), using a rubric devel-

Key

+ = exhibits this behavior all of the time
✓ = need for improvement some of the time
0 = not evident

Child's Name								
Reads with appropriate phrasing (not word by word)								
Reads with appropriate expression and intonation								
Reads at appropriate rate								
Uses punctuation as a meaning tool								
Uses decoding to figure out unknown words								
Rereads if meaning is problematic								

FIGURE 9.1. Oral Reading Checklist.

oped by them and based on their goals for this grade level. Reading specialists can help teachers by talking with them about these data to address two important questions: Are students improving as expected, and, if not, what adjustments in instruction need to be made?

These four types of measures—outcome, initial screening, diagnostic, and progress monitoring—serve different purposes and require different types of assessment tools. Several key resource books that describe specific measures are *Assessing and Correcting Reading and Writing Difficulties* (Gunning, 2005), *Assessment and Instruction of Reading and Writing Difficulties: An Interactive Approach* (Wixson & Lipson, 2009), and McKenna and Stahl's *Assessment for Reading Instruction* (2003).

Principles of Assessment

1. *Facilitate a match between instruction and assessment.* In selecting assessment measures, especially outcome measures over which the school has control, careful attention must be given to the match between the instruction provided in the school and the measure chosen. Tests need to be selected that match the objectives and curriculum of the school. Teachers often bemoan the fact that students are tested on a skill that is not introduced in the curriculum until the following grade level! There is strong evidence that the closer the overlap between curriculum and test items, the better students will perform; this just makes sense. This is not to say that teachers should be teaching to the test, but it is foolish to ignore the demands of a test that students will be taking as a measure of their achievement. At times, this outcome measure is a test developed by the state, based on standards that have been adopted by that state. In that case, it again makes sense for reading specialists and their colleagues to work together to decide how and what the schools are teaching so that students can achieve those standards. Only then will the outcome measure be a fair assessment of students' performance.

Beresik and Bean (2002), in their study of teachers' perceptions about a state assessment test, found that teachers did not feel as though they had received sufficient professional development that would help them implement instruction that addressed state standards as measured by that outcome test. This complaint was especially common among teachers who taught at grade levels below the level at which the test was administered.

2. *Develop or select assessment measures for major components of literacy K–12.* At all levels (i.e., primary, intermediate, middle school, and secondary), reading specialists and their colleagues must make decisions about which components of literacy to assess. In the primary grades,

assessment measures should focus more on basic skills as well as comprehension, vocabulary, and writing. In the upper grades, more emphasis should be placed on comprehension, vocabulary, and writing. The key is for school personnel to select instruments that reflect a logical and realistic progression from level to level and across all of the components. At the same time, instructional colleagues must discuss whether assessment is taking too much time away from instruction and whether some adjustments can be made that would reduce the time taken from the school day for assessment purposes. In each of the vignettes in this book, the reading specialists describe specific assessments that they use at the levels at which they work.

3. *Develop a system of literacy assessment that reflects the goals of the school and use assessment tools that are reliable, valid, and practical to administer.* Too often, there is no agreed-upon system of literacy assessment in the school community. Many different tools are used by school personnel, some of which are disparate with school goals. Other assessment tools may be so complicated that they are not usable by the classroom teacher; or as stated above, they may take so much time for administration that valuable instructional time is lost. Furthermore, published instruments may be selected that are not technically valid or reliable; instruments developed by districts themselves can also lack such technical sophistication. For example, if a school decides to assess students' written retelling of a story, careful attention must be given to the rubric used to score this retelling so that there is *reliability* or consistency in the scoring of that instrument. Otherwise, little use can be made of the scores. Also, the tools employed must be *valid*—that is, they actually measure what they purport to measure. For example, a spelling test is not a measure of composition skill, although spelling, as part of a conventions rubric, could be used as one indicator of performance in composition.

Assessment tools should be usable by the teachers who administer them, whether they are reading specialists or classroom teachers. If teachers see these assessments as a burden that only take time away from the instructional program, and if they are not provided with the training they need to see the value of these measures, there will be little value in administering them.

4. *Teachers need assistance in applying data to instructional decision making.* There is clear evidence that when teachers use data to make instructional decisions, student performance improves. Yet, too often, instruction in the classroom is "activity" or materials based; that is, decisions about instruction are based on the selection that comes next in the book. One of the important roles of the reading specialist is to help teachers make decisions about their instruction, based on the results

of the students in their classroom. As mentioned in Chapter 2, RTI requires school personnel to use data to make decisions about how to differentiate instruction; teachers, reading specialists, and special educators will need to work together to analyze data and think about how each of them can contribute to the instructional program for students in specific classrooms. An example of how a reading specialist worked with one teacher in reviewing assessment data is described below, using data presented in Figure 9.2 that lists scores of students in one third-grade classroom on several literacy assessment measures.

Teacher name (last): _____   Grade _3_____

Student name	Pseudo word %	Sight word %	Fluency		Comprehension	
			Words read	Words correct	Retell n/55	Question n/8
Frank	60	89	52	44	7	3
Juan	55	93	90	86	6	6
Clyde	85	97	90	87	10	5
Melissa	45	93	102	98	13	5
Cindy	60	95	57	53	13	6
Sally	35	76	25	11	0	4
Bob	90	97	87	83	19	6
Jerome	90	98	143	143	11	8
Ralph	95	82	52	48	14	5
Gail	80	96	102	99	7	8
Celeste	20	95	57	52	11	4
Joseph	25	98	65	61	30	7
Tyrone	25	96	63	59	26	6
Henry	45	67	29	18	15	5
Mark	60	92	81	77	19	6
Julie	40	93	75	71	8	6

FIGURE 9.2. Example of a student data collection sheet, third grade, pretests.

Samantha Jones, the reading specialist, and Roberta Reed, the third-grade teacher, were reviewing the scores of some of Roberta's students on the initial screening measures given at the beginning of the year. It was obvious to them that students were doing fairly well with basic sight words; almost all students scored 75% or better. Students were not performing as well on the pseudo-word test, with 11 of them getting less than 75% correct. Many students also were experiencing difficulty with fluent oral reading (reading below 80 correct words per minute). The poor scores on the retelling were also of concern, and students had some difficulty responding to questions after reading. Roberta and Samantha identified two students (Sally and Henry) about whom they had serious concerns.

Samantha and Roberta made the following decisions after a lengthy discussion. First, all students in this third-grade class would benefit from activities that emphasized fluency practice, and Samantha shared with Roberta various ways to facilitate this (e.g., repeated readings, choral reading, etc.). Samantha indicated that she would come into the room 4 days a week to work on decoding with the 11 students who seemed to have the most difficulty; she told Roberta that she would emphasize word-building or manipulation activities to help students apply what they knew about letter–sound matches to identifying new words. All lessons would include opportunities for reading connected text.

Because of the low retelling score, both educators agreed that students did not seem to understand the task of retelling and that the entire group would benefit from lessons that helped them (1) understand the activity of retelling and why it helps them think about a story, and (2) develop strategies to help them with retelling (i.e., story structure or story mapping). They would also be given opportunities to retell orally as well as in writing. Samantha and Roberta agreed that they need to develop comprehension strategy lessons for these students, given the emphasis on reading more challenging and conceptually difficult text at this grade level. However, they decided to begin with a focus on retelling at this time.

Samantha told Roberta that she would do some additional diagnostic testing on Sally and Henry to get a better idea of their specific problems. She agreed to administer an informal reading inventory to see how they responded to different genres of text at varying levels. She also thought it would be helpful to gather additional data on their decoding and writing skills. She suggested to Roberta that it would be a good idea for the two of them to analyze the writing abilities of *all* the students within the next month. Roberta and Samantha agreed to meet in 2 weeks to talk about their instruction and to make adjustments, as needed.

This example provides a description of how one reading specialist worked collaboratively with a classroom teacher in using test results to make instructional decisions. In the vignette in Chapter 3, Jennifer, a high school reading specialist, describes which assessment tools she uses and how she uses them to make decisions about instruction.

At the present time, especially with the RTI initiative, there is emphasis on using data results to inform instruction. Often, reading specialists as well as other specialized personnel meet with teachers at specific grade levels to discuss results across the grade, for example, to determine numbers of students meeting standards or targets, as well as those who are not, and to discuss ways by which the teachers as a group can modify instruction to meet the needs at that grade level. In fact, in our work with Reading First, it was evident that teachers and administrators appreciated the way in which data helped to inform instruction (Zigmond & Bean, 2008). In some schools, "data walls" are posted, showing results for students and also showing changes in scores. I have some reservations about such public posting of student scores, and encourage administrators and teachers to recognize some of the problems inherent in such a display (e.g., embarrassment for individual students and teachers; tendency to overemphasize testing; possibility of negative, public comments about students). Teachers and administrators must discuss the pros and cons of these displays so that they do not have a negative effect on the school and its climate. In some schools, teachers and reading specialists develop charts that indicate where students are in terms of performance so that teachers can visually see the levels at which their students are performing and make some decisions about "next steps." Figure 9.3 shows such a chart for three first-grade classrooms in a school with results from the Developmental Reading Assessment (Beaver, 2006) administered by the classroom teachers early in the year. Notice that in this school a number of students are reading well and teachers will need to make some decisions about how to meet the needs of these high-performing students. And, of course, they will need to consider how to adjust instruction for other students also.

THINK ABOUT THIS

Review Figure 9.3. What sort of curricular and instructional modifications might you have to make for the students in this first-grade classroom? Should some sort of cross-classroom grouping or regrouping be considered? How can the reading specialist be helpful?

School personnel need opportunities to hold frequent, focused conversations about student learning. Moreover, these discussions about assessments should serve as opportunities for problem solving rather than as ones in which teachers feel as though they are being criticized

Grade Equivalent		Level tested on but not passed/ previously passed level		Level tested on but not passed/ previously passed level
Levels A–2 (End kindergarten)	Level A	Level 1	Level 2/1 Sammy Isabel	3/2 Zeke Carlos
Levels 3–4 (Beginning grade 1)	Level 3	4/3 Holly Zach Tom Frank Anna Stephen	Level 4 – below grade level	6/4 Maria Ethan Ava Halley Karen Taquik
Levels 6–8 (Beginning grade 1)	Level 6 – on grade level Mike V. Jerome Shavone Jimmy Stephanie	8/6 Brittany C. Abby Colon Charlie Harry T.	Level 8 Harry W. Melissa Peter Clyde	10/8 Freddy David Carol Eris Miles
Levels 10–12 (Mid grade 1)	Level 10	12/10 Brittany T. Tiffany Chelsea B. Dorin	Level 12 Celeste	14/12 Meredith Marisa S. Mary Dale
Levels 14–18 (Mid grade 1–end grade 1)	Level 14	16/14 Walter Tyrone Arthur Susan M.	Level 16 – above grade level Chelsea P. Benjamin	18/16 Dylan Susan A.
Levels 18–20 (End grade 1–beginning grade 2)	Level 18	20/18 John J. Alberta Shana Irene Becky	Level 20	24/20
Levels 24–28 (beginning grade 2–mid grade 2)	Level 24	28/24 Helen	Level 28 Roberta	30/28 John S.

FIGURE 9.3. Class profiles for grade 1: DRA text reading levels in October.

for the results. Assessment results, as mentioned previously, should serve to improve instruction.

5. *Opportunity for student self-assessment and reflection should be built into the program.* Although assessment and accountability are major concerns in schools today, unfortunately, there is less consideration given to the importance of *self*-assessment by the students. Nevertheless, there is strong support for involving students in the process of evaluating their own work (Hansen, 1998; Weber, 1999). Such self-assessment should enable students to make some decisions about their own learning. In fact, Tierney, Johnston, Moore, and Valencia (2000) predicted the continuation of an increased emphasis on learner-centered assessment that signifies "a shift in why assessments are pursued as well as how and who pursues them" (p. 244).

The use of rubrics in classrooms can promote such self-evaluation. A rubric is a scoring guide, with criteria, for judging the relative quality of assessment products. Figure 9.4 shows a sample rubric for assessing student fluency developed by the National Assessment of Educational Progress (Pinnell et al., 1995). Such a rubric could be modified so that students can self-assess their own oral reading or that of their peers. Teachers might develop a simple rubric that asks students to self-evaluate their oral reading, for example, as follows: Do I read at a speed

Level 4	Reads in primarily large, meaningful phrase groups. Although some regressions, repetitions, and deviations from text may be present, these do not appear to detract from the overall structure of the story. Preservation of the author's syntax is consistent. Some or most of the story is read with expressive interpretation.
Level 3	Reads primarily in three- or four-word phrase groups. Some smaller groupings may be present. However, the majority of phrasing seems appropriate and preserves the syntax of the author. Little or no expressive interpretation is present.
Level 2	Reads primarily in two-word phrases with some three- or four-word groupings. Some word-by-word reading may be present. Word groupings may seem awkward and unrelated to larger context of sentence or passage.
Level 1	Reads primarily word-by-word. Occasional two- or three-word phrases may occur, but these are infrequent and/or do not preserve meaningful syntax.

FIGURE 9.4. The National Assessment of Educational Progress's Integrated Reading Performance Record Oral Reading Fluency Scale. From Pinnell et al. (1995).

that makes it easy for others to understand me (not too slow and not too fast)? Do I know most of the words in the story? Do I reread if something doesn't make sense? Do I read so that others enjoy listening to me? A simple 3-point scale can be used by students to self-evaluate each of the elements (e.g., I do a great job; I'm okay most of the time; I need to improve). When students assess their own work, they become knowledgeable about the demands of the task and become more comfortable with the notion of self-evaluation.

Portfolio assessment also can be used as a means of promoting ownership of work. Such assessment can begin in the early grades with the collection of student work, writing samples, reading attitude forms, and books read, and progress to more complicated portfolios created at the middle and high school levels.

6. *Assessment systems should include more than testing.* Although schools should have a well-designed comprehensive assessment system in place, that system should include more than data obtained from tests. Kapinus (2008) discusses various topics about which data can be collected: attendance, parent involvement and attitude toward school, safety of students, instructional schedule and allotment of time for instruction, curriculum, and attitudes of teachers toward teaching and learning (p. 148). Students' motivation to read, the number of books taken out from the library, and the environment that exists in the school as a whole and in classrooms are also useful indicators of whether a school is an effective place for learning—and of ways by which schools can improve their school reading programs.

THINK ABOUT THIS

How would data such as those described in principle 6 be collected? What questions could school personnel ask about such topics as instructional schedule? Attitudes of teachers? How could such data be used to improve instruction?

Issues in Assessment

Who Should Be Involved in Developing the Assessment Plan?

Although assessment plans can be developed by an individual or a small group of administrators, it is best that such a plan be developed by a team or committee, including teachers, reading specialists, department chairs, principals, and parent representatives. Such a team, led by an administrator knowledgeable about tests and assessments, can deal with the issues that generally face such groups:

Which assessments best match the curriculum in our schools, K–12?

Which assessments are required by the state?

How can we get the best information with the least amount of disruption to the instructional schedule?

What training is necessary if teachers are to be able to administer, score (if necessary), and use the results?

Too often, decisions about assessment are made in isolation, with changes occurring at one or another level, precluding the possibility of continuity. And too often, districts cannot use their assessment tools to make decisions because they have (1) changed them too frequently, or (2) the measures are not comparable from one level to another.

School personnel should be familiar with the assessment tools being used by the district and able to discuss and communicate the results of such assessments to parents and others in the community interested in the work of the school. The emphasis by the federal government (i.e., in the NCLB legislation) on assessment results and accountability certainly makes it imperative that schools be able to explain not only *what* they are doing but *how well* they are doing!

How Are Assessment Results Reported?

Again, reading specialists may find it necessary to assist in developing ways that schools report assessment results. They themselves may also be responsible for such reporting. Different audiences are interested in these results including teachers, students, district administration, parents, and community members (as well as those on the school board). The school district should have an established means of reporting students' scores to each teacher; such reports may be similar to the one in Figure 9.2. The reading specialist should be available to assist the teacher in interpreting and using the results for instructional decision making. The reading specialist may also assist the teacher in deciding how scores of individual students can best be reported and explained to parents or to students themselves. Building principals need to receive reports in many different forms: by class, grade level, and domain or area (e.g., reading comprehension, fluency, etc.), to cite a few. They may wish to have data disaggregated by ethnic group, socioeconomic or ELL status, or special education eligibility. Again, the reading specialist may work with the principal on interpreting the results of the literacy assessment; adjustments in the instruction or curriculum may be indicated. The reading specialist and principal together may decide to make a presentation about test results to the entire faculty.

Reporting to parents is certainly a key responsibility of the schools. Reading specialists should, of course, be aware of the ways by which literacy performance is reported and what the specific scores mean: letter grades, effort scores, and grade-level reporting. In addition, they should be able to interpret those results to parents, especially parents of struggling readers. It is probable that those parents may want to meet with the reading specialist to discuss their children's scores. Test data need to be reported in a simple and clear fashion to parents so that they have an understanding of what the scores mean. Although not all reading specialists will have the responsibility for interpreting assessment results to the school board or community, including the media, some may. It is essential that the district be proactive in sharing assessment results. Not only should results be shared, but information should be provided so that interested stakeholders understand what the school is doing to improve students' achievement.

What Are the Limitations of Standardized Tests?

Reading specialists, because they frequently make use of tests in their work, need to be especially aware of the limitations of those tests, especially those that are high stakes or have the potential to label or affect students' lives in a detrimental manner. Two limitations are discussed here. First, a test is a *sample* of all questions that can be asked about a subject and, in addition, it is a *sample* of a students' performance at a single point in time. Therefore, although test publishers work to ensure that the items selected constitute a representative sample of important knowledge and skills, the fact remains that some students might have done better if a different sample of equally adequate questions had been used on the test. Furthermore, on any given day, an external factor such as illness or a disagreement with a parent may have affected a particular student's performance.

Second, changes in the schools' scores can be caused by changes in student population. If a school is one whose population demonstrates high mobility or attrition, then there can be significant differences in the population that takes the test from one administration date to another. Some students may not have been in the school for more than 2 or 3 months. In fact, Kane and Staiger in Kober (2002) estimated that more than 70% of the year-to-year variations in average test scores for a given school or grade could be attributed to external factors rather than educational factors.

Third, the ways by which scores are reported affect perceptions in terms of positive or negative outcomes. For example, look at the data in Figure 9.5, which illustrate reading achievement proficiency at the

	2005–2006	2006–2007	2007–2008
Oak School	20.7%	38.0%	37.5%
Pine School	56.6%	57.0%	57.5%

FIGURE 9.5. Percent of third-graders scoring at proficiency.

third-grade level for two schools over a 3-year period. Which school do you think is doing better?

If the two schools are compared, it is obvious that Pine School has more students reading at proficiency; most likely Pine School met the requirements for "adequate yearly progress" as required by NCLB. However, if we look at change in performance of students, then we see greater growth or change in Oak School where student performance has improved from a low of 20.7% scoring at proficiency to 36.5% at the proficiency level. Initially, NCLB considered only status or current level of proficiency for making decisions about whether schools were improving satisfactorily. At the present time, some states have been given permission to use evidence of growth or change scores as a means of determining whether schools have improved.

In addition to looking at the results in terms of change or status, those who interpret data need to look at trends in a school. For example, in looking at only 2 years of growth for Oak School, we can be mislead by the data because in 2006–2007, 38% of the students were proficient and in 2007–2008, the proficiency rate was 37.5%; if we use only the previous year's results, we see no improvement, but if we analyze scores from 2005–2006 to 2007–2008, we see significant improvement. In other words, we need to be extremely careful not only in collecting data but in analyzing and interpreting them. Results may be arbitrary; that is, improvement depends on the approach used for analysis. Reading specialists should be familiar with these limitations. Reading specialists who want to know more about high-stakes testing may wish to read the policy brief written by Peter Afferbach (2004) for the National Reading Conference (*www.nrconline.org*).

Summary

Assessment is an important responsibility of the reading specialist, not only for assessing the strengths and needs of individual students but also for making decisions about the performance of classes, schools, and the district as a whole. Assessment should be closely related to instruction, and there should be a sequential, comprehensive assessment system, K–12. In addition, various stakeholders, including teachers and community representatives, should be involved in making decisions about the assessment of literacy. Multiple assessment measures that display established technical adequacy should be used. Reading specialists may have responsibility for working with teachers, administrators, and the community interpreting and applying the results of assessment. They should also be knowledgeable about the strengths as well as the limitations of all assessment measures, especially those that are used for high-stakes purposes.

Reflections

What are the strengths and weaknesses of various assessment instruments with which you are familiar?

Activities

1. Interview a reading specialist in a district about his or her role in assessment. Which assessment tools does he or she use? How does the reading specialist work with teachers to use results in planning instruction?

2. Interview a reading specialist or another school leader to discuss a district's plan of assessment, K–12. Does the district have a plan of assessment, K–12, and if so, what measures are used? How does the assessment differ from level to level?

3. Select an assessment tool used by a district with which you are familiar and investigate whether the instrument meets a standard of technical adequacy.

10

School, Community, and Family Partnerships

It takes a village to raise a child.
—African Proverb

Although this expression is often used, its merit cannot be disputed. When teachers are asked to identify their greatest problem in working with struggling readers, they often mention the lack of parental involvement in providing additional support or attending to the child's behavioral needs, especially in schools where there are large numbers of students from poor or minority backgrounds (National Center for Education Statistics, 1998). Teachers in the early grades decry the fact that students come to kindergarten without the background knowledge/ exposure that enables them to learn to read; these teachers are concerned that children do not have the literacy and language experiences that provide the foundation for learning to read.

In the past, some educators believed that it was their job to teach and that parents had the responsibility of "parenting." This viewpoint has certainly changed; the education of the child is one that requires the effort of both. The research evidence is clear. When there is parental involvement and support, students have a much better chance of success in school (Henderson & Berla, 1995; Morrison, Bachman, & Connor, 2005). When parents are involved in their children's schooling, the children earn higher grades and test scores, and they stay in school longer. In addition, the increased pressure on educators to account for levels of student achievement has generated a need for more parental involvement. In its NCLB (U.S. Department of Education, 2002b) legislation, the federal government gave parents a range of options to pursue if their children are placed in unsuccessful schools. Schools must have supplemental programs for children with special needs, and parents have the choice of transferring their children to better-performing public schools. Whether we agree with this policy or feel that it puts the focus of success solely on schools and teachers, the fact is that all schools and all teachers must think about their involvement in the community in new and different ways.

Epstein's (1995) research-based framework includes six types of parental involvement:

1. Parenting: helping families establish home environments that support children's development.
2. Communicating: designing and using effective forms of communication about programs and children's growth.
3. Volunteering: recruiting and organizing help and support in schools.
4. Learning at home: providing information and ideas to families about how to help students.
5. Decision making: including parents in school decisions.
6. Collaborating with the community.

Reading specialists and their colleagues can implement many different efforts to foster growth in these areas.

This chapter begins with a discussion of the reading specialist's involvement with community agencies and institutions, addressing Epstein's (1995) sixth point of collaborating with the community. Next, guidelines for working with volunteers and paraprofessionals in the schools are provided. Lastly, the role of the reading specialist in working with families and addressing issues of parenting, communicating, learning at home, and decision making is explored.

Involvement with External Agencies

There are many different agencies with which reading specialists might work. Involvement with five important entities is discussed here: preschool providers, libraries, community-based programs, universities and colleges, and volunteers or paraprofessionals in the schools.

Preschool Providers

The 5-year-olds who enter kindergartens come with a variety of experiences, many of them having attended a day-care center, nursery, or preschool. Some arrive having learned not only school and learning behaviors but also literacy skills that enable them to move comfortably into the kindergarten setting. Others seem to struggle with literacy tasks. Research on the cognitive development of young children emphasizes the importance of high-quality early learning experiences. There is evidence of great variability in the quality of the preschool experiences that children receive, especially in preschool programs serving children from poor families (McGill-Franzen, Lanford, & Adams, 2002; Snow et al., 1998). At the same time, the quality of child-care programs has been identified as an important determinant of language acquisition in the form of preliteracy skills (Barnett, 1995; Barnett, Frede, Mobasher, & Mohr 1987).

What can be done to increase the possibility that young children receive adequate preparation in their day-care or preschool setting? Schools may work in a number of ways with preschool providers; three major efforts to increase the collaboration between school districts and preschool providers are described here. First, school districts should work collegially with preschool providers so that there is a clear understanding of what schools expect from entering kindergarteners, and what educational experiences students receive in their preschool settings. Schools also need to know what providers value and why their programs include various activities and experiences. Gathering this information can be accomplished in several ways: (1) Schools can share the list of standards or competencies for entering kindergarten, (2) preschool providers can also share their curriculum, (3) teachers from the two sites can visit each others' classrooms to get a better understanding of students' experiences, and (4) meetings between the two groups of teachers can bridge the gap that often occurs and eliminate, or at least reduce, the "blame" game.

Second, and as important, preschool providers who educate students for a district should be included in the various professional development programs that are available. When school districts convene a professional development meeting in which the speaker is addressing an issue important for the education of young children, invitations can be extended to the preschool providers. It may not be possible for all preschool teachers to attend, but perhaps arrangements can be made so that there is some sharing of information.

Third, when opportunities for working together arise, seize them! At the present time, the interest in early learning is not only creating such opportunities, it is *demanding* them. Possible proposals for funding can be investigated and written, and community collaboration for such endeavors can be cultivated.

Reading specialists can assume an important role in promoting each of these three steps. Indeed, reading specialists are often the ones who can "create" opportunities for working together. They can certainly foster interaction between kindergarten and preschool teachers, especially in the discussion about literacy instruction. They may also be able to provide professional development for the preschool teachers.

Recently, there have been efforts to provide additional professional development on literacy for preschool teachers. Often, agencies or districts receiving these funds have built coaching into their proposals as a means of supporting job-embedded learning for preschool teachers who may not have had extensive learning opportunities about literacy and language development. In these instances, new opportunities are available for reading specialists interested in early childhood education.

Libraries

Reading specialists, of course, can work collaboratively with school librarians to develop experiences for students that create excitement and enthusiasm for reading. The reading specialist should be aware of what resources are available in the school library, and assist the librarian in selecting print and nonprint materials that enhance students' motivation to read and also promote learning across curricular areas. The reading specialist may be able to work with the librarian to identify the various themes and topics addressed in the academic areas. School librarians can also be involved in supporting the school's literacy program. My colleague and I (Bean & Eichelberger, 2007) evaluated a program in a local school district in which school librarians could opt to attend workshops led by district literacy coaches that would increase their knowledge and understanding of the various strategies and approaches used in the literacy program. These librarians were very positive about this experience, indicating that now they had a better understanding of the language of literacy used by teachers and also were able to reinforce in their library classes some of what students were learning in their classrooms.

The community library is also a resource for the school. Most community libraries assign a staff member to interact with personnel from schools who are eager to participate in school–library collaborations. The community librarian may be able to purchase resources that relate to the curriculum emphasized in the school. The reading specialist who takes the time to work with the community librarian is likely to find new ways to enhance student motivation to read. Some of the ways that schools and libraries can work together include the following:

• Librarians can come to school to read books to children and to solicit membership in the community library. After reading a book, it can be left in the classroom for follow-up work by the teacher.

• Students can visit the community library on a field trip; the librarian may lead the students through the various sections of the library, explaining the types of resources offered by each.

• School and library personnel can work together to develop a summer program for students. This program can be promoted in the school and recognition given at the school in the fall for those students who complete the program. Research findings indicate that there is a "summer slide" for children of poverty; that is, children from higher socioeconomic groups do not experience the summer learning loss that characterizes those in lower socioeconomic groups (Alexander, Entwisle, & Olson, 2001). Allington and McGill-Franzen (1989) indicated that it is important for children to have many opportunities to read during the summer. I would encourage reading specialists to work with the community library to create programs that benefit both successful and struggling readers.

• The reading specialist can inform the librarian about special school initiatives; for example, specific reading programs or efforts that require specific books. Often, the librarian will then make certain that those books are included in the library's collections.

During the past several years, a library and school district in an urban setting collaborated to develop a special library program designed to promote reading in schools where there were large numbers of struggling readers. This program, funded by a local foundation, was designed to (1) stimulate motivation to read by exposing students to books about children from various cultures, including their own, and (2) enhance reading achievement by introducing and discussing various vocabulary words from those texts. Personnel from the library went to the third-grade classrooms twice a month to read and discuss a book with the children, and then left the book in the classroom. Evaluation of that program indicated that students enjoyed listening to the book and that they often reread the book that had been read to them. Teachers felt the program enhanced students' reading interest, and they (the teachers) enjoyed learning about new trade books they could then use in their classroom work (Genest & Bean, 2007).

Community-Based Programs

In many communities, especially those in poverty areas, programs operated by churches or community agencies are available. These programs provide a safe place for children whose parents may be working, and, as important, they reinforce school lessons by helping students with homework or providing tutoring and academic support. Recent legislation has deemed faith-based organizations eligible to apply for approval to provide supplemental educational services to low-income students attending underachieving schools. Such services can provide help before or after school, on weekends, or during the summer, in both reading and math.

These organizations, whether faith- or community-based, can support or extend the work of the school. In order to help them achieve their goals in ways that facilitate the work of the school, reading specialists or other school personnel may become involved in two ways. First, schools can communicate with agencies offering these services so that there is an awareness of what additional support students are receiving. Second, schools can increase the effectiveness of these community programs by providing training or guidance about possible strategies or instruction that would best support classroom instruction. For example, if students in a school are working with a specific program or curriculum, the school might suggest that the community-based program use the supplemental books that are aligned with that program. A check sheet might be devised for classroom teachers, so that they can easily communicate the needs of specific students (e.g., "J needs to practice his new sight words; I'm including them in this packet.").

Universities and Colleges

Many schools are close enough to universities to be able to partner with them on various projects that bring preservice teachers, volunteers, or faculty into their schools. Faculty involved with preservice education programs look for ways to form partnerships with schools in which there is quality instruction based on best practice and with mentors who are excellent role models. Many are eager to cooperate in many different ways: teaching classes on site and recruiting classroom teachers willing to participate, providing up-to-date resources and information to schools, and holding meetings in which there is in-depth discussion about what preservice students are learning and its congruence with the instruction occurring in the classrooms.

Many faculty at universities and colleges also appreciate opportunities to participate in professional development efforts of schools, or they are interested in conducting research that will contribute to the understanding of how students learn to read. Although such partnerships need to be entered into thoughtfully, so that there is a clear understanding of the benefits for each partner, these ventures can be the catalyst for much growth for both. In a previous chapter, I described the LEADERS project in which we worked with several school districts on a professional development initiative. The outcome of the project included not only changes in classroom teacher practices and student achievement; in addition, university faculty learned a great deal about what works in schools, what is difficult to implement, and the problems that must be addressed in efforts to improve the quality of literacy instruction.

Because of the work–study portion of the America Reads Challenge Act of 1997 (*www.ed.gov/inits/americareads*), which provided funding for college students who were eligible for work–study to become volunteer tutors in the schools, many colleges and universities sent their students into schools or community agencies to tutor struggling readers. Much has been written about the results of the America Reads efforts (Fitzgerald, 2001; Morrow & Woo, 2000), and various manuals and procedures for implementing programs have been developed (Bader, 1998; Johnston, Juel, & Invernizzi, 1995). Bean, Turner, and Belski (2002) discussed lessons learned from implementing such a program, identifying issues that need to be addressed by university and school or community-based personnel. We found that a successful volunteer tutoring program benefited from a well-structured training program that provides a framework for these novice tutors. Such a program needs to include information about literacy instruction and how best to engage students. Furthermore, because tutors were not always familiar or comfortable with the sites to which they were assigned, they needed experiences and guidance that would help them learn more about the context in which they were going to work. Also, a collaborative program like this requires clear and ongoing communication of expectations and responsibilities between the partners.

For 10 years, I directed a reading specialist intern program in which graduate students in the reading specialist certification program at the University of Pittsburgh, Pennsylvania, were placed in a school site for an entire year to work with students needing reading support and with the teachers of those students; at the same time students were enrolled in courses and applying what they were learning at their schools. This partnership was a win–win for participants. It provided excellent and real experiences for the reading specialist candidates who came to class each week with new issues and ideas. It provided additional support for the struggling readers in these schools, and it provided the classroom teachers and reading specialists in the schools with opportunities to work with teachers new to the profession (see Bean et al., 1999, for a more in-depth description of this initiative). The next section discusses guidelines for working with volunteer tutors and paraprofessionals.

Volunteers and Paraprofessionals in the Schools

Volunteers, of course, can come from many different sources: senior citizens, retired teachers, and parents, as well as college students. They can also come from the business sector. In the past, volunteers came into schools to help teachers. Often they did clerical work—duplicating worksheets, correcting papers—or they assisted in cafeteria or playground duty. Currently, there is much more emphasis on using volunteers or paraprofessionals to assist with instruction, providing opportunities for students to practice reading orally, reviewing sight words, and helping with student writing. Such volunteer programs can be informal, with parents or tutors following the lead or suggestions of teachers to whom they have been assigned, or much more formal, with volunteers or paraprofessionals serving as tutors for children experiencing difficulties or for those students needing supplemental or Tier 2 instruction in schools using an RTI approach. In fact, given the increased number of paraprofessionals in schools to supplement the work of teachers, the International Reading Association (2003) Standards indicated that reading specialists need to work effectively with paraprofessionals by helping them to plan lessons, observing them with students, providing feedback about their performance, providing staff development training, and providing emotional and academic support. The standards also include a list of competencies for paraprofessionals. The 2010 Standards (International Reading Association) currently being developed, also include a list of competencies and identify expected qualifications for educational support personnel who work with students.

Often, the reading specialist is responsible for recruiting, training, and directing the work of paraprofessionals and volunteers in the school. One reading specialist in a local school was responsible for directing the work of more than 17 tutors who worked with primary children in her building. She had a massive job of coordinating schedules, training these tutors, and then monitoring their work and the progress of students. Lapp, Fisher, Flood, and Frey (2003) described a tutoring program in which reading specialists train, monitor, and support aides who provide one-to-one instruction to struggling readers. What is critical, however, is that the work of these individuals be closely monitored to ensure that they are working effectively with students, and especially struggling readers. In one of the Reading First schools in Pennsylvania, retired teachers were recruited to provide differentiated, supplemental instruction for all students in a lab setting. In this Reading First school, volunteers or paraprofessionals who had expertise as teachers were given more instructional responsibilities than less experienced individuals. In other words, although volunteers or paraprofessionals can be helpful, there is justifiable concern about using less qualified personnel to provide instruction for those who need the most help! The following guidelines may be helpful to those interested in initiating such programs in their schools.

1. *Provide adequate training for volunteers or paraprofessionals.* Wasik (1998) reported that in successful tutoring programs, reading specialists (1) trained and provided feedback to volunteer tutors, and (2) wrote and supervised lessons. In other words, tutoring programs may not be successful if careful supervision of tutors is lacking. Indeed, an unsupervised program can result in wasted time and money. On the other hand, Baker, Gersten, and Keating (2000) described a volunteer tutoring program in which community volunteers were given brief training and a broad framework from which to plan. Students in the experimental group exhibited greater growth on several dimensions of reading, compared to students in the comparison group who received no tutoring. This study suggested that even minimally trained tutors can facilitate progress in struggling readers. The Baker study, and a later one by Fitzgerald (2001), indicated that there is much we do not know about tutoring by volunteers. The caring relationship that is built between the volunteer and the child may be a key element in motivating the child to do better in school. The gains, of course, may have been greater with additional training of volunteers. However, in instances where fiscal or logistical restrictions limit the amount of training or supervision, leaders can still develop a tutoring program that can have a positive effect on students and their reading performance.

Tutoring programs currently available, such as Reading One-to-One (Farkas, Warrren, & Johnson, 1999), provide specific directions and materials for tutors so that they understand what they need to do to work successfully with children. As mentioned earlier, in our work with America Reads tutors who came with little or no experiences with students or with literacy instruction, we found that they needed assistance in how to motivate and keep children interested in learning. We also found that they needed a structured lesson plan to guide them in their work (Bean, Turner, & Belski, 2002). A successful program may require a literacy coordinator who is responsible for the training, monitoring, and evaluation of that program.

THINK ABOUT THIS

What are your thoughts about using minimally trained tutors with struggling readers? As a reading specialist, how would you use paraprofessionals or volunteers in the school in which you work?

---

2. *Help tutors understand the school culture, school procedures, and regulations.* Many volunteer tutors have little understanding or experience with schools, other than the ones they attended, often many years ago! Volunteers need to be given specific information about school rules and regulations, appropriate dress, and behavior. They need assistance in understanding how to communicate with the classroom teacher and the rules to be followed if the child is not behaving (i.e., what are the specific disciplinary procedures followed by the school or the classroom teacher?) The time spent on these topics is appreciated by tutors and creates a better atmosphere for cooperation and collaboration between school personnel and tutors.

3. *Seek input from and provide feedback to classroom teachers.* Classroom teachers can provide useful information about children and their reading needs. They can also provide information as to whether there are changes in the child's performance as the tutoring progresses. At the same time, the classroom teacher should be informed about the tutoring, its emphasis, and given feedback as to how the child is performing in the tutoring session. Teachers may be more receptive to the tutoring, which may pull students from classroom instruction, if they have input into the tutoring plan. Or if the tutoring takes place in the classroom, the classroom teacher needs to take a leadership role in how the volunteer works with students. Classroom teachers should have occasions to meet and talk with tutors; in fact, the reading specialist may choose to work with the students while the classroom teacher meets for a brief time with tutors. Often, the classroom teachers can provide ideas to tutors about working with specific children.

4. *Monitor and evaluate the program.* The reading specialist responsible for the tutoring program should monitor the work of each tutor and determine whether a child is making progress. If there is little or no progress, changes need to be made. The reading specialist should have a system for evaluating the overall program. If the program is successful, great! But if the program is showing little in the way of results, there must be discussion about how it can be improved.

One of the criticisms of tutoring programs is that they are not aligned with the classroom instruction. This is a legitimate concern that should be addressed by those responsible for the tutoring program. In evaluating the program, the reading specialist can develop and send questionnaires to teachers and parents to determine program effects. Student outcomes can also be investigated by using formal or informal assessment measures.

Working with Families

Given the requirements in Title 1 regulations, many reading specialists have a special role in promoting family involvement. They have had to keep parents apprised of the supplemental instruction received by students who have reading difficulties. They also communicated with parents in various ways and on a regular basis to help them understand what they can do to enhance the reading performance of their children. Specialists may also need to develop comprehensive family literacy programs in which parents also receive literacy instruction.

The awareness of the importance of family involvement has generated policies and procedures at all levels of government—federal, state, and local—and has affected school programs and practices. The following sections discuss various ways in which reading specialists can work with parents and families to ensure greater literacy performance for children. First, several important guidelines are described:

1. *School personnel must have an understanding and appreciation for the families whose children they serve.* In today's schools, many teachers do not live in the communities they serve, and for that reason may lack an in-depth understanding of the culture and experiences of their students. Teachers may believe that children are not learning because of their backgrounds or the lack of support from home. And although the educational task may be more difficult when children do not arrive at the school door with expected literacy experiences or skills, teachers with an understanding and appreciation of the talents and experiences that children *do* bring can be more effective in working with them. Some schools have asked teachers to conduct home visits; others schedule parent conferences in neighborhood agencies that are close to children's homes (especially necessary when children are bused to schools a far distance from their homes). The reading specialist can serve as a catalyst for helping teachers gain knowledge, and an understanding of, and appreciation for students, their background, and their culture.

2. *School personnel must help parents understand their academic and behavioral goals and expectations for children.* Although schools continue to

communicate through written materials, others have begun to develop telephone networks or computer hotlines where parents can find information online.

3. *School personnel should create an environment that welcomes parents into the schools.* Too many parents, especially those who themselves were not successful in school, are not comfortable going into classrooms. As mentioned above, parents may serve as volunteers and paraprofessionals in providing direct service to students. These parents then know a great deal about the schools! Parents can also assist by making presentations to classes about their professions, serving as reader-of-the-day or week, and serving as supervisors on field trips. In one school, the coordinator of a special reading project developed a program in which parents were responsible for reading a book and then presenting a craft or art activity to the children. The coordinator helped parents select the book and the activity, and the teacher assisted with the lesson and any management problems. Parents were delighted with the teaching experience and the added bonus of seeing their child in the classroom context. Children were excited that their mom or dad was going to teach (and other children often acknowledged the fact that "Billy's mom is teaching today!"). At a celebration breakfast these parents talked about their increased appreciation for the teaching profession—and the teachers of their children! (Teaching is not as easy as they thought.)

In another school, the individual responsible for federal programs held four evening meetings a year to which students brought their families. These meetings were based on a theme; for example, teachers had read *Where the Wild Things Are* (1988) by Maurice Sendak and then each class constructed a large monster drawing to be hung in the school gym. Children and parents arrived at the gym in the early evening to construct masks, to listen to another reading of the book, and to sample light refreshments. The local bookstore sent a "monster" to walk around the gym and decide which of the classes' monsters was the very best. Attendance at these events ranged from 100 to 250 participants and included parents, children and their siblings, grandparents, and interested relatives!

Results of a survey on family and school partnerships (National Center for Education Statistics, 1996) indicated that parents are more likely to attend meetings if there is some possibility of interacting with their child's teachers. It is necessary to know the community and families and to provide what works. Parents can also serve on a school advisory team or participate in committees that are working to improve the school; for example, a playground committee or after-school programming.

4. *Parent involvement should extend through the grades.* It is true that parent involvement declines with each grade level, showing the most dramatic decrease at the point of transition into the middle grades (Billig, 2002). Nevertheless, opportunities to build parent involvement in the middle grades are available. Billig suggests that too often the communication during the middle and high school years tends to be one-way—from the school to the family—and recommends the following five guidelines for schools seeking to form strong partnerships with parents (2002, pp. 43–45):

    a. Use the challenges of the middle school years to build parent involvement programs. Students will now face more demanding academics and be asked to assume more responsibility.

    b. Build on the need and value that middle schoolers place on strong relationships.

    c. Encourage parent and student participation in decision making. Parents and students can be involved in curriculum decisions (e.g., selection of textbooks).

    d. Train school faculty to work well with parents, how to communicate, how to report student progress, work with volunteers, and become involved with community partnerships.

    e. Keep families informed about what students are learning.

Practical Ideas for Increasing Parent Involvement in the Schools

This section describes ideas for increasing parent involvement in the schools and resources that may be helpful.

1. *Create a parent involvement program that is an integral part of the school reading program.* Too often, parent involvement efforts are idiosyncratic; that is, they differ from teacher to teacher. Effective programs, however, require procedures for reflecting on what is being done and a systematic effort to involve parents in their children's educational process. This effort includes involving parents in the decision making about the plan itself (i.e., what do parents need and want?) and securing a long-term commitment to the plan on the part of teachers and parents alike. Sometimes it is necessary to educate teachers about how to work effectively with families; often it means rethinking what parent involvement means in a specific school or community. In other words, teachers,

administrators, and reading specialists should decide as a group what means will be used to communicate with and inform parents. Such a plan may include ideas for formal events such as parent workshops or conferences. It may also include ideas for communicating with parents on a regular basis about the accomplishments of their children. The plan may also indicate who is responsible for the various activities (e.g., the reading specialist will plan a meeting that provides suggestions for parents on how they can help their children become better readers, all teachers will send home a "positive" note to parents at least once a semester).

2. *Take every opportunity to communicate with parents, and use many different approaches to communication.* Effective teachers have always reinforced the positive. They send home notes telling parents what their child has done well, reinforced a child's behavior with stickers or a certificate, or even called parents to tell them how "Johnny made my day." In today's world, we need to take advantage of the technology available to communicate with parents. One kindergarten teacher creates a photograph album of her class, with digital pictures and a caption dictated by the child. At the end of the year, this teacher holds a kindergarten graduation at which she shows these photos to the attending parents. Each parent also receives a copy of the album. Student success is celebrated! This teacher has no difficulty with parent attendance. She also communicates on a weekly basis with parents, sending a letter that tells them what students have learned that week and how parents can reinforce the learning. Other teachers communicate via e-mail messages; some have cell phones, and parents are told that they can call a designated number at a specific time to raise questions or address concerns.

In addition to these individual efforts that teachers make, there should be a systematic plan for communicating with parents, K–12. Newsletters and bulletins are useful, especially if they include many practical ideas for parents. Some schools send home a calendar over the summer that suggests a literacy activity that children can do each day or week.

Reading specialists can develop their own material to send home to parents, or they can select from material that is available. Figure 10.1 is a handout for parents with tips for reading to their child that was distributed by the Keystone State Reading Association, Families and Reading Committee (*www.ksra.org*). Figure 10.2 is a list of references for adults interested in learning more about literacy for children or appropriate books for children of different ages.

In one community, foundations provided support to place large billboards near major highways, displaying a picture of a mother read-

- Read aloud to your child every day, even an older child. Reading aloud provides a good model, expands vocabulary, stimulates curiosity and imagination, lengthens attention span, and motivates the child to want to read better books independently. Most important of all, it helps to develop a lifetime reader! Be sure to "ham it up" when reading aloud.

- Share reading *with* your child by alternate reading. You read a page and then your child reads a page. Or you read a paragraph and your child reads a paragraph.

- Be aware that reading level and listening level are different.
  –Read easy books *with* your child.
  –Read more advanced books *to* your child to instill motivation and a love of books.

- For an older child, read aloud the first few chapters of a book to get him or her started. This is where the characters are introduced, the plot is set up, and the setting is described. You'll be offering a jump start!

- Discuss the book you're reading together:
  –Predict what the book will be about before reading it.
  –Talk about the pictures.
  –Periodically stop and predict what will happen next.
  –Consider what else could have happened.
  –Relate the story to your own experiences.
  –Stop to explain things you think your child does not know.
  –Talk about the author and illustrator.

- Carry books with you wherever you go; read to your child while waiting for appointments, for example.

- Tape-record favorite books so your young child can listen to them over and over, even in the car.

- Choose repetitive, rhythmic books for younger readers, and look for interesting illustrations that help to tell the story.

- Take time each day for everyone in the family to read silently; show you value reading by allowing your child to see you read.

- Encourage your child to keep a journal by recording the day's happenings, his or her feelings, etc.

- Provide pencils, pens, crayons, markers, paper, and other materials for your child to use to express feelings and thoughts about what is read.

- Give your child his or her own library card for the public library; visit the library often.

- Encourage your child to read easy books to improve fluency.

- Subscribe to children's magazines.

- Write notes to your child and tuck them into a lunch box or pocket.

- Enjoy reading with your child.

FIGURE 10.1. Tips for reading with your child (from Keystone State Reading Association).

Books

Book Crush for Kids and Teens: Recommended Reading for Every Mood, Moment, and Interest by Nancy Pearl. Seattle, WA: Sasquatch, 2007.

Gotcha for Guys!: Nonfiction Books to Get Boys Excited about Reading by Kathleen Baxter and Marcia Agness Kochel. Santa Barbara, CA: Libraries Unlimited, 2006.

Hey! Listen to This!: Stories to Read Aloud by Jim Trelease. New York: Penguin, 1992.

Raising Bookworms: Getting Kids Reading for Pleasure and Empowerment by Emma Walton Hamilton. Sag Harbor, NY: Beech Tree, 2008.

Raising Readers: Helping Your Child to Literacy by Steven Bialostok. Winnipeg, Canada: Peguis, 1992.

Reading Begins at Home: Preparing Children for Reading before They Go to School (2nd ed.) by Dorothy Butler with Marie Clay. Portsmouth, NH: Heinemann, 2008.

Reading Magic: Why Reading Aloud to Our Children Will Change Their Lives Forever (2nd ed.) by Mem Fox. Boston: Mariner, 2008.

The Read-Aloud Handbook (6th ed.) by Jim Trelease. New York: Penguin, 2006.

Websites for Parents and Teachers

www.ed.gov

www.funbrain.com

www.pbs.org/parents

FIGURE 10.2. References for adults.

From *The Reading Specialist: Leadership for the Classroom, School, and Community* (2nd ed.) by Rita M. Bean. Copyright 2009 by The Guilford Press. Permission to photocopy this form is granted to purchasers of this book for personal use only (see copyright page for details).

---

ing to her young child. The goal was to generate awareness of the importance of reading and to motivate families to read to their children.

Reading specialists can develop and hold workshops and meetings that increase parents' understanding of how important they are to the literacy learning of their children. Ideas about how to help children develop a love of reading and providing an environment that encourages reading can be shared. Parents can be given specific ideas about how to read effectively to their children and how to listen to their children read to them.

3. *Provide training that improves teachers' ability to talk or confer with parents.* Some guidelines that may be helpful include the following:

• Be prepared. Have examples of student work easily at hand so that parents can be shown what their child can and cannot do. As noted, it is important to talk about what the child *can* do and to emphasize the positive.

• Refrain from using school talk or jargon. Parents may not be familiar with such terms as "phonemic" or "phonological awareness," "fluency," or concepts about print. It is best to *show* parents what is challenging their child.

• Establish a friendly but professional atmosphere in the conference. It is preferable for the reading specialist to avoid sitting behind his or her desk; a table is more welcoming and still provides the surface area for various materials and work samples.

• Talk only about the child and what he or she can do. Do not compare the child to others.

• Be a good listener. Reading specialists learn so much more if they solicit information from parents, who, after all, may be able to provide additional understanding of how to work with their child. No matter how divergent their point of view, it will enhance the reading specialist's understanding of the child, especially relative to the home and parents' expectations for that child.

It is a rare parent who does not want his or her child to be successful. It is the teachers' responsibility to solicit parents' participation in their children's learning process.

Summary

This chapter discussed the rationale for building partnerships with communities and families and described various ways in which reading specialists can work to build relationships with community agencies, including preschool providers, universities, libraries, those who offer supplemental programs to students, and volunteers. In addition, the importance of parents' involvement, and ways of enhancing that involvement in their children's education were discussed.

Reflections

1. Why would some parents feel uncomfortable about meeting with a teacher? How could this discomfort be alleviated?
2. What activities and programs does your local library offer that enhance reading performance of students in the school? How could your school partner with the local library?

Activities

1. Develop a friendly newsletter for parents that provides them with ideas about how they can work effectively with their children. The newsletter can be one for parents of students in a specific age group (i.e., preschool, primary, intermediate, middle school, or secondary).

2. Using the guidelines in this chapter, practice holding a conference with a parent, using one of the scenarios described below. Role-play in threes—one person is the family member, the other is the teacher or reading specialist, and the third is the observer who provides feedback about the conference.

    Scenario 1: Sally. Sally's mom is concerned about her daughter's performance in school. She does not understand why Sally is receiving help from the reading specialist. Sally is a fourth-grader at an urban elementary school. She is coming to the reading specialist because she is having difficulty in her social studies and science classes. She received all A's in reading and spelling in grades 1, 2, and 3, but this year she seems to be having trouble with her content subjects. She complains to her mom that she can read the words but she does not know what they mean, and that when she gets to the end of a passage or chapter, she cannot remember anything she has read.

    Sally, an only child, has always lived with her mother and grandmother, who both work. Finances are limited, and Sally has not had many opportunities that might enrich her literacy background. Although her caregivers have tried to take her to the museum, the local zoo, and so on, time is limited (given their work schedules). There are few books in the home, and although the mother indicates that she would love to read to Sally, she is tired at the end of the day, and somehow there never seems to be time. Sally has good health; she wears glasses (although she forgets them much of the time). She loves school and her teachers (except for the social studies teacher—who keeps asking her difficult questions). She also loves books—especially storybooks. She hates her content subjects, though, because "everything is just too hard" (or so she tells her mom). She has always received praise from her reading teachers for her excellent reading; she loves to read orally, and with expression. She cannot understand why she is unable to comprehend her new books in fourth grade.

    Scenario 2: Henry. Henry's parents have come for a consultation about Henry's poor grades. They are eager to help him. Henry is a ninth-grade student at a suburban high school. He is getting D's and F's in courses such as American literature and history. He does fairly well in algebra and biology. Henry moved to this high school from a small rural school this past year. He had always been an average student in school. He knows that he is a slow reader and that he often has difficulty figuring out the words. Once he knows the words, he realizes that he does know the meaning. Henry does not read much, but when he does read, he chooses material about dog care (he has a Labrador retriever that he trains) or magazines dealing with the outdoors. He cannot remember reading a book that was not required reading. Henry likes classes where he does not have to read much—and he hates to write. (His handwriting is slow and laborious.) He does love working on the computer, though, and his parents have agreed to get one (he is really excited about that). Math is his favorite subject, and he likes science too (especially biology).

Henry is the oldest boy of four children (he has an older sister and younger twin brothers). All of his siblings are excellent readers, and Henry realizes that he is the one who has the most difficulty in school. His parents try to help him with his schoolwork, but he does not like to bother them because they have lots of things to do with his younger brothers. The family is very supportive of all the children. Henry has decided to go out for the track team, and he knows that his family will attend all of the games.

Henry has good vision and hearing. He had one serious illness in second grade, when he missed a great deal of school and was tutored at home for almost 3 months. Since that time, he has not had any difficulty with his health. He has always had difficulty with reading, especially after his return to school in second grade.

11

Writing Proposals

- The superintendent is excited about the potential of obtaining additional funds from the state to develop a summer school for struggling readers. The Title 1 proposal is due soon, and the reading specialist has the responsibility for writing it.
- There is an opportunity to obtain funds from a local foundation to upgrade computers in the school, if a proposal is submitted that demonstrates how the use of such computers will be integrated into classroom instruction.
- Teachers can obtain mini-grants by writing a proposal for a special classroom project.

In today's world, there are many opportunities for obtaining additional funds to support schools' efforts to provide instruction to its students. At times, reading specialists in the schools may be required to write proposals to obtain Title 1 funds, special state funding, or foundation grants. Reading specialists may also take the initiative and write a proposal because they see the possibility of improving the reading program with additional support. There are many different types of proposals, and requirements differ. For example, some research proposals often require lengthy submissions, with a review of literature and research that supports the plan. On the other hand, some proposals for obtaining materials or developing a special program may be quite short, requiring only the rationale, the plan for use or implementation, and a budget. All proposals have some characteristics in common, however. This chapter presents general guidelines for writing a proposal, describes the various parts of a proposal, and makes suggestions for developing each part.

General Guidelines for Proposal Writing

1. *Develop a great idea!* No matter how well written or how elaborate a proposal is, without a great idea, it will not be an effective outreach

214

tool for obtaining funding. Reviewers look for an idea that is creative, well developed, and addresses an important topic. For example, if there is concern about the fact that primary students are regressing in their reading performance over the summer, coming up with a creative idea for motivating children and families to read over the summer may be the key to obtaining funds from a local foundation. Or, a secondary reading specialist may want to purchase novels that support a specific unit being taught in a content field; for example, study of the Civil War in history class.

Just as authors stress the importance of writing about a topic known well to the writer, so too do great ideas for grants come from immersion in the work that needs the funding. The content or ideas in a proposal should be based on reading specialists' expertise, interests, and knowledge of the field (i.e., what has been done and what has worked). Often these ideas come from discussions with colleagues, attendance at a conference, or from reading an article in a professional journal. At other times, ideas come from an identified need in the school; for example, more parental involvement, greater number of multicultural books in the school library, or a Saturday school for struggling readers.

2. *Locate a good match.* Funds may be available from federal, state, or local agencies, from corporate foundations, or from private foundations. A reading specialist seeking funds to undertake a specific project must try to locate funders whose priorities match the proposed activities or initiative. The reading specialist would not, for example, send a proposal for a professional development project to a funding agency that indicates they are seeking proposals for summer programs for children.

Several useful resources are available for those who wish to write proposals to seek additional funds to support their efforts:

> *Designing successful grant proposals* by Donald C. Orlich. Alexandria, VA: Association for Supervision and Curriculum Development, 1996.
>
> *Grants for K–12 hotline* (biweekly report published by Quinlan Publishing Group, Boston).
>
> *www.schoolgrants.org*

Often, reading specialists are encouraged by school leadership to write proposals for grants that are available from the state, because many times a state department of education has monies that they can allocate to districts (e.g., Pennsylvania has accountability block grants for which districts can apply). Or, at times, a local foundation may encourage school districts to write a proposal for funding (i.e., support for additional after-school programming for students in a high-poverty school who need additional literacy support). Reading specialists who have grant-writing responsibilities may find the book, *Getting the Grant: How Educators Can Write Winning Proposals and Manage Successful Projects* (Gajda & Tulikangas, 2005) a useful resource.

3. *Proposal should be well written.* This is, of course, easy to say but more difficult to do. Funders do not look favorably on proposals that have grammatical errors or are difficult to read (e.g., they are difficult to follow or lack meaningful transitions between parts). The following tips may be helpful in thinking about this guideline:

• Use the terminology and organization suggested in the proposal application. If the application calls for a discussion of objectives followed by a plan of implementation, use those terms to identify those two sections of the proposal. If the application requires two specific types of evaluation (e.g., formative and summative), write the proposal to address those two dimensions. This is a place where creativity may count against the writer!

• Follow the rules. The submission should not have more than the required number of pages, it should arrive on or before the designated closing date, it should display the appropriate font size, and so on. The writer also needs to address the priorities mentioned in the proposal. If the funding is offered for students who have been identified as coming from high-poverty areas, receiving a proposal in which the population of students does not qualify as such will immediately disqualify it from consideration by the funding agency.

4. *Talk to funders.* It is appropriate to call and ask questions of those who want to fund proposals. After all, they have put out a call, wanting to give funds to worthy recipients. Generally, they are more than willing to answer questions about the proposal before the closing date. Grant writers should feel free to call or e-mail the funder to discuss their ideas or to raise questions about the proposal application itself. If there is a preproposal session, held for potential writers, it would be beneficial to attend those sessions. In one instance, I was able to collaborate with two educators from other universities in writing a professional development proposal, because we had all attended the preproposal session and had an opportunity to sit and talk about our ideas.

5. *Solicit feedback.* Writing is a lonely task, and, too often, writers think that what they have written is very clear! Soliciting feedback from a colleague is an excellent way to determine whether the content makes sense, whether there is enough detail, and whether there are any technical problems with the writing. The goal is to obtain constructive feedback based on a thoughtful, critical evaluation.

6. *Use effective formatting.* Although a great idea is very important, even it can lose its luster in a poorly formatted presentation. A well-formatted proposal containing a great idea catches the eye and the mind of reviewers. Providing a table of contents and using section headings that guide the reader are important techniques to use. Likewise, use bold, italic, or underlining to highlight the important ideas. If possible, use graphics to amplify points made in the narrative text.

7. *Become familiar with the review criteria.* Proposal guidelines often include the criteria for proposal review (e.g., indicating the number of points designated for each section). A smart proposal writer makes certain that each criterion is addressed and emphasizes the sections that are worth a significant number of points.

Elements of a Proposal

Most proposals require each of the elements or parts discussed below. When preparing to write a proposal, it is helpful to read all of the proposal guidelines, and then, after writing various sections, reread them as a means of determining whether each of the elements has been clearly addressed. At the end of this chapter is a short proposal written by a graduate student for a course assignment. It illustrates many of the elements discussed below, although a few differences exist because the writer followed the guidelines of the funding agency.

Goals and Objectives

Although some of the other elements may not be required in a specific proposal application, all proposals require statements of goals or objectives for the potential project or program. In some proposals, only broad goals are required (e.g., increase teachers' use of computer technology in teaching reading). In other applications, however, the writer must write objectives that indicate specifically what is going to change and by how much and when:

> By the end of 5 years, we will improve the average comprehension performance of Title 1 students from 30 Normal Curve Equivalents to 50.

Review of Literature

Not all proposals call for a review of the literature; the funding source, the amount of funding offered, and the type of proposal (e.g., research) are the common determinants of this component. When there is a requirement for such a review, the key is to identify the relevant and current literature that (1) supports the need for the project being described, and (2) summarizes what is known to date about the proposed issue or project. For example, if a reading specialist wants to develop a project for working with preschool providers, a review of literature about the importance of early learning for young students and its impact on later reading achievement would be beneficial. Such literature should include information about the need for additional knowledge in this area. The sample proposal in Figure 11.1, written by a graduate student for a class assignment, contains no literature review because such a review was not required. However, the writer does use research to introduce her project and highlight its importance, given research evidence about the need for exposing young children to informational text.

Project Activities or Methods

In some proposal applications, this section is referred to as the design of the project. It is here that the writer explains what he or she plans to do. The activities or design must relate to the identified objectives or goals, and there must be clear evidence that the plan will enable the writer to meet them. The writer must be certain that readers know exactly what will be done, when, and how. Examples are critical—let the readers know, by example, what will occur. Described below is an example of part of a methods section:

> We plan to work with preschool providers in two ways. First, we will invite them to visit our kindergartens and then participate in a 2-hour discussion with the kindergarten teachers. Second, kindergarten teachers will visit the preschool programs and, again, participate in a 2-hour discussion. Our expectation is that participants will have opportunities to address issues such as the following: What are the literacy expectations and standards in kindergarten and in what ways can preschool teachers prepare students for their kindergarten experience? What experiences and activities are currently occurring in preschool programs, and how do they address the literacy needs of students?

Creating a time line for various activities is helpful not only to readers but also to the writer as a means of determining exactly how the entire project or activity will be implemented. Likewise, graphics or visuals can aid readers in understanding the plan of operation.

Personnel

Funders want to know who will work on the project and what skills and experiences they have that will enable them to accomplish the planned work. So, for example, if the reading specialist writing the proposal cited above has taught in a preschool or has already implemented such a program in another district, this experience should be described. Providing specifics about qualifications helps to assure funders that the expertise needed to undertake the project is available. Likewise, the application may call for an iteration of the resources or capabilities of the organization or institution with which the writer is affiliated. What computer resources are available to assist in data analysis? Does the institution have a testing department that can assess the success of the project? Are there other personnel who might be helpful with the project (e.g., a supportive director of curriculum, librarian, etc.)?

Evaluation

Almost all proposals call for some form of evaluation that indicates to what extent the writers have accomplished their goals. Evaluation plans run the gamut of simple to complex. The two types of evaluation that may be required—formative and summative—are described below:

Formative

Formative evaluation requires ongoing documentation of what occurs. This type of evaluation is often used to make mid-project corrections or adjustments; in other words, to learn from what has transpired. In the preschool proposal example described above, formative evaluation might include documentation logs of various meetings (i.e., when they occurred and who attended) and evaluation forms completed by attendees.

Summative

The summative evaluation provides the results of the project; in this case, the effects of the preschool–kindergarten project on participants (e.g., students, teachers, parents). The evaluation may also call for "deliverables"; a manual or listing of activities developed as a result of the project. Often, with summative evaluation, we think of effects as "changes" that have occurred. For example, a writer might propose the possibility of specific changes in teacher classroom practices. Likewise, various pretests and posttests can be administered to students to determine whether there are differences in reading performance, or attitudes toward reading, after the implementation of the project. The writer of the proposal in Figure 11.1 includes both summative and formative evaluation. In addition to documenting ongoing efforts, the writer administers a final questionnaire to teachers and parents and also analyzes results of reading tests.

Budget

All proposals naturally require a budget (i.e., because the writer is applying for funds to do something), which can be a simple or complex matter, as is the case with evaluations. For example, a budget submission may be as simple as requesting $200 to purchase books to conduct literature circles, or as in the proposal in Figure 11.1 somewhat more complex, in that the writer had to identify costs for staff development in addition to hiring substitute teachers to cover classrooms while teachers attended meetings. Large proposals may require budgets that include costs for personnel, supplies, materials, travel, and so on. In some instances, the writer must include indirect or overhead costs; that is, the amount the institution will charge for housing the grant. This item covers such necessities as lighting, office space, and computer accessibility. Generally, in a school context, the school district or institution has a specific amount identified. Sometimes the funding agency supplies a ceiling amount or indicates that they do not pay overhead costs at all. Often this is the case with foundations.

Dissemination Plan

Some proposals require that writers discuss how they will share the information they learn with others. Writers might indicate that they will present at conferences, write papers, or produce a deliverable that will be distributed to various institutions and educators.

Continuation Plans

Although not invariably a required part of a proposal application, many funding agencies (especially foundations) ask for continuation plans because they are interested in the sustainability of various projects. Can they be assured that if they provide monies for a special project, such as a summer program, that the institution will then find a way to continue such an effort? Often, funders are discouraged that various projects are disbanded as soon as the funding is gone.

Abstract

The all-important abstract, which is the beginning of the proposal submission, is best written after the writing is complete. Only now is the writer ready to summarize, in a few lucid paragraphs, exactly what he or she is planning to do. The abstract must catch the reader's eye (the value of a first impression) and identify the goals and activities of the proposed plan succinctly and clearly. It may also include an overview of the evaluation approaches.

Sources for Funding

Many different sources of funding can be investigated to determine whether various grant possibilities exist. Generally, the education department in the state posts announcements about various state or federal funding possibilities on its website. Newsletters and websites of various professional organizations are also excellent sources for obtaining information about support (e.g., Association for Supervision and Curriculum Development, International Reading Association, National Council of Teachers of English). Local and national foundations often have calls for proposals on websites; foundation directories that describe goals and purposes of these philanthropic organizations are also available.

One of the best ways to seek funding is to work collaboratively with another institution in the area, such as a local university, library, or community agency. Funding agencies look favorably upon such collaborative efforts because the unique contributions that can be made by each partner strengthen a proposal. For example, a university can assist in the evaluation of a project designed by a school district. Or the school district and library can work together to design a summer reading program for struggling readers.

Rejection

A chapter on proposal writing should not end on a negative note. However, the reality is that not all proposals are funded. All of us who have written proposals have most likely received one or more rejection notices. Another reality, however, is that the key to getting a project funded is to write *and* submit a proposal! Furthermore, rejection notices can be very helpful. I have learned that reviewers' comments can be used to rewrite and resubmit—either in a different funding cycle or to a different funding agency. Believe it or not, the second time around can be successful! Moreover, writing the proposal enables the writer to cultivate a relationship with the funding agency, thereby increasing the potential for later success.

Summary

This chapter discussed reasons why the reading specialist may be involved in proposal writing. Guidelines for writing proposals and the various elements of a proposal were then described.

Reflections

What opportunities to become involved with proposal writing are available to you in your current position? What grants has your school received, for what, and from what agencies?

Activities

1. Go to your state's department of education website. Locate available grant possibilities to see what is being funded at the state level. Read one of the RFP's (request for proposals) and compare its elements with those described in this chapter. Be prepared to discuss what you learned with colleagues.
2. Interview someone who writes proposals to get his or her ideas about what it takes to write a successful one. Be prepared to discuss what you learned in class or with your colleagues.
3. Locate several proposals that have been submitted and critique them, using the ideas in this chapter (i.e., elements of a successful proposal).
4. Review the proposal in Figure 11.1 that follows and discuss each of its features with your colleagues or classmates.

READING INFORMATIONAL TEXTS IN PRIMARY CLASSROOMS

Mission Statement:

We believe each person has value and the capability to achieve success. Through the commitment of a quality staff and the partnership with home and community, the mission of the Green Valley School District is to educate all students to ethically meet the challenges of a global society through positive life-role performances (Green Valley School District Strategic Plan, 2000).

Introduction:

According to Duke (2000), "In this Informational Age the importance of being able to read and write informational texts critically and well cannot be overstated. Informational literacy is central to success, and even survival, in schooling, the workplace and the community" (p. 213). Typically in today's classrooms, children are not given the opportunity to explore informational/nonfiction literature until the second- or third-grade year. This omission leaves a lapse of 7 to 8 years during which children are not exposed to this type of literature. Upon entering high school and throughout their lives, most of what these children will be reading and writing is informational text. More often than not, adults read material such as newspapers, magazines, manuals, recipes, menus, directions, and brochures far more frequently than a book of fictional literature. For this reason, children should be given the opportunity to see and read informational literature as another genre available to them before they reach high school age. As a representative of Madison Primary School in the Green Valley School District, I propose to create a program that supplies the classroom libraries of our primary school teachers with informational/nonfiction literature. This literature will be available for children in kindergarten through grade 3 to take home and read independently or with family members and to supplement the content area instruction provided in the classroom.

I am asking the Literacy Link Foundation to become a part of this project to introduce a new literature genre to our young children by donating funds to purchase books, magazines, and other necessary materials to be placed in every classroom library in Madison Primary School. As a sponsor, the Literacy Link Foundation will assist this district's educators in helping the students become knowledgeable and productive citizens through the introduction of and exposure to informational/nonfiction text. Through the early introduction of this type of text, our students will be better prepared to comprehend the informational literature they will be expected to read throughout their adult lives.

Goals of Project:

The goals and purpose of this program are to

- Expose primary school children to informational/nonfiction literature in their classrooms.
- Encourage the reading of informational/nonfiction literature by primary school children.
- Support primary classroom teachers in their content area instruction.

(cont.)

FIGURE 11.1. An example of a brief proposal.

The goals of this program correlate directly with the mission of the Literacy Link Foundation by providing quality learning opportunities to children at a time in their lives when this opportunity is not usually given.

The educators responsible for achieving the success of these goals and objectives are part of a district comprised of 95 professionals with an average of 15 years teaching experience. In this group, 33% has received a master's degree, and 1% has received a doctorate degree. At Madison Primary School, 354 students are guided by 18 teachers, two reading specialists, and one principal. Each member of this teaching community feels this program would be an added benefit to those attending school in the Green Valley School District. The mission of the district is met by partnering quality staff with family and community members to give each student the capability to succeed within the challenges of a global society. By exposing children to the genre of literature they will be expected to read and understand in their adult lives, this program will improve their chance of success as they develop into knowledgeable and productive citizens.

Project Activities:

The following activities will support each of the three goals listed above:

- All teachers at Madison Primary School will introduce and read aloud to their classes at least two informational/nonfiction books each month.
  1. The teachers will select two books to be read to their classes each month.
  2. Planning for the reading of the selected books will involve writing them in their weekly lesson plans.
  3. The principal will verify that the books to be read are included in the weekly plans.
  4. Teachers will maintain a list of books read to their classes.

- Each classroom will receive copies of informational/nonfiction literature equal to the number of students in the classroom.
  1. By September 1 of each school year, a box for donated books will be placed in the libraries of the upper elementary and middle schools to be given to the primary classrooms.
  2. With book fair profits (a book fair is held each year in March), each teacher will select $25 worth of informational/nonfiction literature to be placed in his or her classroom libraries (district contribution).
  3. Grant funds received will be used to purchase informational/nonfiction literature for each classroom (purchase to be completed by August 1).

- Each child will be required to read at least two informational/nonfiction books each month.
  1. Beginning the second week of school, the classroom teacher or school reading specialist will place one informational/nonfiction book in each child's "Book-in-a-Bag," to be read every 2 weeks.
  2. A classroom chart is maintained with titles of the books read by each child.

(cont.)

FIGURE 11.1. *(cont.)*

- Each classroom teacher will offer an incentive for each child to meet the above objective.
  1. Incentives for reading two informational/nonfiction books each month will become part of the classroom behavior incentive.
  2. The classroom teacher will give stickers or awards if the objective is met each month (actual reward is at the discretion of the teacher).
- The reading specialist will offer at least one staff development course to each grade level, to focus on using informational/nonfiction literature in the classroom.
  1. The reading specialist will gather instructional methods/materials to be used by the classroom teachers. (Topics to be discussed the following school year must be submitted to the principal or reading specialist by June 1.)
  2. The reading specialist will present the content area materials at a staff development class to be held in August or September of each year.
- All reading specialists employed at Madison Primary School will assist their assigned classroom teachers with instruction, materials, and resources needed for content area instruction.
  1. The school reading specialists will discuss available materials with their teachers (in progress).
  2. The reading specialists will provide a list of materials and resources that can be used as part of instruction (in progress).
  3. The reading specialist will model at least one whole-class lesson, emphasizing the use of informational/nonfiction literature (the total number of lessons should be decided by teacher and reading specialist).

The success of this program will rely on the following actions and processes:

- All children receiving instruction at Madison Primary School will be exposed to informational/nonfiction literature in two ways: (1) easily accessible books will be placed in the classroom library, and (2) books will be read weekly to the class by the classroom teacher.
- All children receiving instruction at Madison Primary School will be encouraged to read two informational/nonfiction books each month. The "Book-in-a-Bag" program and the monthly incentives given to those who achieve this goal will support this encouragement.
- All Madison Primary School classroom teachers will be supported by the reading staff through regular discussions, staff development courses, and the modeling of effective research-based instruction.

Evaluation:

The project will be evaluated as follows:

1. Teachers and parents will be asked to complete a questionnaire to determine the extent to which they valued this program and why.
2. All staff development meetings will include a written evaluation form in which teachers indicate their response to the activities.

(cont.)

FIGURE 11.1. *(cont.)*

3. Reading specialists will document which reading strategies and materials they have introduced in the classrooms.
4. Students' comprehension scores on the standardized reading test given at the end of the year will be compared to scores of the previous year.

Program Budget and Narrative:

Category	Expense	Credit
Supplies	$6,044.46	
Staff Development	1,120.00	
Transportation	200.00	
Total	$7,364.46	
District Contribution		($450.00)
Grant Request Total	$6,914.46	

Supplies: Informational/nonfiction literature, as quoted by *Scholastic and Scholastic.com.* Include additional bookcases, as needed, for additional literature.

Staff Development: Four substitute teachers to provide coverage in classrooms while teachers meet for staff development.

Transportation: Transportation costs to collect donated materials from both the upper elementary and middle schools. Transportation costs to collect materials from Scholastic warehouse.

MARSHA TURNER
Graduate Student
Reading Specialist Certification Program
University of Pittsburgh, Pennsylvania

FIGURE 11.1. An example of a brief proposal.

12

The Reading Specialist as Lifelong Learner
Meeting Challenges and Changes

Marshall McLuhan once remarked about the hazards of driving "into the future using only our rearview mirror" (*www.thinkexist. com/English/Author/x/Author_3619?2.htm*). This statement also applies to reading specialists who have served students in schools in many different ways throughout the years—as supervisors of reading programs, remedial teachers, resource teachers, and literacy coaches. Currently, the role of reading specialist is too diverse to define it in a narrow way. Not only is the role different but so, too, are the labels: *reading specialist, literacy coach, reading consultant, literacy consultant,* among others. Yet the underlying premise for reading specialists remains one of promoting reading achievement for *all* students, and especially for struggling readers (International Reading Association, 2000b). Fulfilling these goals can be accomplished in a number of ways, depending on school needs, funding for specialists, and their own experiences and strengths.

The chapters in this book address the many functions that reading specialists may be fulfilling on a daily or regular basis, and also those that they may be asked to fulfill in the future, as responsibilities and roles change. For example, many reading specialists who worked only with students are currently being asked to assume the role of reading or literacy coach in their schools. The greatest challenge for reading specialists is to be prepared for those changes that may occur. Indeed, change may be generated or initiated by specialists themselves, who see that they can affect student performance more effectively in new and different ways. This chapter focuses on the reading specialist as learner, on the premise that those who stay abreast of developments in the literacy field and in education, in general, will be able to meet the challenges and changes that are sure to occur. This chapter concludes with a section on becoming a reading specialist, providing potential reading specialists with some ideas of what to expect in reading specialist certification programs, and how they might prepare for interviews for reading specialist positions.

Professional Development for Reading Specialists

Professional development for reading specialists, as for teachers, can occur in many different ways, from reading professional materials to formal participation in classes (i.e., face-to-face and online courses), workshops held by the district or state, conferences and sessions of professional groups, or network meetings with other reading specialists or coaches. Chapter 5 discusses professional development for teachers and reading specialists' role in leading such efforts. As they spearhead such efforts, reading specialists learn as they investigate and study topics that are to be addressed. In many schools, teachers now participate in study groups in which they discuss a specific book pertinent to educational concerns or goals. Certainly, participation in groups in which teachers and reading specialists discuss a particular book (e.g., *Is Literacy Enough?: Pathways to Academic Success for Adolescents*; Snow, Porche, Tabors, & Harris, 2007), generates new ideas and expands knowledge of specific topics.

Many reading specialists choose to continue their formal education by taking classes at a university or attending professional meetings. Reading specialists can also join, and become active in, one or more professional organizations; becoming a member of the network of educators involved in an organization promotes ongoing learning and sustained motivation. Reading specialists may become members of their local and state reading associations as well as the International Reading Association (*www.reading.org*), whose professional journals, website, and other resources are invaluable to practicing reading specialists. Other groups that may be appropriate, depending on the grade level and responsibilities of specific reading specialists, include:

- American Library Association (*www.ala.org*)
- Association for Supervision and Curriculum Development (*www. ascd.org*)
- Association of Literacy Educators (formally College Reading Association) (*www.aleronline.org*)
- International Reading Association (*www.reading.org*)

- International Society for Technology in Education (*www.iste.org*)
- National Association for Education of Young Children (*www. naeyc.org*)
- National Council of Teachers of English (*www.ncte.org*)
- National Middle School Association (*www.nmsa.org*)
- National Reading Conference (*www.nrc.org*)

In addition to attending meetings of professional groups and professional development sessions in schools, reading specialists must continue to read professional journals and books as a means of keeping current, not only about reading instruction and assessment, but to understand the political and social climate in which they work. In addition, reports from the U.S. government or other agencies that synthesize the research on various aspects of literacy can provide important information about current trends or research emphases. Some examples include:

- *Report of the National Reading Panel* (National Institute of Child Health and Human Development, 2000)
- *Put Reading First* (Armbruster & Osborn, 2001)
- *Reading Next* (Biancarosa & Snow, 2004)
- *Adolescent Literacy* (Ippolito, Steele, & Samson, 2008)
- Developing Early Literacy: Report of the National Early Literacy Panel (2008) (*www.nifl.gov/nifl/publications/pdf/NELReport09. pdf*)

Online resources provide much useful information to specialists for their own professional development. The Literacy Coaching Clearinghouse (*www.literacycoachigonline.org*), funded by the International Reading Association and National Council of Teachers of English, on its website provides briefs of pertinent articles and a list of published articles on topics related to reading specialists/coaches; opportunities to blog and participate in a forum are also included. The websites of each of the professional organizations also makes available position statements, articles, and reference lists that may be useful to reading specialists. For example, on the International Reading Association website, one can find position statements on important topics; for example, literacy in preschools, adolescent literacy, and evidence-based reading instruction.

The reading specialists whose vignettes appear in this book are examples of educators who are lifelong learners. All have participated in formal education to obtain advanced degrees, all attend and present at various conferences and workshops, and all are readers who keep abreast of what is occurring in their field. Most of all, they are passionate about their profession and eager to learn all they can to improve instruction for the students in their schools.

Local, State, and Federal Guidelines

Educators in today's schools face many challenging and complex political and social issues. Reading specialists must keep current about the various school-related legislative actions at local, state, and federal levels. As described in Chapter 9, the No Child Left Behind legislation has certainly had an impact on schools. It has influenced the assessment tools being used, has made accountability a key issue for individual teachers and for schools, and has affected curriculum and instruction at all levels. Because there most likely will be changes in the law, given the results of the U.S. presidential election in 2008, reading specialists must not only keep abreast of the discussions in Congress, but also work with their professional groups to bring to the attention of legislators issues that are critical to the reauthorization of this legislation. Moreover, because so many reading specialists are funded with monies from Title 1 legislation, there is certainly a need for reading specialists to be aware of the regulations of that program.

Likewise, rules and regulations of each state influence the literacy curriculum. The emphasis on standards creates a real need for reading specialists to be aware of how to assist their teacher colleagues in implementing an instructional program that addresses those standards. Standards developed by individual states and the English/Language Arts Standards formulated by the International Reading Association and National Council of Teachers of English are also important resources for reading specialists.

As mentioned in Chapter 5, reading specialists should share information with teachers with whom they work. In addition to the professional development opportunities described above, one helpful source that provides an update about many trends in education is the publication *Education Week* (*www.edweek.org*). A school subscription to that resource keeps educators aware of what is happening at the national level in the field of education.

Lifelong Learning: A Necessity for Reading Specialists

All those who work in schools must be lifelong learners; there is always something new to learn—new materials, new approaches, and even students new to the educator! Moreover, given the many variables that affect the position of reading specialist and the changes that may occur from year to year within a school—some prescribed by legislation or school needs, others from recommendations by reading specialists themselves—reading specialists must remain lifelong learners. Ideas that may be helpful follow.

Set Learning Goals

Perhaps the specialist wants to involve parents more actively in school programs; perhaps the specialist wants to become more involved with teachers of content. Whatever the specific goal, the reading specialist needs to set a goal, identify activities that facilitate its achievement, and set a deadline for accomplishment. Attending one or more conferences, reading several articles or books about the selected topic, and then meeting and sharing the information with teachers (e.g., possibly forming a study group) are examples of lifelong learning activities. Goals can be *personal* ones; for example, enrolling in a program to obtain literacy coaching endorsement or attending the research conference at the national meeting of the International Reading Association to stay abreast of current research efforts. Goals can also be ones related to school efforts or needs; for example, in one middle school, there may be an effort to enhance literacy instruction across the academic disciplines, or in a primary school, the goal may be to increase teachers' understanding of the best ways to instruct ELLs. In these cases, reading specialists may choose to identify professional development activities that enable them to assist teachers and other professionals in the schools to achieve those goals.

Be Prepared to Change or Modify Past or Current Behavior

One of the most difficult steps for all of us is to realize that we may have to give up what we have been doing if we are going to make changes that will make us more effective in our roles. Reading specialists who have always worked in a pullout setting may find it difficult to switch to working in the classroom. They may even grieve a little as they lose what they have always found to be a comfortable and rewarding approach to instruction. Grieving is fine, but it is important to *move on* and experience the rewards of the new and different. Change is inevitable as we learn more about how to improve reading instruction and assessment. Indeed, reading specialists can serve as models for teachers who may also find it necessary to modify classroom practices while confronting notions that are in conflict with their beliefs about teaching or learning.

Self-Recognition

All of us appreciate the rewards and recognition that come from others—the principal who commends the work that I have done with struggling readers, the parent who tells me of the positive effect that I have had on her child. Similarly, reading specialists need to "pat themselves on the back" for what they have accomplished regarding their own learning. After finishing a professional book on assessment approaches for classroom teachers, it may be time for a special dinner, a week without any professional reading (just a good mystery), or some other activity or experience that serves as a reward for "a job well done."

See Problems as Friends

There will always be demands and problems within the school setting that need the attention of the reading specialist (e.g., working with a teacher who is resistant to change, improving writing scores, planning a professional development program for middle school content teachers). These demands or problems should not be seen as burdens or obstacles but as problems that generate active thinking, the opportunity for group interaction, and the possibility of new and exciting ventures in the school. Large-scale efforts that involve large numbers of people will produce disagreements and questions, but as indicated by Fullan, Bertani, and Quinn (2004), productive conflict is to be expected! Being receptive and listening to divergent ideas can be helpful in solving problems and moving the school in a positive direction.

Self-Reflection

Chapter 5 discusses the importance of teacher reflection to personal learning. Likewise, reading specialists need to take time to reflect on, and think about, what they have been doing, what they have learned, and what this learning means for future behavior. Recently, a teacher who had just completed a professional development experience expressed this thought: "It's more than learning a lot of strategies. It's thinking in a different way." In essence, her statement revealed that she was taking the time to reflect not only on her teaching methods—on what worked and what did not work—but also to consider the paradigm underlying those old methods and allow a new paradigm to form in support of the new methods. That reflection provided her with the impetus to seek new solutions to classroom problems. Taking the time for reflection means setting time aside, perhaps at the end of the day, to think about what happened and why, and the impact of that experience on future behavior. Some reading specialists and coaches keep logs as a means of self-reflection; they can then look back and think about how they allocated their time, their responses to various events, and use these written records as a means of making what they consider to be positive changes. Figure 12.1 illustrates a partial log of one elementary reading specialist.

By being a lifelong learner, the reading specialist models for others in the school the behavior that is necessary for the school as an organi-

Harry

What I Did Today	Comments/Reflections
Morning Pull-out class of five fourth-graders (using expository text; focus on "during text" understandings and inferences)	Group works well together (good discussion and thinking). Science text on reptiles worked well because of their interest; get similar text specific to snakes (they were fascinated).
Met with sixth-grade teachers to discuss results of writing samples from their classes; what can we do to improve students' ability to summarize from their reading? Teachers felt need for some "input" and were very receptive to this.	I need to check my books and do some research, get some material that they can read. What about Beers's SWBS strategy? Check her book (Beers, 2003, p. 147). Others?
Worked in classroom of fifth-grade social studies teacher; how to introduce vocabulary and set a purpose (we actually co-taught this introduction)	Sam is excited about this; he wants me to continue working with him (wonder if he would be willing to do more with small group to get kids engaged). Will discuss with him and get his ideas; what are his goals for students (important!).
Afternoon Planning for workshop on differentiation of instruction for all intermediate teachers	Yikes! I need to focus on what my goals are. What do I want teachers to know and be able to do? What are they ready to do—next steps?
Meeting with principal to go over test results (that I discussed with sixth-grade teachers this morning)	She is concerned about writing test coming up in several months. Wants me to be sure to work with these sixth-grade teachers (I need time—and they do too!). Asked her whether the workshop on differentiation should be postponed; should we focus on writing? Too many directions for teachers. She agreed!

FIGURE 12.1. Partial log of a reading specialist.

zation to change in order to become more effective. Leaders within a school provide the impetus for others to also become lifelong learners.

Becoming a Reading Specialist

When I ask those who enter the reading specialist certification program at my institution why they have chosen to do so, they often tell me that they have become curious about students in their classrooms who have reading difficulties and wonder how they can better help them to achieve. Some tell me that they feel unprepared to teach reading, given the few courses they received in their teacher preparation programs. Some want to work especially with struggling readers, whereas others are clear that they do not really want to leave the classroom; rather they want to become more proficient at teaching reading and meeting the needs of all students in their classrooms.

These are all good reasons for entering a reading specialist preparation program. Most universities have well-developed programs that meet the Standards required of their state and of the International Reading Association (2003). Such programs require students to become knowledgeable about the underlying theoretical bases for literacy development and acquisition, literacy assessment and instruction, and issues related to leadership and working with others. They usually require students to participate in practica or clinical experiences in which they demonstrate that they can fulfill the requirements of the position. Most offer many practical experiences as an integral part of their programs, so that reading specialist candidates become proficient in working with struggling readers and with teachers. As completion of the program draws near, candidates begin to think about applying for positions as a reading specialist. They are curious about possible questions that they may be asked and how they can prepare for the interviews that generally are part of the application process. Questions that may be part of an interview are discussed in Appendix C. Candidates for a reading specialist position may wish to think about the questions and how they would answer them. Those in a reading specialist certification program may role-play an interview in class, using some of the questions identified there.

In addition to acquiring the knowledge and understanding needed to become a reading specialist, another important attribute of any candidate for such a position is enthusiasm. School district personnel want to employ individuals who are excited and enthusiastic about becoming a reading specialist and having the opportunity to make a difference for all the students in a school.

Before an interview, candidates for positions may want to reread the notes that they have taken in their coursework. They may also want to read several articles in which roles of reading specialists are described. The Bean, Swan, and Knaub (2003) article, in which the many roles of reading specialist in exemplary reading programs are listed, or the one by Lapp and colleagues (2003) that describes the dual role of reading specialists in an urban setting may be helpful. Dole's (2004) article, in which she discusses the coaching role of specialists may be useful to those who may have responsibility for coaching. And again, some of the briefs available on the Literacy Coaching Clearinghouse (*www.literacy-coachingonline.org*) would be useful to those applying for a literacy coaching position. Rereading the vignettes of the reading specialists found in this book may also provide candidates with a better idea of what reading specialists may be asked to do. Each of these reading specialists exhibits passion and enthusiasm for her position, regardless of the challenges or problems faced.

Summary

This chapter described ways in which reading specialists can continue their learning and become lifelong learners. What reading specialist candidates might expect in a preparation program and ideas for participating in a job interview for the reading specialist position were also discussed.

Reflections

1. Which type of learning—formal or informal—is most appealing to you, given where you are in your professional career? How can you take advantage of the opportunities that are available to you?
2. Think about the ideas suggested for those who are lifelong learners. Identify something you want to learn and develop a plan for doing so. Set a goal, develop a plan of action, set a deadline—and plan for a reward.

Activities

1. Organize a study group in which you and several others agree to read and discuss a specific book that addresses an issue or problem in your school or setting.
2. Participate in a role-play of a job interview, using the questions in Appendix C.

Appendix A

Sample Observation Form

Teacher's name: _____ Grade Level: _____ Date: _____

Start time: _____ End time: _____ Number of students: _____

Focus of lesson: _____

Grouping: Whole class _____ Small group _____ Individual _____

Overall impressions of environment:

Teacher	Students

Appendix B

Observation Protocol
for Content Area Instruction

Teacher: _____ **Grade Level:** _____

Date: _____ **Time Begin:** _____ **End:** _____

 # Students Present: _____ **Content Area:** _____

Lesson Focus: _____

Materials: (Check all that apply)

☐ Textbook   Grouping: (Check all that apply)

☐ Board/Chart   ☐ Whole Class

☐ Computer   ☐ Small Group

☐ Worksheet   ☐ Pairs

☐ Student Work   ☐ Individual

☐ Other

Protocol to be used as a guide. Scale to be completed after the observation has been completed.

Scale:	Great Extent	Some Extent	Minimal Extent	Not Observed
	(4)	(3)	(2)	(1)
Classroom Environment				
Materials supporting literacy are available *Books, visuals, print and nonprint materials about topic are evident*	☐	☐	☐	☐
Provides for social interaction *Areas for small-group/partner work*	☐	☐	☐	☐
Strategies for learning are displayed *Informative, positive strategies (e.g., why and how of summarizing)*	☐	☐	☐	☐

(cont.)

Scale:	Great Extent	Some Extent	Minimal Extent	Not Observed
	(4)	(3)	(2)	(1)

Instruction

Before Reading

Sets purpose, makes connections, development of vocabulary	☐	☐	☐	☐
Small-group discussion	☐	☐	☐	☐
Engages in coaching/scaffolding, teacher models strategies	☐	☐	☐	☐

During Reading

Think-alouds by teacher, connects to students' experiences, points out text features	☐	☐	☐	☐
Questioning that requires high-level thinking, engages in coaching/scaffolding	☐	☐	☐	☐

After Reading

Small-group discussion or writing activities that require responding to text	☐	☐	☐	☐
Activities require high-level thinking	☐	☐	☐	☐
Opportunities for differentiation to meet student needs	☐	☐	☐	☐
Teacher monitors and supports student work	☐	☐	☐	☐

Scale:	Great Extent	Some Extent	Minimal Extent	Not Observed
	(4)	(3)	(2)	(1)

Classroom Climate/Engagement of Students

High level of student participation *Students are actively engaged*	☐	☐	☐	☐
Positive learning environment *Interactions are respectful and supportive, encourages risk taking*	☐	☐	☐	☐
Students use strategies to learn *Evidence of students knowing when, how, and which strategies to use (e.g., note taking, summarizing)*	☐	☐	☐	☐
Students show evidence of being able to think about their own learning *Provide justification for thinking, evidence of being able to organize own learning*	☐	☐	☐	☐

Notes:

Appendix C

Preparation for Job Interviews

Candidates for positions as reading specialists often raise questions about how to prepare for job interviews. The questions identified below are some that may be asked by school personnel. Often interviewers ask basic questions to get a sense of the experiences and education of candidates. In addition, they ask questions that elicit candidates' beliefs and perspectives regarding students, literacy teaching, and learning. These questions tend to be more difficult to answer because the interviewer probably has his or her own beliefs and values regarding each area. Be as honest and tactful as possible. The interviewer needs to know whether the reading specialist is a "match" for the district. At the same time, the reading specialist needs to determine whether the district is a place in which he or she will enjoy working.

Basic Questions

1. Tell us about your past teaching experiences, especially those that prepare you for this position.
2. What certifications do you have? Where did you receive your reading specialist certification? What were the strengths of the program?

Questions Eliciting Knowledge, Beliefs, and Understandings

1. What are your beliefs about reading instruction? Specifically, what are your beliefs about beginning reading instruction? Phonics instruction (primary position)? What are your beliefs about intermediate reading instruction? Secondary reading instruction?
2. What assessment instruments have you had experience administering and interpreting? Talk about them and their possible uses.
3. What do you think about pullout and in-class reading programs? Is one better than the other? Why?

4. What do you think is important in working effectively with teachers whose students you will be teaching? Why?
5. In addition to teaching struggling readers, what other kinds of contributions can you make to the reading program?
6. Have you had any experience in conducting professional development? If so, what?
7. What strengths (qualifications) do you think you would bring to this position? Why do you want this position?

Questions the Reading Specialist Should Ask

The interview should also provide an opportunity for the reading specialist to obtain information about the position. Interviewers often ask if the interviewee has any questions, so the reading specialist should go into the interview with several questions important to him or her. Broad categories of topics follow:

1. *Duties required:* What are the expectations of the position regarding teaching, assessment, and so on?
2. *Resources:* What materials and resources are available for teaching reading?
3. *Opportunities for collaboration:* In what ways can I collaborate with teachers, parents, and community entities such as libraries, and so on?
4. *Professional opportunities:* Does the district encourage continuing education and provide opportunities for teachers to attend conferences?

The following guidelines might also be helpful in an interview:

1. *Listen carefully before answering any question.* Be certain you know what is being asked.
2. *Answer questions honestly.* If you do not know a specific answer, it is best to say so (or qualify your answer by saying that you are not certain, but to the best of your ability, you think ...).
3. *Show enthusiasm and interest in the position.* Indicate why you want to work in that specific school and why you believe you would be an excellent candidate for the job.

Appendix D

Ideas for Course or Workshop Instructors

In this section are additional ideas for activities that can be used by those using this book with a class or leading professional development sessions. Although I suggest activities immediately after each chapter, these additional activities are ones that may be useful to those wishing to expand upon the ideas in various chapters.

Chapter 1

1. Have participants work in small groups to brainstorm issues faced by educators, especially those involved with literacy instruction. Begin by talking briefly with them about some current issues that you believe are important ones; for example, literacy across the curriculum, or issues about how to assess student learning in literacy. After participants identify the issues, share across groups to look for commonalities and differences. (This list can be used for further group work later in the term, if desired.)

2. Ask participants to read the latest issue of a survey conducted by Cassidy and Cassidy, "What's Hot, What's Not" (2009), and discuss whether they agree with experts in the field who have identified specific reading topics as "hot" or "not."

3. Ask participants to download and read the Position Statement on the Role of the Reading Specialist (2000) from the website of the International Reading Association (*www.reading.org*). Assign various sections to small groups of participants to read and identify important ideas. Discuss with the whole group.

Read and discuss one of the following articles:

> Dole, J. A. (2004). The changing role of the reading specialist in school reform. *The Reading Teacher, 57*(5) 462–471.
>
> Quatroche, D. J., & Wepner, S. B. (2008). Developing reading specialists as leaders: New directions for program development. *Literacy Research and Instruction, 47,* 99–115.

Chapter 2

1. Read and discuss the following article discussed in this chapter:

Foorman, B. R., & Torgeson, J. (2001). Critical elements of classroom and small-group instruction promote reading success in all children. *Learning Disabilities Research and Practice, 16*(4), 203–212.

2. Ask participants to conduct a survey at a school in which they work or a school with which they are familiar to determine whether the school is attempting to implement an RTI approach to instruction, and if so, how the school addresses the following:

1. Is there a core reading program for Tier 1 students, and if so, what is it?
2. What additional support do Tier 2 students get (e.g., who teaches them)? What materials are used? Any additional time?
3. What additional support do Tier 3 students get (e.g., who teaches them)? What materials are used? Any additional time?
4. What problems does the school have in accomplishing its RTI objectives?

Participants who are working at a middle or high school level should conduct a survey to determine whether this school is attempting to implement an RTI approach to instruction, and how students who are experiencing difficulties with literacy are being supported. What problems does this school face in accomplishing its RTI objectives?

Participants should be prepared to discuss their findings in a class session, comparing results from the various schools.

Chapter 3

1. Divide the class into three groups (primary, elementary/middle school, and secondary). Have each group read and discuss one of the sample cases of reading specialists in this chapter, using the questions in the Think about This sections. Have each group share the results of their discussion with the entire group.
2. Have participants read and discuss Jennifer's vignette, using the questions provided in the text. Ask participants to think about how prepared they feel to take on such a position. What skills, abilities, and knowledge would they need? What questions does Jennifer's vignette raise in their minds?

Chapter 4

1. Ask participants to write a paper describing themselves as leaders: What do they see as their strengths, limitations, and how might they change? What

experiences have they had in their homes or education that have prepared them for a leadership role? Participants can save their papers until the conclusion of the course or workshops and reflect on what they had written.

2. Have participants work on a T-chart in which they list attributes of an effective meeting and an ineffective meeting. This can be done individually or in small groups and then shared with the entire group.

3. Have participants read and discuss Toni's vignette, using the questions provided in the text. Ask participants to think about how prepared they feel to take on such a position. What skills, abilities, and knowledge would they need? What questions does Toni's vignette raise in their minds?

4. Divide group into two smaller groups. Do fishbowl activity in which those in one group role-play being a member of a group. The outer group (sitting in a circle around the inner group) serves as observers, watching the other group as it goes through the role-playing experience. They then provide feedback to the group, responding to the following: What are some examples of active listening? Effective group behaviors (task behaviors, relationship behaviors)? Feedback from observers should be positive and encouraging. Here are examples of some possible role-playing scenarios:

> *Scenario 1:* A group of teachers has to decide how to reward students who achieve the goal of reading 25 books per year. They must decide what the reward will be and who will handle responsibility for deciding that students have met the goal. They must also decide what they will do with students who haven't met the goal. There are issues that they must address in terms of whether they should provide an extrinsic reward for students who have met this goal.

> *Scenario 2:* A group of fourth-grade teachers has reviewed their assessment data and found that students' vocabulary scores are low. The principal has asked them to address two questions: What are the reasons for the low scores? How do they think they can improve student vocabulary learning? (Some of the teachers think that the students come from such poor backgrounds that vocabulary will always be low; others think that perhaps the textbooks don't provide enough rich vocabulary teaching.)

Chapter 5

1. Assign this article to participants to read and then discuss in class:

> Walpole, S., & Beauchat, K. A. (June, 2008). *Facilitating teacher study groups.* Denver, CO: Literacy Coaching Clearinghouse. Retrieved March 30, 2009, from *www.literacycoachingonline.org*

2. Ask participants to use Figure 5.2 to assess the culture of the school in which they work or with which they are familiar. Have participants discuss the results of their assessment with others.

3. Ask participants to think about presentations that they have heard and thought to be effective. Ask them to describe the ways in which the presenter kept them interested. Some ideas for discussion: How did the speaker begin the presentation? End the presentation? Was the audience involved and if so, how? In what ways did the presenter help the audience connect with the topic? Ask participants to generate a list of guidelines for making effective presentations.

Chapter 6

1. Form triads to discuss the activities in Figure 6.2. Have triads group the activities into one of three categories: low risk, medium risk, or high risk (in terms of what would be difficult for them to do—and then discuss what might be perceived as more "threatening" to teachers and more difficult for coaches to do. Discuss commonalities and differences in a large group.

2. Using the interview questions developed by the group (see Chapter 6), ask each participant to meet with and interview a literacy coach. Group members should be encouraged to locate literacy coaches working at the preschool, elementary, or secondary levels. Share responses to these interviews. The group can also arrange for a conference call and interview a literacy coach by telephone.

3. Discuss this scenario in small groups and then share across groups:

> Your superintendent has told you that as a coach you are to spend your time with teachers who have low achievement scores and shouldn't spend any time with other teachers whose kids are doing well. You don't think this is the way to establish a relationship with teachers, believing that teachers will not want to work with you. They will realize that "only those having problems" work with the coach! So what are some ways of addressing this? What actions can you take?

Chapter 7

1. Below are some coaching scenarios that can be used for discussion. Each addresses situations at different grade levels. Meet in small groups to discuss. In the discussion, consider the following:

1. What are some ideas for working with the teacher?
2. What roadblocks might arise and how might you address them?

> *Scenario 1.* Kindergarten teacher asked the coach to observe her classroom. Although she has taught before (fourth grade), she has never taught kindergarten. She told the coach that she is having difficulties with classroom management. Coach observes and sees "chaos." Teacher is teaching a small group, but has to stop frequently to reprimand students for their behavior: "J, get back in your seat," "S, stop hitting H,"

and so on. The students are not working in their centers (as they were told), but are wandering around the room. Coach and teacher are now going to meet for a feedback session. How does the coach begin? What are some important points that need to be made?

Scenario 2. Although the students in this ninth-grade English classroom have "high" test scores, the teacher lectures most of the time and is not attempting to use the classroom discussion approaches that are part of the new literacy framework for use in content-area classrooms. She has indicated to other teachers and to the coach that she sees no need to do this because her students are "doing well." As the coach, you have been charged with helping teachers implement these new discussion techniques. What should and could you do?

Scenario 3. Josh, an experienced eighth-grade social studies teacher, was transferred to the elementary school where he was assigned to a third-grade classroom. He says, "I have never taught reading. All I know is that there are a number of students in my classroom who can't read the materials we use in reading class. I've been trying to use strategy instruction but the kids are having trouble summarizing information." He has asked to meet with the coach to discuss this problem. The coach wants to get some idea of what Josh knows and believes about "teaching reading," and how he is actually facilitating the work of the students.

THINK ABOUT THIS

Types of questioning you might use.

The strategies that might be helpful.

The roadblocks that might arise and how you might address them.

---

2. Assume that you have just been hired as a literacy coach for a school (you decide on the level). Write a letter that you could send to teachers about you and your role. Share the letter with other participants. Compare similarities and differences across letters.

Chapter 8

1. Ask participants to meet in small groups to discuss factors that positively or negatively affect change in their own schools. Have them think about the six factors described in this chapter on pages 155–158 (Fullan & Hargreaves, 1996). Are any of these factors present in their schools? Others? Is the culture of their school one in which teachers would be receptive to change and why?

2. Ask participants to interview an administrator or school leader at a local school to discuss the reading program (K–12). Questions that might be asked include:

What is the process for decision making in curriculum development?

What materials or documents are available to explain the program?

What materials are used in the program to meet the needs of students of differing abilities and needs?

What professional development is provided for teachers to help them implement the program?

3. Ask participants to retrieve the policy document *Keeping Our Promise to All Students* (International Reading Association, 2008/2009) from the International Reading Association website (*www.reading.org*). Read the document to get a better understanding of how a large professional organization hopes to influence policy and ultimately education of teachers and students. Discuss the document with others and think about the following questions: What ideas do you believe are most important to improving student learning? Are there recommendations about which you have concerns?

Chapter 9

1. Ask participants to identify and discuss specific assessment measures that can be used at various levels. You may choose to group participants by level (i.e., primary, intermediate/middle school, high school). Share results of discussion with the entire group. Ask them to indicate purposes of the instruments: initial screening, diagnostic, progress monitoring, or outcomes. You can provide participants with a chart similar to the following:

	Primary	Intermediate	Middle School	High School
Initial Screening				
Diagnostic				
Progress Monitoring				
Outcomes				

2. Have students obtain and read either the summary of the policy brief by Peter Afferbach (*www.nrconline.org*) or the entire paper of the policy brief (*www. nrconline.org/publications/HighStakesTestingandReadingAssessment.pdf*). Hold a discussion of this brief. Ask students to relate to their experiences in the schools in which they work.

Chapter 10

1. Form small groups and then ask participants to discuss one of the following scenarios. Have them share with the entire group.

Scenario 1. The parents of Natalie, a kindergarten child, ask for an appointment with the reading specialist to talk about their child. They tell the reading specialist that the child is reading chapter books, similar to those that a second- or third-grader would read. She is now getting "homework" in kindergarten, which consists of activities like the following: Cut out pictures of things that start with the letter *B* and glue to a large sheet of paper; practice two new letters (*A* and *I*); practice writing your name (which Natalie has been doing since she was age 3). Her parents indicate that this homework has not been "very exciting" and it's hard to get her interested. She would rather spend time reading independently or working on the computer, doing some first- and second-grade programs. Her parents are concerned that Natalie will find school boring. Should they be considering options (e.g., a private school, skipping a grade, etc.)? They are seeking help from a reading specialist.

Scenario 2. The reading specialists in one district recognize that their student population is changing and that they now have a large number of students from many different countries in their schools. They would like to take advantage of this cultural diversity; in addition, they would like to help all parents understand the value of "culturally responsive" instruction. They are meeting to discuss whether they should pull together some material that would be "parent-friendly" to address this topic, hold some workshops, have an ethnic fair, etc. How should teachers be involved? Is this something that should be done only at the elementary level, or at higher levels?

2. Ask participants to interview the school librarian to determine in what ways she or he collaborates with teachers in the schools. Providing related materials? Coordinating instruction with the content teachers? How aware is the librarian about the literacy program in the school? Are there opportunities to collaborate with teachers? What does the librarian think should be done to improve the ways in which he or she works with teachers to improve instruction?

Chapter 11

Have students write a proposal that addresses the following mini-grant opportunity. This could be an individual assignment, or could be done in small groups. Opportunity to share the finished product can be provided.

A local foundation is willing to provide $500 to classroom teachers who wish to implement a creative project for their classroom that will enhance the reading performance of their students. The proposal should include the following elements: goals and objectives, plan of activities, time line, personnel, evaluation, and budget (describe the funds you will need and how they will be used).

Chapter 12

1. Use a fishbowl activity to role-play a candidate applying for a reading specialist position. Two participants should volunteer to be in the fish bowl, one who is the candidate for a reading specialist or literacy coach position, and the other, the interviewer (perhaps a principal or curriculum director). The outer group (sitting in a circle around the two participants who have agreed to role-play an interview situation) observes and then provides feedback about the interview to the participants.

2. Ask participants to keep a reflection log for several days in which they describe their activities and also write a reflective statement about those activities. After keeping the log for several days, have them discuss in a small group setting the benefits of such a self-reflective process, and any limitations or challenges to keeping such a log.

3. Ask participants to go to a website of a professional organization (e.g., *www.reading.org, www.ncte.org*) or to the Literacy Coaching Clearinghouse website (*www.literacycoachingonline.org*). Have them identify and share with others the possible opportunities for professional learning that are available on that site.

References

Afferbach, P. (2004). National Reading Conference policy brief: High stakes testing and reading assessment. Oak Creek, WI: National Reading Conference. Retrieved January 10, 2009, from *www.nrconline.org/publications/HighStakesTestingandReadingAssessment.pdf*

Alexander, K. L., Entwisle, D. R., & Olson, L. S. (2001). Schools, achievement, and inequality: A seasonal perspective. *Educational Evaluation and Policy Analysis, 23*(2), 171–191.

Alexander, S. H. (1990). *Mom can't see me.* New York: Macmillan.

Allington, R. L. (1986). Policy constraints and effective compensatory reading instruction: A review. In J. Hoffman (Ed.), *Effective teaching of reading and research and practice* (pp. 261–289). Newark, DE: International Reading Association.

Allington, R. L. (2006). *What really matters for struggling readers: Designing research-based programs.* New York: Pearson.

Allington, R. L., & McGill-Franzen, A. (1989). School response to reading failure: Instruction for Chapter 1 and special education students in grades 2, 4, and 8. *Elementary School Journal, 89,* 529–542.

Allington, R. L., & Shake, M. C. (1986). Remedial reading: Achieving curricular congruence in classroom and clinic. *The Reading Teacher, 39*(7), 648–654.

Alvermann, D. E. (2001). *Effective literacy instruction for adolescents.* Executive Summary and paper commissioned by the National Reading Conference. Retrieved March 20, 2003, from *nrconline.org*

Alvermann, D. E. (2002). Effective literacy instruction for adolescents. *Journal of Literacy Research, 34*(2), 189–208.

Alvermann, D. E., & Phelps, S. F. (2002). *Content reading and literacy: Succeeding in today's diverse classrooms* (3rd ed.). Boston: Allyn & Bacon.

American Educational Research Association. (2005). *Research points. Teaching teachers: Professional development to improve student achievement* (Vol. 3, Issue 1) [Brochure]. Washington, DC: Author.

Anonymous. (1986). Where have all the children gone? *Scanner, Shaler Area Education Association, 13*(2), 3.

Armbruster, B. B., & Osborn J. (2001). *Put reading first: The research building blocks for teaching children to read.* Washington, DC: National Institute for Literacy and the Partnership for Reading.

Au, K. H., Raphael, T. E., & Mooney, K. C. (2008). Improving reading achievement in elementary schools: Guiding change in a time of standards. In S. B. Wepner & D. S. Strickland (Eds.), *Administration and supervision of reading programs* (pp. 71–89). New York: Teachers College Press.

August D., & Shanahan, T. (2006). *Report of the National Literacy Panel on Language Minority Children and Youth.* Philadelphia: Erlbaum.

Bader, L. A. (1998). *Read to succeed: Literacy tutor's manual.* Upper Saddle River, NJ: Prentice-Hall.

Baker, L., Dreher, M., & Guthrie, J. (2000). *Engaging young readers: Promoting achievement and motivation.* New York: Guilford Press.

Baker, S., Gersten, R., & Keating, T. (2000). When less may be more: A 2-year longitudinal evaluation of a volunteer tutoring program requiring minimal training. *Reading Research Quarterly, 35*(4), 494–519.

Barnett, W. S. (1995). Long-term effects of early childhood programs on cognitive and school outcomes. *The Future of Children, 5*(3), 25–50.

Barnett, W. S., Frede, E. C., Mobasher, H., & Mohr, P. (1987). The efficacy of public preschool programs and the relationship of program quality to efficacy. *Educational Evaluation and Policy Analysis, 10*(1), 37–49.

Barone, D., & Wright, T. E. (2008–2009). Literacy instruction with digital and media technologies. *The Reading Teacher, 62*(4), 292–303.

Bean, R. M. (2001). Classroom teachers and reading specialists working together to improve student achievement. In V. Risko & K. Bromley (Eds.), *Collaboration for diverse learners: Viewpoints and practices* (pp. 348–368). Newark, DE: International Reading Association.

Bean, R. M. (2002). Developing an effective reading program. In S. B. Wepner, D. S. Strickland, & J. T. Feeley (Eds.), *The administration and supervision of reading programs* (3rd ed., pp. 3–15). New York: Teachers College Press.

Bean, R. M. (2004). Promoting effective literacy instruction: The challenge for literacy coaches. *The California Reader, 37*(3), 58–63.

Bean, R. M. (2008). Developing an effective reading program. In S. B. Wepner and D. S. Strickland (Eds.), *The administration and supervision of reading programs* (4th ed., pp. 11–29). New York: Teachers College Press.

Bean, R, M., Belcastro, B., Jackson, V., Vandermolen, J., & Zigmond, N. (2008, December). *Literacy coaching in reading: The blind men and the elephant.* Paper presented at the National Reading Conference, Orlando, FL.

Bean, R. M., Cassidy, J., Grumet, J. V., Shelton, D., & Wallis, S. R. (2002). What do reading specialists do?: Results from a national survey. *The Reading Teacher, 55*(8), 2–10.

Bean, R. M., Cooley, W., Eichelberger, R. T., Lazar, M., & Zigmond, N. (1991). In-class or pullout: Effects of setting on the remedial reading program. *Journal of Reading Behavior, 23*(4), 445–464.

Bean, R. M., & DeFord, D. (n.d.). *Do's and don'ts for literacy coaches: Advice from the field.* Denver, CO: Literacy Coaching Clearinghouse. Retrieved March 29, 2009, from *www.literacycoachingonline.org/briefs*

Bean, R. M., & Eichelberger, R. T. (2007). *Evaluation of improving literacy through school libraries grant.* Unpublished technical report.

Bean, R. M., Eichelberger, R. T., Turner, G., & Tellez, F. (2002). *Evaluation of four parochial elementary schools.* Pittsburgh, PA: Extra Mile Foundation.

Bean, R. M., & Eisenberg, E. (2009). Literacy coaching in middle and high schools. In K. D. Wood & W. E. Blanton (Eds.), *Literacy instruction for adolescents: Research-based practices* (pp. 107–124). New York: Guilford Press.

Bean, R. M., Fulmer, D., & Zigmond, N. (2009). *Reading First Observation Checklist and Rating Scale.* Unpublished instrument, University of Pittsburgh, Pennsylvania.

Bean, R. M., Grumet, J. V., & Bulazo, J. (1999). Learning from each other: Collaboration between classroom teachers and reading specialist interns. *Reading Research and Instruction, 38*(4), 273–287.

Bean, R. M., & Morewood, A. (2007). Best practices in professional development for improving literacy instruction. In L. Gambrell, L. Morrow, & M. Pressley (Eds.), *Best practices in literacy insruction* (3rd ed., pp. 373–394). New York: Guilford Press.

Bean, R. M., Swan, A. L., & Knaub, R. (2003). Reading specialists in schools with exemplary reading programs: Functional, versatile, and prepared. *The Reading Teacher, 56*(5), 446–455.

Bean, R. M., Swan, A. L., & Morris, G. (2003). *Providing professional development for teachers of beginning reading: Tinkering or transforming?* Manuscript submitted for publication.

Bean, R. M., Trovato, C. A., & Hamilton, R. (1995). Focus on Chapter 1 reading programs: Views of reading specialists, classroom teachers, and principals. *Reading Research and Instruction, 34*(3), 204–221.

Bean, R. M., Turner, G. H., & Belski, K. (2002). Implementing a successful America Reads Challenge tutoring program: Lessons learned. In P. E. Linder, M. B. Sampson, J. Dugan, & B. Brancato (Eds.), *24th yearbook of the College Reading Association* (pp. 169–187). Easton, PA: College Reading Association.

Bean, R. M., & Wilson, R. M. (1981). *Effecting change in school reading programs: The resource role.* Newark, DE: International Reading Association.

Beaver, J., & Carter, M. (2003). *Developmental Reading Test Grades 4–8.* Upper Saddle River, NJ: Pearson.

Beaver, J. M. (2006). *Developmental Reading Assessment Test.* Upper Saddle River, NJ: Pearson.

Beck, I. L., & Hamilton, R. (1996). *Beginning reading module.* Washington, DC: American Federation of Teachers.

Beck, I. W., & McKeown, M. G. (2001). Text-talk: Capturing the benefits of read-aloud experiences for young children. *The Reading Teacher, 55,* 10–20.

Beers, K. (2003). *When kids can't read: What teachers can do (A guide for teachers 6–12).* Portsmouth, NH: Heinemann.

Beresik, D. L., & Bean, R. M. (2002). Teacher practices and the Pennsylvania system of school assessment. *Pennsylvania Reads: Journal of the Keystone State Reading Association, III*(II), 16–29.

Biancarosa, G., & Snow, C. E. (2004). *Reading next: A vision for action and research in middle and high school literacy: A report to Carnegie Corporation of New York.* Washington, DC: Alliance for Excellent Education. Retrieved January 14, 2009, from *www.all4ed.org/publication_material/reports*

Billig, S. H. (2002). Involving middle-graders' parents. *Education Digest, 67*(7), 42–45.

Blanchard, K., Bowles, S., Carew, D., & Parise-Carew, E. (2001). *High five: The magic of working together.* New York: HarperCollins.

Borman, G. D. (2002–2003). How can Title 1 improve achievement? *Educational Leadership, 60*(4), 49–53.

Borman, G. D., & D'Agostine, J. V. (2001). Title 1 and student achievement: A quantitative synthesis. In G. D. Borman, S. C. Stringfield, & R. E. Slavin (Eds.), *Title I compensatory education at the crossroads* (pp. 25–58). Mahwah, NJ: Erlbaum.

Briggs, D. A., & Coulter F. C. (1977). The reading specialist. In W. Otto, N. A. Peters, & C. W. Peters, *Reading problems: A multidisciplinary perspective* (pp. 215–236). Reading, MA: Addison-Wesley.

Brown, D., Reumann-Moore, H. R., Christman, J. B., Riffer, M., duPlessis, P., & Maluk, H. P. (2007, October). *Making a difference: Year two report of the Pennsylvania High School Coaching Initiative.* Philadelphia: Research for Action.

Brozo, W. G., & Gaskins, C. (2009). Engaging texts and literacy practices for adolescent boys. In K. D. Woods & W. E. Blanton (Eds.), *Literacy instruction for adolescents: Research-based practices* (pp. 170–186). New York: Guilford Press.

Buehl, D. (2009). *Classroom strategies for interactive learning* (3nd ed.). Newark, DE: International Reading Association.

Buly, M., & Valencia, S. (2002). Below the bar: Profiles of students who fail state reading assessments. *Educational Evaluation and Policy Analysis, 24*(3), 219–239.

Burkins, J. M. (2007). *Coaching for balance: How to meet the challenges of literacy coaching.* Newark, DE: International Reading Association.

Cassidy, J., & Cassidy, D. (2009, February/March). What's hot for 2009: National Reading Panel influence wanes in 13th annual survey. *Reading Today, 26*(4), 1, 8, 9.

Center for Education Policy. (2007). *Moving beyond identification: Assisting schools in improvement.* Washington, DC: Author.

Center for the Improvement of Early Reading Achievement. (1998). *Every child a reader: Applying reading research in the classroom* [Online]. Ann Arbor, MI: Author. Available from *www.learningfirst.org/publications.html*

Clay, M. (1985). *The early detection of reading difficulties* (3rd ed.). Portsmouth, NH: Heinemann.

Cochran-Smith, M., & Lytle, S. L. (1993). *Inside/outside: Teacher research and knowledge.* New York: Teachers College Press.

Cook, L., & Friend, M. (1995). Co-teaching: Guidelines for creating effective practices. *Exceptional Children, 28*(3), 1–16.

Costa, A. L., & Garmston, R. J. (2002). *Cognitive coaching: A foundation for Renaissance schools* (2nd ed.). Norwood, MA: Christopher-Gordon.

Covey, S. (1989). *The 7 habits of highly effective people.* New York: Simon & Schuster.

Covey, S. R. (2004). *The 8th habit: From effectiveness to greatness.* New York: Free Press.

Cunningham, P. M., & Hall, D. P. (1994). *Making words.* Torrance, CA: Good Apple.

Desimone, L. M., Porter, A. C., Garet Yoon, K. S., & Birman, B. F. (2002). Effects of professional development on teachers' instruction: Results from a three-year longitudinal study. *Educational Evaluation and Policy Analysis, 24*(2), 81–112.

Diller, D. (2005). *Practice with purpose: Literacy work stations for grades 3–6.* Portland, ME: Stenhouse.

Dole, J. A. (2004). The changing role of the reading specialist in school reform. *The Reading Teacher, 57*(5), 462–471.

Duffy, G. G. (2009). *Explaining reading: A resource for teaching concepts, skills, and strategies* (2nd ed.). New York: Guilford Press.

Duffy, H. (2009). *Meeting the needs of significantly struggling learners in high school: A look at approaches to tiered intervention.* Washington, DC: National High School Center. Retrieved February 9, 2009, from *www.betterhighschools.org/docs/NHSC_RTIBrief_08-02-07.pdf*

Duke, N. K. (2000). 3.6 minutes per day: The scarcity of informational texts in first grade. *Reading Research Quarterly, 35*(2), 202–224.

Elbaum, B., Vaughn, S., Hughes, M. T., & Moody, S. W. (2000). How effective are one-to-one tutoring programs in reading for elementary students at risk for reading failure?: A meta-analysis of the intervention research. *Journal of Educational Psychology, 92*(4), 605–619.

Elementary and Secondary Education Act of 1965, Pub.L.No. 89-10, 29 Stat.27.

Epstein, J. (1995). School/family community partnerships: Caring for the children we share. *Phi Delta Kappan, 76*(9), 701–712.

Farkas, G., Warren, M., & Johnson, A. (1999, July). *Tutor manual: Reading one-to-one.* Dallas: University of Texas at Dallas, Center for Education and Social Policy, School of Social Sciences.

Fawson, P. C., & Reutzel, D. R. (2000). But I only have a basal: Implementing guided reading in the early grades. *The Reading Teacher, 54,* 84–97.

Fitzgerald, J. (2001). Can minimally trained college student volunteers help young at-risk children to read better? *Reading Research Quarterly, 36*(1), 28–47.

Foorman, B. R., & Torgeson, J. (2001). Critical elements of classroom and small-group instruction promote reading success in all children. *Learning Disabilities Research and Practice, 16*(4), 203–212.

Frost, S., & Bean, R. M. (2006, September 27). *Qualifications for literacy coaches: Achieving the gold standard.* Denver, CO: Literacy Coaching Clearinghouse. Retrieved January 8, 2009, from *www.literacycoachingonline.org*

Fullan, M. (1991). *The new meaning of educational change.* New York: Teachers College Press.

Fullan, M. (2001). *The new meaning of educational change* (3rd ed.). New York: Teachers College Press.

Fullan, M., Bertani, A., & Quinn, J. (2004). New lessons for districtwide reform. *Educational Leadership, 61*(7), 42–46.

Fullan, M., & Hargreaves, A. (1996). *What's worth fighting for in your school?* New York: Teachers College Press.

Gajda, R., & Tulikangas, R. (2005). *Getting the grant: How educators can write winning proposals and manage successful projects.* Alexandria, VA: Association for Supervision and Curriculum Development.

Gamse, B. C., Jacob, R. T., Horst, M., Boulay, B., & Unlu, F. (2008, November). *Reading First Impact Study: Final report* (NCEE 2009-4038). Washington, DC: National Center for Educational Evaluation and Regional Assistance, Institute of Education Sciences, U.S. Department of Education.

Genest, M., & Bean, R. M. (2007). *Bringing libraries and schools together (blast): A collaborative program between Carnegie library of Pittsburgh and the Pittsburgh Public School District (Year 5).* Unpublished technical report.

Glazer, S. M. (1998). *Assessment is instruction: Reading, writing, spelling, and phonics for all learners.* Norwood, MA: Christopher-Gordon.

Glickman, C. D. (1990). *Supervision of instruction: A developmental approach.* Boston: Allyn & Bacon.

Globe Fearon's Secondary Reading Assessment Inventory. (2000). Upper Saddle River, NJ: Globe Fearon Publishing.

Good, C. V. (1973). *Dictionary of education* (3rd ed.). New York: McGraw-Hill.

Good, R. H., & Kaminski, R. A. (2002) *Dynamic indicators of basic literacy skills.* Eugene: University of Oregon.

Good, R. H., Simmons, D. C., & Kame'enui, E. J. (2001). The importance and decision-making utility of a continuum of fluency-based indicators of foundational reading skills for third-grade high-stakes outcomes. *Scientific Studies of Reading, 5*(3), 257–288.

Goodman, K. (Ed.). (2006). *The truth about DIBELS: What it is; what it does.* Portsmouth, NH: Heinemann.

Green, J. F. (1996). *Language!™: A literacy intervention curriculum* (2nd ed.). Longmont, CO: Sopris West.

Gunning, T. (2005). *Assessing and correcting reading and writing difficulties* (3rd ed.). New York: Allyn & Bacon.

Guskey, T. R. (1986). Staff development and the process of teacher change. *Educational Researcher, 15*(5), 5–12.

Guskey, T. R. (2000). *Evaluating professional development.* Thousand Oaks, CA: Corwin Press.

Guthrie, J. (2008). *Engaging adolescents in reading.* Thousand Oaks, CA: Corwin Press.

Hall, B. (2004, Fall). Literacy coaches: An evolving role. *Carnegie Reporter, 3*(1), 10–19.

Hall, G. E., & Hord, S. M. (1987). *Change in schools: Facilitating the process.* Albany: State University of New York Press.

Hamilton, R. L. (1993). *Chapter I reading instruction: Exemplary reading specialists in an in-class model.* Unpublished doctoral dissertation, University of Pittsburgh, Pennsylvania.

Hampton, S., & Resnick, L. B. (2008). *Reading and writing with understanding: Comprehension in fourth and fifth grades.* Newark, DE: International Reading Association.

Hansen, J. (1998). *When learners evaluate.* Portsmouth, NH: Heinemann.

Harari, O. (2002). *The leadership secrets of Colin Powell.* New York: McGraw-Hill.

Hasbrouck, J., & Denton, C. (2005). *The reading coach: A how-to manual for success.* Boston: Sopris West Educational Services.

Henderson, A., & Berla, N. (1995). *The family is critical to students' achievement* (2nd ed.). Washington, DC: Center for Law and Education.

Henwood, G. F. (1999–2000). A new role for the reading specialist: Contributing toward a high school's collaborative educational culture. *Journal of Adolescent and Adult Literacy, 43*(4), 316–325.

Hersey, P., & Blanchard, K. (1977). *Management of organizational behavior: Utilizing human resources* (3rd ed.). Englewood Cliffs, NJ: Prentice-Hall.

Hoffman, A. R., & Jenkins, J. (2002). Exploring reading specialists' collaborative interactions with school psychologists: Problems and possibilities. *Education, 122*(4), 751–758.

Hoffman, J. V., McCarthy, S. J., Elliott, B., Bayles, D. L., Price, D. P., Ferree, A., et al. (1998). The literature-based basals in first grade classrooms: Savior, Satan, or same-old, same-old? *Reading Research Quarterly, 33*, 168–197.

Hord, S. M. (2004). *Learning together: Leading together.* New York: Teachers College Press.

Individuals with Disabilities Education Improvement Act of 2004 (IDEA), Pub.L. No. 108-446, 118 Stat.2647 (2004).

International Reading Association. (1968). *Guidelines for reading specialists.* Newark, DE: Author.

International Reading Association. (1999). *Adolescent literacy: A position statement.* Newark, DE: Author.

International Reading Association. (2000a). *Making a difference means making it different: A position statement.* Newark, DE: Author.

International Reading Association. (2000b). *Teaching all children to read: The roles of the reading specialist.* Newark, DE: Author.

International Reading Association. (2002a). *Buyer be wary: A resolution of IRA Board* [Online]. Newark, DE: Author. Available from *www.reading.org*

International Reading Association. (2002b). *Evidenced-based reading instruction: Putting the National Reading Panel Report into practice.* Newark, DE: Author.

International Reading Association. (2003). *Standards for reading professionals.* Newark, DE: Author.

International Reading Association. (2004). *The role and qualifications of the reading coach in the United States.* Newark, DE: Author.

International Reading Association. (2006). *Standards for middle and high school literacy coaches.* Newark, DE: Author.

International Reading Association. (2008/2009). IRA offers policy recommendations to U.S. President-elect Barak Obama: Keeping our promises to all students. *Reading Today, 26*(3), 1, 4, 5. Available from *www.reading.org*

International Society for Technology in Education. (2007). *ISTE's educational technology standards for students.* Washington, DC: Author. Retrieved from *www.iste.org/Content/Navigationmenu/NETS/forStudents/2007standards/ NETS_for_students_2007.htm*

Ippolito, J., Steele, J. L., & Samson, J. F. (2008, Spring). Adolescent literacy. *Harvard Education Review, 78,* 1.

Jacobs, H. H. (1997). *Mapping the big picture integrating curriculum and assessment K–12.* Washington, DC: Association for Supervision and Curriculum Development.

Johnson, D. W., & Johnson, F. P. (2003). *Joining together: Group theory and group skills* (8th ed.). Boston: Allyn & Bacon.

Johnston, F., Juel, C., & Invernizzi, M. (1995). *Guidelines for volunteer tutors of emergent and early readers.* Charlottesville: University of Virginia.

Jolles, R. L. (2001). *How to run seminars and workshops* (2nd ed.). New York: Wiley.

Joyce, B., & Showers, B. (1995). *Student achievement through staff development: Fundamentals of school renewal.* White Plains, NY: Longman.

Joyce, B., & Showers, B. (2002). *Student achievement through staff development* (3rd ed.). Alexandria, VA: Association for Supervision and Curriculum Development.

Kamil, M. L., Mosenthal, P. B., Pearson, P. D., & Barr, R. (Eds.). (2000). *Handbook of reading research* (Vol. 3). Mahwah, NJ: Erlbaum.

Kaner, S., Lind, L., Toldi, C., Fisk, S., & Berger, D. (1996). *Facilitator's guide to participatory deicsion-making.* Gabriola Island, BC, Canada: New Society Publishers/Canada.

Kapinus, B. A. (2008). Assessment of Reading Programs. In S. A. Wepner & D. Strickland (Eds.), *The administration and supervision of reading programs* (4th ed., pp. 144–156). New York: Teachers College Press.

Kaser, J., Mundry, S., Stiles, K. E., & Loucks-Horsley, S. (2002). *Leading every day: 124 actions for effective leadership.* Thousand Oaks, CA: Corwin Press.

Kindler, A. L. (2002). *Survey of the states' limited English proficient students and available educational programs and services. 2001–2002 summary report.* Washington, DC: National Clearinghouse for English Language Acquisition.

Kise, J. A. (2006). *Differentiated coaching: A framework for helping teachers change.* Thousand Oaks, CA: Corwin Press.

Kloo, A. (2006). *The decision-making utility and predictive power of DIBELS for students' reading achievement in Pennsylvania's reading first schools.* Unpublished doctoral dissertation, University of Pittsburgh.

Knaub, R. (2002). *The nature and impact of collaboration between reading specialists and classroom teachers in pullout and in-class reading programs.* Unpublished doctoral dissertation, University of Pittsburgh, Pennsylvania.

Kober, N. (2002, November). What tests can and cannot tell us. *The Forum,* pp. 1–2, 11–16.

Lambert, L. (1998). *Building leadership capacity in schools.* Alexandria, VA: Association for Supervision and Curriculum Development.

Lapp, D., Fisher, D., & Flood, J. (2008). Selecting instructional materials for the literacy program. In S. B. Wepner & D. S. Strickland (Eds.), *Administration and supervision of reading programs* (pp. 105–107). New York: Teachers College Press.

Lapp, D., Fisher, D., Flood, J., & Frey, N. (2003). Dual role of the urban reading specialist. *Journal of Staff Development, 24*(2), 33–36.

Leana, C. R., & Pil, F. K. (2006). Social capital and organizational performance: evidence from urban public schools. *Organization Science, 17*(3), 353–366.

Leslie, J., & Caldwell, J. (2006). *Qualitative Reading Inventory.* New York: Allyn & Bacon.

Leu, D. J., Jr., Kinzer, C. K., Coiro, J. L., & Cammack, D. W. (2004). Toward a theory of new literacies emerging from the internet and other information and communication technologies. In R. B. Ruddell & N. J. Unrau (Eds.), *Theoretical models and processes of reading* (5th ed., pp. 1570–1613). Newark, DE: International Reading Association.

Leu, D. J., Jr., Mallette, M. H., Karchmer, R. A., & Kara-Soteriou, J. (2005). Contextualizing the new literacies of information and communication technologies in theory, research, and practice. In R. A. Karchmer, M. H. Mallette, J. Kara-Soteriou, & D. J. Leu, Jr. (Eds.), *Innovative approaches to literacy education: Using the internet to support new literacies* (pp. 1–10). Newark, DE: International Reading Association.

Little, J. W. (1993). Teachers' professional development in a climate of education reform. *Educational Evaluation and Policy Analysis, 15,* 129–151.

Lyons, C. A., & Pinnell, G. S. (2001). *Systems for change in literacy education: A guide to professional development.* Portsmouth, NH: Heinemann.

Manset-Williamson, G., & Nelson, J. M. (2005). Balanced strategic reading instruction for upper-elementary and middle school students with reading disabilities: A comparative study of two approaches. *Learning Disability Quarterly, 28*(1), 59–74.

Matsumura, L. C. (2006). *Creating high-quality classroom assignments.* Lanham, MD: Scarecrow Education.

McGill-Franzen, A., Lanford, C., & Adams, E. (2002). Learning to be literate: A comparison of five urban early childhood programs. *Journal of Educational Psychology, 94*(3), 443–464.

McKenna, M. C., & Stahl, S. A. (2003). *Assessment for reading instruction.* New York: Guilford Press.

McVee, M. B., & Dickson, B. A. (2002). Creating a rubric to examine literacy software for the primary grades. *The Reading Teacher, 55*(7), 635–639.

Mesmer, E. M., & Mesmer, H. E. (2009). Response to intervention (RTI): What teachers of reading need to know. *The Reading Teacher, 62*(4), 280–290.

Moats, L. (1999). *Teaching reading is rocket science: What expert teachers of reading should know and be able to do* [Online]. Washington, DC: American Federation of Teachers. Retrieved May 5, 2004, from *www.aft.org*

Moje, E. B. (2008). Foregrounding the disciplines in secondary literacy teaching and learning: A call for change. *Journal of Adolescent and Adult Literacy, 52*(2) 96–107.

Morrison, F. J., Bachman, H. J., & Connor, C. M. (2005). *Improving literacy in America: Guidelines from research.* New Haven, CT: Yale University Press.

Morrow, L. M., & Woo, D. G. (Eds.). (2001). *Tutoring programs for struggling readers: The America Reads challenge.* New York: Guilford Press.

Myers, W. D. (2005). *Autobiography of my dead brother.* New York: HarperCollins.

Nater, S., & Gallimore, R. (2006). *You haven't taught until they have learned: John Wooden's teaching principles and practices.* Morgantown, WV: Fitness Information Technology.

National Assessment of Educational Progress. (2005). *The national report card.* Washington, DC: National Center of Educational Progress. Retrieved November 1, 2007, from *nces.ed.gov/nationalreportcard/nrc/reading_2005/*

National Association of Secondary School Principals. (2005). *Creating a culture of literacy: A guide for middle and high school principals.* Reston, VA: Author.

National Center for Education Statistics. (1996). *Parents and schools: Partners in student learning.* Washington, DC: Author.

National Center for Education Statistics. (1998). *Parent involvement in children's education: Efforts by public elementary schools.* Washington, DC: Author.

National Center for Education Statistics. (2003). *Nation's report card: Reading 2002.* Washington, DC: U.S. Government Printing Office. Retrieved October 3, 2007, from *nces.ed.gov/pubsearch/pubsinfo.asp?pubid=2003521*

National Institute of Child Health and Human Development. (2000). *Report of the National Reading Panel. Teaching children to read: An evidence-based assessment of the scientific research literature on reading and its implications for reading instruction* (NIH Publication No. 00-4769). Washington, DC: U.S. Government Printing Office. Available from *www.nichd.nih.gov/publications/nro/smallbook.pdf* (This document can be downloaded or ordered from the National Institute for Literacy at ED Pubs, 800-228-8813.)

National Staff Development Council. (2001). *Standards for staff development* [Online]. Oxford, OH: Author. Available from *www.nsdc.org*

Neuman, S. B., & Dickinson, D. K. (Eds.). (2001). *Handbook of early literacy research* (Vol. 1). New York: Guilford Press.

Newmann, F. M., & Wehlage, G. G. (1995). *Successful school restructuring: A report to the public and educators.* Madison: Center on Organization and Restructuring of Schools, Wisconsin Center for Education Research, University of Wisconsin.

O'Connor, R. E., Bell, K. M., Harty, K., Larkin, K. R., Sackor, S. M., & Zigmond, N. (2002). Teaching reading to poor readers in the intermediate grades: A comparison of text difficulty. *Journal of Educational Psychology, 94,* 474–485.

Ogle, D. (1986). K-W-L: A teaching model that develops active reading of expository text. *The Reading Teacher, 39,* 564–572.

Ogle, D., & Fogelberg, E. (2001). Expanding collaborative roles of reading specialists: Developing an intermediate reading support team. In V. Risko & K. Bromley (Eds.), *Collaboration for diverse learners: Viewpoints and practices* (pp. 152–167). Newark, DE: International Reading Association.

Paris, S. G. (2005). Reinterpreting the development of reading skills. *Reading Research Quarterly, 4*(2), 184–202.

Parrott, L., III. (1996). *How to handle impossible people: High-maintenance relationships.* Carol Stream, IL: Tyndale House.

Parsad, B., & Jones, J. (2005). *Internet access in U.S. public schools and classrooms: 1994–2003 (NCES 2005-015).* Washington, DC: U.S. Department of Education, National Center for Education Statistics.

Pearson, P. D., & Gallagher, M. C. (1983). The instruction of reading comprehension. *Contemporary Educational Psychology, 8,* 337–344.

Pikulski, J. (1994). Preventing reading failure: A review of five effective programs. *The Reading Teacher, 48,* 30–39.

Pinnell, G. S., Pikulski, J. J., Wixson, K. K., Campbell, J. R., Gough, P. B., & Beatty, A. S. (1995). *Listening to children read aloud.* Washington, DC: Office of Educational Research and mprovement, U.S. Department of Education.

Put Reading First. (2001). Washington, DC: Center for the Improvement of Early Reading Achievement.

Quatroche, D. J., Bean, R. M., & Hamilton, R. L. (2001). The role of the reading specialist: A review of research. *The Reading Teacher, 55*(3), 282–294.

Rasinski, T. V. (2000, October). Speed does matter in reading. *The Reading Teacher, 54,* 146–151.

Reeves, D. B. (2005). High performance in high-poverty schools: 90/90/90 and beyond. In J. Flood & P. Anders (Eds.), *Literacy development of students in urban schools: Research and policy* (pp. 362–388). Newark, DE: International Reading Association.

Robbins, P. (1991). *How to implement a peer coaching program.* Washington, DC: Association for Supervision and Curriculum Development.

Sackor, S. (2001). *Three-to-one tutoring: Strategies to enhance the reading comprehension of poor intermediate readers.* Unpublished doctoral dissertation, University of Pittsburgh, Pennsylvania.

Salinger, T., Zmach Tanenbaum, C., Thomsen, K., & Lefsky, E. (2008, December). *Examining the impact of adolescent literacy interventions.* Paper presented at the National Reading Conference, Orlando, FL.

Samuels, C. A. (2009). High schools try out RTI. *Education Week, 28*(19), 20–22.

Sanders, W. L., & Horn, S. P. (1994). The Tennessee Value-Added Assessment System (TVAAS): Mixed-model methodology in educational assessment. *Journal of Personnel Evaluation in Education, 8*(3), 299–311.

Sanders, W. L., & Rivers, J. C. (1996). *Cumulative and residual effects of teachers on future student academic achievement.* Knoxville: University of Tennessee Value-Added Research and Assessment Center.

Schoenbach, J., Greenleaf, C., Cziko, C., & Hurwitz, L. (1999). *Reading for understanding: A guide for improving reading in middle and high school classrooms.* San Francisco: Josey-Bass.

Scholastic. (2002). *Scholastic's READ 180: A heritage of research.* New York: Author. Retrieved January 11, 2003, from *teacher.scholastic.com/read180/research/pdf/heritage_of_research.pdf*

Schumm, J. S., & Mangrum, C. T. (1991). FLIP: A framework for fostering text-book thinking. *Journal of Reading, 35,* 120–124.

Scribner, J. D., & Reyes, P. (1999). Creating learning communities for high-performing Hispanic students: A conceptual framework. In P. Reyes, J. D. Scribner, & A. Scribner (Eds.), *Lessons from high-performing Hispanic schools: Creating learning communities* (pp. 188–210). New York: Teachers College Press.

Sendak, M. (1988). *Where the wild things are.* New York: Harper & Row.

Shanahan, T. (2008). Implications of RTI for the reading teacher. In D. Fuchs, L. S. Fuchs, & S. Vaughn (Eds.), *Response to intervention: A framework for reading educators* (pp. 105–122). Newark, DE: International Reading Association.

Shanahan, T., & Shanahan, C. (2008). Teaching disciplinary literacy to adolescents: Rethinking content-area literacy. *Harvard Educational Review, 78*(1), 40–59.

Simmons, D. C., & Kame'enui, E. T. (2002). *A consumer's guide to evaluating a core reading program grades K–3: A critical elements analysis.* Eugene: University of Oregon, National Center to Improve the Tools of Educators and Institute for the Development of Educational Achievement.

Slavin, R. E. (1987). Making Chapter 1 make a difference. *Phi Delta Kappan, 69*(2), 110–119.

Slavin, R. E., Madden, N. A., Dolan, L. J., & Wasik, B. A. (1996). *Every child, every school success for all.* Thousand Oaks, CA: Corwin Press.

Slosson, R., & Nicholson, C. (2002). *Slosson Oral Reading Assessment Test.* East Aurora, NY: Slosson Educational Publications.

Snow, C., Burns, M. S., & Griffin, P. (Eds.). (1998). *Preventing reading difficulties in young children.* Washington, DC: National Research Council.

Snow, C. E., Porche, M. V., Tabors, P. O., & Harris, S. R. (2007). *Is literacy enough? Pathways to academic success for adolescents.* Baltimore: Brookes.

Sparks, D., & Loucks-Horsley, S. (1990). Models of self-development. In R. Houston (Ed.), *Handbook of research on teacher education* (pp. 234–250). New York: Macmillan.

Stauffer, R. G. (1967). Change, BUT—. *The Reading Teacher, 20,* 474–499.

Stigler, J. W., & Hiebert, J. (1999). *The teaching gap: Best ideas from the world's teachers for improving education in the classroom.* New York: Free Press.

Sturtevant, E. (2003). *The literacy coach: A key to improving teaching and learning in secondary schools.* Washington, DC: Alliance for Excellent Education. Retrieved June 4, 2004, from *www.all4ed.org/publications/LiteracyCoach.pdf*

Tatum, A. W. (2005). *Teaching reading to black adolescent males: Closing the achievement gap.* Portland, ME: Stenhouse.

Taylor, B. M., & Pearson, P. D. (2002). *The CIERA school change classroom observation scheme.* Minneapolis: University of Minnesota.

Taylor, B. M., Pearson, P. D., & Rodriguez, M. C. (2005). The CIERA school change framework: An evidence-based approach to professional development and school reading improvement. *Reading Research Quarterly, 40*(1), 40–69.

Taylor, B. M., Pressley, M., & Pearson, P. D. (2002). Research-supported characteristics of teachers and schools that promote reading achievement. In B. M. Taylor & M. Pearson (Eds.), *Teaching reading: Effective schools, accomplished teachers* (pp. 361–374). Mahwah, NJ: Erlbaum.

Thibodeau, G. M. (2008). A content literacy collaborative study group: High school teachers take charge of their professional learning. *Journal of Adolescent and Adult Literacy, 52*(1), 54–84.

Tierney, R. J., Johnston, P., Moore, D. W., & Valencia, S. W. (2000). Snippets: How will literacy be assessed in the next millennium? *Reading Research Quarterly, 35*(4), 244–250.

Toll, C. (2006). *Lenses on literacy coaching: Conceptualizations, fuctions, and outcomes.* Norwood, MA: Christopher-Gordon.

University of Texas at Austin. (2003). *Preventing reading difficulties: A three-tiered intervention model.* Retrieved May 16, 2007, from *www.texasreading.org/3tier*

U.S. Department of Education. (2002a, April). *Guidance for the Reading First Program.* Washington, DC: Office of Elementary and Secondary Education. Available from *www.ed.gov/programs/readingfirst/guidance.pdf*

U.S. Department of Education. (2002b). *No Child Left Behind: A Desktop Reference.* Washington, DC: Office of Elementary and Secondary Education. Available from *www.ed.gov/admins/lead/account/nclbreference/page_pg5.html#i-b1*

Walp, T. P., & Walmsley, S. A. (1989). Instructional and philosophical congruence: Neglected aspects of coordination. *The Reading Teacher, 42*(6), 364–368.

Walpole, S., & Beauchat, K. A. (2008, June 2). *Facilitating teacher study groups.* Denver, CO: Literacy Coaching Clearinghouse. Retrieved January 20, 2009, from *www.literacycoachingonline.org.*

Walpole, S., & McKenna, M. (2008). *Differentiated reading instruction: Strategies for the primary grades.* New York: Guilford Press.

Warschauer, M. (2006). *Laptops and literacy: Learning in the wireless classroom.* New York: Teachers College Press.

Wasik, B. A. (1998). Volunteer tutoring programs in reading: A review. *Reading Research Quarterly, 33,* 266–292.

Wasik, B. A., & Slavin, R. E. (1993). Preventing early reading failure with one-to-one tutoring: A review of five programs. *Reading Research Quarterly, 28*(2), 178–200.

Weber, E. (1999). *Student assessment that works: A practical approach.* Boston: Allyn & Bacon.

Wilson, B. A. (1996). *Wilson Reading System.* Millbury, MA: Wilson Language Training Corporation.

Wixson, K., & Lipson, M. (2009). *Assessment and Instruction of reading and writing difficulties: An interactive approach* (4th ed.). New York: Allyn & Bacon.

Zigmond, N., & Bean, R. M. (2008). *External evaluation of Reading First in Pennsylvania.* Annual report, University of Pittsburgh.

Zygouris-Coe, V., Yao, Y., Tao, Y., Hahs-Vaugh, D. & Baumbach, D. (2004). *Qualitative evaluation of facilitator's contributions to online professional development.* (ERIC Document Reproduction Service No. ED485072)

Index

The Series on Social Emotional Learning

Teachers College Press
in partnership with the Center for Social and Emotional Education and the
Collaborative to Advance Social and Emotional Learning (CASEL)

Jonathan Cohen, *Series Editor*

CONSULTING EDITORS:
Maurice Elias, Norris M. Haynes, Roger Weissberg, and Joseph Zins

EDITORIAL ADVISORY BOARD:
J. Lawrence Aber, Diana Allensworth, Michael Ben-Avie, Robert Coles,
James P. Comer, Ann Lieberman, Pearl R. Kane, Catherine Lewis,
Karen Marschke-Tobier, John O'Neil, Nel Noddings,
Seymour B. Sarason, Thomas Sobol

Higher Expectations:
Promoting Social Emotional Learning and Academic Achievement in Your
School
RAYMOND J. PASI

Educating Minds and Hearts:
Social Emotional Learning and the Passage into Adolescence
JONATHAN COHEN, EDITOR

Caring Classrooms/Intelligent Schools:
The Social Emotional Education of Young Children
JONATHAN COHEN, EDITOR

Social emotional learning is now recognized as an essential aspect of children's
education and a necessary feature of all successful school reform efforts. The
books in this series will present perspectives and exemplary programs that foster social and emotional learning for children and adolescents in our schools,
including interdisciplinary, developmental, curricular, and instructional contributions. The three levels of service that constitute social emotional learning
programs will be critically presented: (1) curriculum-based programs directed
to all children to enhance social and emotional competencies, (2) programs and
perspectives intended for special needs children, and (3) programs and perspectives that seek to promote the social and emotional awareness and skills of educators and other school personnel.

HIGHER EXPECTATIONS

Promoting
Social Emotional Learning and
Academic Achievement in Your School

RAYMOND J. PASI

Foreword by Maurice Elias

Teachers College
Columbia University
New York and London

Published simultaneously by Teachers College Press, 1234 Amsterdam Avenue, New York, NY 10027 and by the National Association of Secondary School Principals, 1904 Association Drive, Reston, VA 20191

Library of Congress Cataloging-in-Publication Data

Pasi, Raymond J.
   Higher expectations : promoting social emotional learning and academic achievement in your school / Raymond J. Pasi.
     p. cm. — (The series on social emotional learning)
   Includes bibliographical references (p.   ) and index.
   ISBN 0-8077-4091-8 (paper : alk. paper)
    1. Affective education.   2. Social learning.   3. Emotional intelligence.
   I. Title. II. Series.
   LB1073 .P37 2001
   370.15′3—dc21   2001035580

ISBN 0-8077-4091-8 (paper)

Printed on acid-free paper
Manufactured in the United States of America

08 07 06 05 04 03 02 01   8 7 6 5 4 3 2 1

This book is dedicated to my parents,
Irene and Raymond J. Pasi,
and to
The Marist Brothers of the Schools.

Throughout my life, they taught me,
by word and by example,
the importance of educating the mind and heart.